ASIAN ECONOMIC INTEGRATION REPORT 2017

THE ERA OF FINANCIAL INTERCONNECTEDNESS
How Can Asia Strengthen Financial Resilience?

50 YEARS

ADB

ASIAN DEVELOPMENT BANK

CONTENTS

Foreword vi
Acknowledgments vii
Definitions viii
Abbreviations ix
Highlights xi

1. **REGIONAL OUTLOOK, LINKAGES, AND VULNERABILITIES** 1
   Regional Outlook, Integration, and Challenges 2
   Transmission Mechanism 4
   Emerging Vulnerabilities 6
   Coping Mechanisms 8
   Concluding Remarks 11
   References 11

   Box
   1.1: Trade Volume Outlook For Asia 5

2. **TRADE AND THE GLOBAL VALUE CHAIN** 13
   Recent Trends in Asia's Trade 14
   Asia's Intraregional Trade 16
   Progress of Global and Regional Value Chains 18
   Updates on Regional Trade Policy 19
   References 23

   Box
   2.1: Gravity Model Estimation of Bilateral Exports 17

3. **CROSS-BORDER INVESTMENT** 25
   Trends and Patterns of FDI in Asia 26
   Outward FDI 30
   References 36

   Box
   3.1: Outward Investments from Selected Asian Economies 33

4. **FINANCIAL INTEGRATION** **37**
   Progress in Cross-border Financial Transactions 38
   Analysis using Price Indicators. 49
   Financial Spillovers. 52
   References. 55

   Box
   4.1: Asia's Cross-border Collateral Agreements. 47

5. **REMITTANCES AND TOURISM RECEIPTS** **57**
   Remittance Flows to Asia 58
   Tourism Receipts 62
   References. 64

   Box
   5.1: Understanding the Sources of Fluctuations
        in Remittance Inflows. 61

6. **SUBREGIONAL COOPERATION INITIATIVES** **65**
   Central and West Asia: Central Asia Regional Economic
   Cooperation Program 66
   Southeast Asia: Greater Mekong Subregion Program. 69
   East Asia: Support to CAREC and GMS Programs. 73
   South Asia: South Asia Subregional Economic Cooperation. . . . 75
   The Pacific: Regional Approach to Renewable Energy
        Investments 79
   Toward Regional Connectivity. 81
   References. 83

7. **ASIA-PACIFIC REGIONAL COOPERATION
   AND INTEGRATION INDEX**. **85**
   References. 91
   Annex 92

   Box
   7.1: Constructing the Asia-Pacific Regional Cooperation
        and Integration Index 87

8. **THEME CHAPTER**
 THE ERA OF FINANCIAL INTERCONNECTEDNESS:
 HOW CAN ASIA STRENGTHEN FINANCIAL
 RESILIENCE? **95**
 Introduction 96
 Experiences and Lessons from Past Crises 97
 Financial Conditions, Vulnerabilities, and Cycles in Asia........ 101
 New Global Financial Conditions and Vulnerabilities 108
 Asia's Financial Interconnectedness, Transmission, and
   Spillovers of Shocks and Risks 110
 Conclusions and Policy Considerations....................... 125
 Background Papers... 130
 References... 131
 Annex 134

Boxes
 8.1: The Influence of US Dollar Funding Conditions on
    Asia's Financial Markets................................... 106
 8.2: Deriving Asia's Financial Sector Network: Data,
    Methodology, and Model 111
 8.3: Assessing Interbank Contagion During the Global
    Financial Crisis: Data, Methodology, and Model........... 117
 8.4: Estimating Macrofinancial Implications of
    Nonperforming Loans: Data, Methodology, and Model 122

9. **STATISTICAL APPENDIX** **137**

FOREWORD

This year's *Asian Economic Integration Report (AEIR)* continues to chronicle progress in regional cooperation and integration (RCI) in Asia and the Pacific. Despite an improved global economic outlook, elevated uncertainty in the international policy environment continues to weigh on global trade. Although world trade is expected to recover this year, its growth remains weaker than income growth following further deceleration in 2016. Foreign direct investment (FDI) worldwide also dropped 2% last year. Yet, the trend of RCI in Asia and the Pacific is gaining momentum, providing a buffer against the fallout from increasingly inward-looking policies around the world. Asia's intraregional trade share—measured by value—rose to 57.3% in 2016 from 56.9% in 2015, up from an average 55.9% during 2010–2015. Intraregional FDI share also grew to 55.3% in 2016 from 47.6% in 2015. Asia's cross-border bank claims increased to $4.4 trillion from $4.1 trillion. Asia's international tourism receipts are increasingly sourced from other Asian economies, with more than 70% of Asia's outbound tourists traveling within the region.

To better monitor this progress, *AEIR 2017* introduces the Asia-Pacific Regional Cooperation and Integration Index (ARCII), a newly created composite index that allows comparative analysis of six RCI dimensions across subregional groups and economies. Its six component indexes cover: (i) trade and investment, (ii) money and finance, (iii) regional value chains, (iv) infrastructure and connectivity, (v) movement of people, and (vi) institutional and social integration. RCI in Asia and the Pacific, while significantly behind the European Union, ranks above both Africa and Latin America. Within the region, ARCII shows RCI is most advanced in East Asia and Southeast Asia, drawing on the expansion of regional trade and FDI networks linked to global supply chains.

AEIR 2017 includes a Theme Chapter on how best to enhance regional financial resilience as global financial systems become more interconnected. "The Era of Financial Interconnectedness: How Can Asia Strengthen Financial Resilience?" examines the structural weaknesses of the region's financial systems, existing and emerging vulnerabilities, and the implications of increasingly more pronounced and procyclical financial cycles and financial interconnectedness. It investigates the evolution of financial networks and various channels through which financial shocks can be transmitted. And it specifically cites the region's overreliance on external funding (largely denominated in US dollars) as one of many sources of potential vulnerability should the global financial cycle reverse and dollar liquidity tighten.

However, the Theme Chapter also shows that—20 years after the 1997/98 Asian financial crisis—wide-ranging reforms helped build national and regional financial resilience and safety net systems against the impact of external shocks—as seen by Asia's relative resilience to and rapid recovery from the 2008/09 global financial crisis. The chapter reviews crisis lessons and remaining policy gaps for further structural reforms needed to further strengthen financial resilience. The region's policy makers need to continue reforms that ensure good macroeconomic fundamentals, build strong regulatory and supervisory frameworks, deepen alternative sources of market financing such as local currency bond market transactions, and further strengthen financial safety nets. Finally, the region's continued cooperation to ensure financial stability will allow authorities in Asia and the Pacific to respond promptly, decisively, and collectively should global risks and financial volatility pose risks to the region's continued robust economic development.

Yasuyuki Sawada
Chief Economist and Director General
Economic Research and Regional Cooperation Department
Asian Development Bank

ACKNOWLEDGMENTS

The *Asian Economic Integration Report* (AEIR) 2017 was prepared by the Regional Cooperation and Integration Division (ERCI) of the Economic Research and Regional Cooperation Department (ERCD) of the Asian Development Bank (ADB), under the overall supervision of ERCI Director Cyn-Young Park. Jong Woo Kang coordinated overall production assisted by Mara Claire Tayag. ERCI consultants under Technical Assistance 9121: Asian Economic Integration—Building Knowledge for Policy Dialogue contributed data compilation, research, and analysis.

Contributing authors include James Villafuerte and with data support from Joy Blesilda Sinay and Pilar Dayag (Regional Outlook, Linkages, and Vulnerabilities); Jong Woo Kang, Mara Claire Tayag, Suzette Dagli, Dorothea Ramizo, and Paul Mariano (Trade and the Global Value Chain); Fahad Khan, Ma. Concepcion Latoja, Suzette Dagli, and Cindy Jane Justo (Cross-border Investment); Junkyu Lee, Kijin Kim, Satoru Yamadera, Ana Kristel Molina, and Racquel Claveria with data support from Clemence Fatima Cruz (Financial Integration); and Aiko Kikkawa Takenaka with data support from Grendell Vie Magoncia and Ma. Concepcion Latoja (Remittances and Tourism Receipts). The chapter "Subregional Cooperation Initiatives" was consolidated by Paulo Rodelio Halili based on contributions by regional departments of ADB: Shaista Hussain, Guoliang Wu, and Ronaldo Oblepias (Central and West Asia); Greater Mekong Subregion Secretariat (Southeast Asia); Ying Qian and Yuebin Zhang (East Asia); Rose McKenzie and Jesusito Tranquilino (South Asia); and Paul Curry and Rommel Rabanal (Pacific). The chapter on Asia-Pacific Regional Cooperation and Integration Index was written by Cyn-Young Park—based on a background paper by Cyn-Young Park and Hyeon-Seung Huh—with data support from Racquel Claveria. Junkyu Lee and Peter Rosenkranz coordinated and contributed to the production of the theme chapter, "The Era of Financial Interconnectedness: How Can Asia Strengthen Financial Resilience?" Background papers were provided by Ross Buckley, Stijn Claessens, Mardi Dungey, Junkyu Lee, Cyn-Young Park, Peter Rosenkranz, Kwanho Shin, and James Villafuerte. Monica Melchor, Jesson Pagaduan, Hoang Pham, and Alyssa Villanueva provided research support.

Guy Sacerdoti edited the report. Ariel Paelmo typeset and produced the layout. Erickson Mercado created the cover design and assisted in typesetting. Paulo Rodelio Halili and Aleli Rosario helped in proofreading. Support for *AEIR 2017* printing and publishing was provided by the Printing Services Unit of ADB's Office of Administrative Services and by the Publishing and Dissemination Unit of the Department of External Relations. Carol Ongchangco, Pia Asuncion Tenchavez, Maria Criselda Aherrera, and Marilyn Parra provided administrative and secretarial support, and helped organize the AEIR workshops, launch events, and other AEIR-related seminars. Harumi Kodama and Erik Churchill of the Department of External Relations coordinated dissemination of *AEIR 2017*.

DEFINITIONS

The economies covered in the *Asian Economic Integration Report 2017* are grouped by major analytic or geographic group.

- Asia refers to the 48 Asia and the Pacific members of the Asian Development Bank (ADB), which includes Japan and Oceania (Australia and New Zealand) in addition to the 45 developing Asian economies.

- Subregional economic groupings are listed below:

  - Central Asia comprises Armenia, Azerbaijan, Georgia, Kazakhstan, the Kyrgyz Republic, Tajikistan, Turkmenistan, and Uzbekistan.
  - East Asia comprises the People's Republic of China; Hong Kong, China; Japan; the Republic of Korea; Mongolia; and Taipei,China.
  - South Asia comprises Afghanistan, Bangladesh, Bhutan, India, Maldives, Nepal, Pakistan, and Sri Lanka.
  - Southeast Asia comprises Brunei Darussalam, Cambodia, Indonesia, the Lao People's Democratic Republic, Malaysia, Myanmar, the Philippines, Singapore, Thailand, and Viet Nam.
  - The Pacific comprises the Cook Islands, Fiji, Kiribati, the Marshall Islands, the Federated States of Micronesia, Nauru, Papua New Guinea, Palau, Samoa, Solomon Islands, Timor-Leste, Tonga, Tuvalu, and Vanuatu.
  - Oceania includes Australia and New Zealand.

Unless otherwise specified, the symbol "$" and the word "dollar" refer to US dollars, and percent changes are year-on-year.

ABBREVIATIONS

ABMI	Asian Bond Markets Initiative
ADB	Asian Development Bank
AEIR	Asian Economic Integration Report
AFC	Asian financial crisis
AMRO	ASEAN+3 Macroeconomic Research Office
ARCII	Asia-Pacific Regional Cooperation and Integration Index
ASEAN	Association of Southeast Asian Nations (Brunei Darussalam, Cambodia, Indonesia, the Lao People's Democratic Republic, Malaysia, Myanmar, the Philippines, Singapore, Thailand, and Viet Nam)
ASEAN+3	ASEAN plus Japan, the People's Republic of China, and the Republic of Korea
BCP	border crossing point
BEZ	border economic zone
BIS	Bank for International Settlements
BOJ	Bank of Japan
BOP	balance of payments
BOT	Bank of Thailand
BRI	Belt and Road Initiative
CAGR	compounded annual growth rate
CAREC	Central Asia Regional Economic Cooperation
CBCA	cross-border collateral arrangement
CBTA	Cross-Border Transport Facilitation Agreement
CCBM	correspondent central banking model
CI	CAREC Institute
CMI	Chiang Mai Initiative
CMIM	Chiang Mai Initiative Multilateralisation
CSD	central securities depositories
DCC	dynamic conditional correlation
DMC	developing member country
DVA	domestic value added
ECB	European Central Bank
ECD	economic corridor development
EDC	European sovereign debt crisis
EPA	Economic Partnership Agreement
EU	European Union (Austria, Belgium, Bulgaria, Croatia, Cyprus, Czech Republic, Denmark, Estonia, Finland, France, Germany, Greece, Hungary, Ireland, Italy, Latvia, Lithuania, Luxembourg, Malta, the Netherlands, Poland, Portugal, Romania, Slovak Republic, Slovenia, Spain, Sweden, and the United Kingdom)
euro area	Austria, Belgium, Cyprus, Estonia, Finland, France, Germany, Greece, Ireland, Italy, Latvia, Lithuania, Luxembourg, Malta, the Netherlands, Portugal, Slovak Republic, Slovenia, and Spain
FDI	foreign direct investment
FSM	Federated States of Micronesia
FTA	free trade agreement
GCF	Green Climate Fund
GDP	gross domestic product
GFC	global financial crisis
GMS	Greater Mekong Subregion
GVC	global value chain
HRD	human resource development
ICT	information and communication technology

IMF	International Monetary Fund
M&A	merger and acquisition
MW	megawatt
NPL	nonperforming loan
OECD	Organisation for Economic Co-operation and Development
OFDI	outward foreign direct investment
PCA	principal components analysis
PIREIP	Pacific Islands Renewable Energy Investment Program
PRC	People's Republic of China
PVAR	panel vector autoregression
QE	quantitative easing
RCEP	Regional Comprehensive Economic Partnership
RCI	regional cooperation and integration
ROW	rest of the world
RTGS	real-time gross settlement
SASEC	South Asia Subregional Economic Cooperation
SASEC OP	SASEC Operational Plan
SEZ	special economic zone
SIFI	systemically important financial institution
SME	small and medium-sized enterprise
SPS	sanitary and phytosanitary
SSM	Single Supervisory Mechanism
TFA	Trade Facilitation Agreement
TPP	Trans-Pacific Partnership
TTF	transport and trade facilitation
TTFS	Transport and Trade Facilitation Strategy
TUTAP	Turkmenistan–Uzbekistan–Tajikistan–Afghanistan–Pakistan
UK	United Kingdom
US	United States
VAR	vector autoregression
VCIC	Visakhapatnam–Chennai Industrial Corridor
WTO	World Trade Organization

Highlights

Trade and Investment

- **Asia and the Pacific is leading a recovery in world trade amid the continued uncertainty surrounding the global trade policy environment.** In 2016, Asia's trade (by volume) grew faster than global trade, but remained below its economic growth.[1] Asia's trade growth picked up to 1.7% in 2016 from 1.4% in 2015, while the world trade growth decelerated to 1.3% from 2.6%. Ongoing global economic recovery lifted demand for the region's exports, particularly from Japan; Taipei,China; Hong Kong, China; and Viet Nam. The region's import growth has also accelerated recently due to robust demand from the People's Republic of China (PRC) and India, among others. Asia's trade growth accelerated further to 7.4% during the first half of 2017 and will likely continue to gain momentum as global economic recovery gathers pace. However, potential bilateral trade friction and policy uncertainties among the world's major trading partners remain downside risks.

- **Asia's intraregional trade continued to strengthen in 2016.** Asia's intraregional trade share—measured by value—rose to 57.3% in 2016 from 56.9% in 2015, up from an average 55.9% during 2010–2015. Strong intraregional trade offers a buffer against potential headwinds from global trade and policy uncertainties. Subregionally, trade integration—measured by the share of intra-subregional trade to total trade—is strongest in East Asia, followed by Southeast Asia and Central Asia.

- **Amid a slowdown in total inward foreign direct investment to Asia, intraregional investment flows continue to rise.** Global foreign direct investment (FDI) into the region (measured by gross inward FDI) fell 6% in 2016—to $492 billion from $525 billion in 2015. The region's share of global inward FDI dropped to 28% from 30%. Nonetheless, intraregional FDI rose in both absolute value (to $272 billion in 2016 from $250 billion in 2015) and its share in total (to 55% from 48%). Intra-Asian FDI is geared more toward global and regional value chains, mainly going to greenfield investments in manufacturing. This should help strengthen the region's trade globally as well as regionally.

- **Asia's outward foreign direct investment rose 11% in 2016—to $482 billion from $434 billion in 2015.** The region's outward FDI accounted for 33% of global FDI, up from 27% in 2015. In 2016, the PRC; Japan; and Hong Kong, China were among the world's top 10 global investors. Combined, their outward FDI reached $391 billion, or 81% of total outward FDI from Asia. Emerging Asian investors such as India, the Republic of Korea, Malaysia, Singapore, and Thailand are also expanding their global presence in such areas as renewable energy, semiconductors, natural resources, information technology, and food, among others.

---

[1] In this report, Asia refers to the 48 Asia and the Pacific members of the Asian Development Bank (ADB), including the region's three advanced economies —Australia, Japan, and New Zealand, while developing Asia refers to ADB's 45 developing member economies.

Financial Integration

- **Asia's portfolio investors continue to invest more outside the region.** Outward debt investment from Asian economies stood at $4.0 trillion in 2016, up from $3.6 trillion in 2015, driven largely by the region's higher investments in the European Union (EU) (up $110 billion) and the United States (US) (up $224 billion). Outward equity investment outstanding also rose to $3.5 trillion from $3.2 trillion. Asia's continued portfolio investment bias toward outside the region has led to a lower intraregional outward debt (equity) investment share—at 15.3% (19.0%) in 2016 from 16.7% (20.0%) in 2015.

- **Cross-border banking activity in Asia is steadily increasing.** Asia's cross-border bank claims stood at $4.4 trillion in 2016, up from $4.1 trillion in 2015. Japan accounted for 88.7% of the increase due to its increased overseas lending especially to the US and the EU. Japan's cross-border bank claims outstanding rose from $3.2 trillion to $3.4 trillion (driven by an increase of $19.8 billion to the region, $59.2 billion to the EU, and $131.3 billion to the US). The intraregional share of Asia's cross-border bank claims also increased from 17.8% in 2011 to 21.4% in 2016.

- **The volatility of Asian equity market returns is explained more by variations in global than regional equity market returns.** Asian equity market return volatility is more prone to global impact, with the trend strengthening further since 2015. This suggests Asia's equity markets remain more globally than regionally integrated. On the other hand, after the 2008/09 global financial crisis (GFC), a greater portion of volatility in Asian local currency bond returns is explained by variation in regional bond market returns, partly reflecting the growing participation of Asian investors in local currency bond markets. The impact of global shocks on local currency bond return volatility picked up, however, since the US Federal Reserve began to normalize monetary policy in 2015.

Movement of People

- **Remittances to the region dropped to $259 billion in 2016 from $269 billion in 2015—the largest drop since 2009.** Central Asian countries saw inflows decline for the third consecutive year, mainly due to weak economic recovery in the Russian Federation, the subregion's top migrant destination. Low global oil prices also affected remittances to countries (like India and Pakistan) with a large number of workers in the Middle East. Around 45% of global remittances flow into Asia, the world's largest source of international migrants. Empirical analyses suggest that remittance inflows are more stable when there is a higher proportion of female migrants. Quality institutions such as the rule of law and creditor protection in a migrant's home country can also help stabilize remittance inflows, likely due to more reliable and efficient money transfer systems.

- **Tourism is growing rapidly in the region, with an increasing number of tourists traveling within the region.** Asia is the second largest beneficiary of tourism receipts after Europe. Tourism receipts reached $398.6 billion in 2015 after growing an average 10.1% yearly since 2012. More than 70% of Asia's outbound tourists traveled within the region. The number of tourists from the PRC rose 11.8% in 2015, with 61.0% staying within the region. The PRC; Thailand; and Hong Kong, China earned most from tourism. However, as a proportion of gross domestic product (GDP), Maldives tops the list with 83.5% of GDP coming from tourism. The Pacific developing member countries earn an average 18.5% of GDP from tourism.

Asia-Pacific Regional Cooperation and Integration Index

- **This year's *Asian Economic Integration Report* introduces a new composite index to gauge the progress of regional cooperation and integration in Asia and the Pacific.** Regional cooperation and integration (RCI) plays an important role in supporting economic growth and poverty reduction, and has been high on the development agenda for many Asian economies in recent years. Supporting RCI is one of ADB's key strategic priorities for development assistance in the region. An index that calibrates the status of RCI can be a useful policy tool for assessing the progress of RCI efforts especially by various subregional initiatives.

- **The Asia-Pacific Regional Cooperation and Integration Index is constructed from 26 socioeconomic indicators grouped into six dimensions to capture the diversity of regional cooperation and integration.** The six dimensions cover: (i) trade and investment, (ii) money and finance, (iii) regional value chains, (iv) infrastructure and connectivity, (v) movement of people, and (vi) institutional and social integration (based on indicators for trade agreements, diplomatic ties, and cultural relations).

- **The indicators are expressed as a ratio of a country's intraregional sum (or average) to total sum (or average) of cross-border economic activities and are aggregated into a single composite index following a two-step procedure.** The first step involves minimum-maximum scaling to normalize indicators with different measurement units to a uniform range between 0 and 1, with higher values denoting greater regional integration. The second step is to perform principal component analysis to estimate the weights used in aggregating individual indicators into a composite index: (i) first for each of the six dimensions and (ii) then again to combine the six composite indexes into the overall Asia-Pacific Regional Cooperation and Integration Index (ARCII).

- **The ARCII allows Asian economies to keep track of the progress in their regional integration.** The index allows comparative analysis of RCI by measuring the degree of RCI in the six dimensions as well as their collective contributions to overall regional integration across subregional groups or countries. The six dimensional indexes are designed to reflect the core socioeconomic components of the regional integration process. The ARCII allows each subregional group or economy to identify their strengths and weaknesses across the six RCI dimensions.

- **The ARCII, by the nature of its construction, measures an Asian economy's integration with the other regional economies relative to its integration with the world.** As such, a low score in an economy's ARCII does not necessarily mean the economy is not regionally integrated defined in some absolute terms, but it would simply reflect the economy's higher interregional rather than intraregional integration. For example, Singapore, one of the region's top performers in ARCII, scores high across all six dimensions, but its regional money and finance integration is weaker relative to other dimensions. This stems largely from the fact that Singapore is a global financial center and more globally integrated than regionally. Both Japan and Hong Kong, China are equally regarded as global financial centers and also have relatively low scores for regional money and finance integration.

- **The EU has the highest regional integration score on all but one dimensional indexes; but Asia outranks both Africa and Latin America.** The EU broadly outperforms Asia across all dimensions—Asia's trade and investment integration index is the only one comparable in magnitude. Asia's institutional and social integration is particularly weak. Asia's composite ARCII index is 0.448, below the EU's 0.617. Latin America follows close behind at 0.423, with Africa at 0.395. Regional value chain and movement of people are Asia's most regionally integrated components, while institutional and social integration is least.

THEME CHAPTER

The Era of Financial Interconnectedness: How Can Asia Strengthen Financial Resilience?

- **Twenty years after the Asian financial crisis, Asia stands strong—with more flexible exchange rates, higher foreign reserves, healthier financial systems, stronger regulations, deeper capital markets, and better regional financial cooperation mechanisms.** Nonetheless, the region's economic growth and financial stability were briefly disrupted by the GFC. Significant challenges remain, along with unresolved financial market and system weaknesses. Remaining regulatory policy gaps also leave room for a buildup of financial vulnerability through excessive leverage and risk-taking. Asia's policy makers must remain vigilant and be ready to act when necessary, while continuing to deepen financial reforms.

- **Structural weaknesses continue to permeate Asian financial markets and systems.** In particular, when combined with increased procyclicality of financial cycles and growing regional and global financial interconnectedness, these weaknesses present new challenges. They include how: (i) increased financial interconnectedness helps speed international transmission of financial risks; (ii) foreign currency-(especially US dollar-)denominated debt continues to rise, reflecting limited domestic capital market-based financing solutions; (iii) rising private-sector debt and leverage—combined with the rapid growth of shadow banking (including wealth management products issued in some Asian economies)—increase financial fragility; and how (iv) deteriorating bank asset quality and its potential macrofinancial feedback effects pose risks to Asia's economic and financial stability.

- **Over the past 20 years, Asian financial markets have become more interconnected—both globally and intraregionally.** Empirical analysis of 42 equity markets (15 within Asia) from 1996 to 2016 shows a deepening and growing complexity in Asian financial market interconnectedness. The results also reveal that interconnectedness increased during financial crises and decreased during recoveries.

- **Growing financial interconnectedness can increase vulnerabilities to external shocks, financial contagion, or liquidity risks stemming from cross-border bank lending.** Analyzing bilateral data on cross-border bank liabilities suggests that an economy's banking exposure to crisis-affected economies can affect the size of capital outflows from the economy during a crisis. The analysis highlights how cross-border bank borrowing can become a global transmission channel when liquidity tightens.

- **Continued high reliance on US dollar-denominated funding has significant implications for the transmission of global financial conditions to domestic financial and macroeconomic conditions.** In the first quarter of 2017, 79% of total outstanding international debt securities for Asia's major emerging economies were denominated in US dollars, with shares recently rising. The concentration of foreign borrowing in a single currency leaves the region's financial systems vulnerable to external shocks through unexpected changes in foreign currency liquidity conditions and related capital flow reversals. Empirical evidence shows that a change in bilateral US dollar exchange rates has a significant impact on sovereign credit risk premiums (widening sovereign bond market spreads), which can affect financial conditions in some emerging Asian economies.

- **The recent rise in nonperforming loans in several emerging Asian economies is a concern due to potential macrofinancial feedback effects.** Nonperforming loans (NPLs) have increased in the PRC, India, Bangladesh, Indonesia, and Mongolia, among others. Empirical findings show that while macroeconomic conditions and bank-specific factors—such as rapid credit growth and excessive bank lending—contribute to the buildup of NPLs, a sustained increase can likewise lead to a reduction in credit supply and slowdown in overall economic activity.

Policy Considerations for Enhancing Financial Resilience

- **A key lesson drawn from recent crises is the urgent need to strengthen macroprudential regulation and supervision in the region.** Authorities should consider establishing and implementing an effective macroprudential policy framework to address two dimensions of system-wide risk: (i) a buildup of systemic risk over time (the "time dimension"), and (ii) a spillover and contagion of risk across different financial sectors and systems (the "cross-sectional dimension"). Macroprudential policy tools—such as countercyclical provisions, capital and liquidity buffers, and other balance sheet instruments—can be useful in mitigating financial system procyclicality.

- **Further developing local currency bond markets across the region is key to enhancing financial resilience and mobilizing stable long-term finance.** While local currency bonds outstanding in Association of Southeast Asian Nations plus the PRC, Japan, and the Republic of Korea (ASEAN+3) tripled from $6.6 trillion in 2002 to $19.8 trillion at end-2016, challenges remain. To meet the region's financing needs, local currency bond markets must improve market efficiency, broaden their investor base, deepen secondary markets, and integrate more regionally.

- **Growing cross-border banking activities and systemic importance of some large regional financial institutions underscore the need to discuss regional regulatory cooperation, including resolution mechanisms for interconnected regional banks.** Supervisory colleges for regionally active foreign banks can be an effective regional cooperation tool to strengthen cross-border supervision in Asia. Regional cooperation to develop effective resolution mechanisms for distressed assets of cross-border financial institutions can also complement national efforts to address NPLs efficiently and sustainably.

- **The region should consider reviewing and strengthening existing financial safety nets against potential contagion and spillover effects.** Asia's financial markets are increasingly open, interconnected, and vulnerable to external shocks. Strengthening the Chiang Mai Initiative Multilateralisation and its regional macroeconomic surveillance unit, the ASEAN+3 Macroeconomic Research Office, can help monitor potential liquidity risks and slow the spread of shocks across the region's economies.

01

Regional Outlook, Linkages, and Vulnerabilities

Regional Outlook, Linkages, and Vulnerabilities

Regional Outlook, Integration, and Challenges

Developing Asia's economic output is expected to grow 5.9% in 2017 from 5.8% in 2016—0.2 percentage point above the projection in the *Asian Economic Integration Report 2016*.

A rebound in global trade, recovery in major industrial economies, and stronger-than-expected growth in the People's Republic of China (PRC) are expected to support the better growth outlook. Gross domestic product (GDP) in the PRC is now expected to grow 6.7% in 2017—0.3 percentage point above the *Asian Economic Integration Report 2016*

forecast—led by expansionary fiscal policy and an unanticipated rise in external demand.

More than 70% of the region's economies should see faster growth compared with 2016, with higher rates in all subregions except East Asia and South Asia, where growth this year is stable (Table 1.1). A better external environment and strong domestic demand generally support the forecast. After 2 years of lower export receipts, the value of the region's exports surged 10.1% year-on-year in the first 7 months of 2017. Moderately rising oil prices are giving some fiscal relief to oil and gas exporters without destabilizing oil importers. Excluding the PRC, Asia's eight largest developing economies also saw real manufacturing exports rebound—particularly electronics, where foreign direct investment has been increasing (ADB 2017).

Table 1.1: Regional GDP Growth[a] (%, year-on-year)

	2014	2015	2016	Forecast[c]	
				2017	2018
Developing Asia[b]	6.4	6.0	5.8	5.9	5.8
Central Asia	5.2	3.1	2.2	3.3	3.9
East Asia	6.6	6.1	6.0	6.0	5.8
People's Republic of China	7.3	6.9	6.7	6.7	6.4
South Asia	6.9	7.3	6.7	6.7	7.0
India	7.5	8.0	7.1	7.0	7.4
Southeast Asia	4.6	4.6	4.6	5.0	5.1
The Pacific	9.4	8.4	2.4	2.9	3.2
Major industrialized economies					
euro area	1.2	1.9	1.7	2.0	1.8
Japan	0.2	1.1	1.0	1.5	1.1
United States	2.4	2.9	1.5	2.2	2.4

GDP = gross domestic product.

[a] Aggregates weighted by gross national income levels (Atlas method, current $) from World Development Indicators, World Bank.

[b] Refers to the 45 ADB developing member economies.

[c] Forecasts based on ADB's *Asian Development Outlook Update 2017*.

Sources: ADB calculations using data from ADB (2017); and CEIC (accessed September 2017).

Risks to the outlook have become more balanced, both positive and negative.

There are three main risks to the outlook: (i) lower-than-expected oil prices; (ii) United States (US) monetary policy surprises; and (iii) uncertain US fiscal policy reform. While softening oil prices would benefit importers, it would also hit oil exporters. A sharper-than-expected tightening of the US Federal Funds rate could still induce large capital outflows from developing Asia, although better communication of US Federal Reserve intentions has so far averted market overreaction. And while US tax reform and spending on public works could have positive global spillover effects, intense debate and possible political stalemate over budget details could unsettle currently buoyant business expectations of a boost in domestic demand, thereby increasing market uncertainty.

Recently, developing Asia's growth cycle has moved more synchronous with the US than intraregionally.

Developing Asia's growth cycle has recently become more correlated with the US than internally. This is evident from business cycle correlation analysis that shows the degree of co-movement between business cycle fluctuations in the US, the euro area, Japan, and across developing Asia (Figure 1.1). The region's business cycle correlation with the US has turned positive since first quarter of 2017. The increased business cycle synchronicity could arise from a common global factor—such as resurging trade growth—or a demand spillover from advanced economies to the region. By contrast, intraregional business cycle correlation has weakened—still but remain in positive territory—since the third quarter of 2016, partly reflecting the limited spillover effect of the PRC slowdown.

Slowdown in global demand and the PRC growth moderation continue to affect the region's business cycle.

Examining changes in GDP growth during previous recessions in the US and euro area show that global shocks are having an increasing impact on developing Asia (Figure 1.2). For example, the ratio of change between GDP contractions in the US with those in developing Asia—for the same period—has increased over time. It is more closely aligned for export-oriented newly industrialized economies than for middle-income Association of Southeast Asian Nations (ASEAN)

Figure 1.1: Developing Asia's Business Cycle Correlations

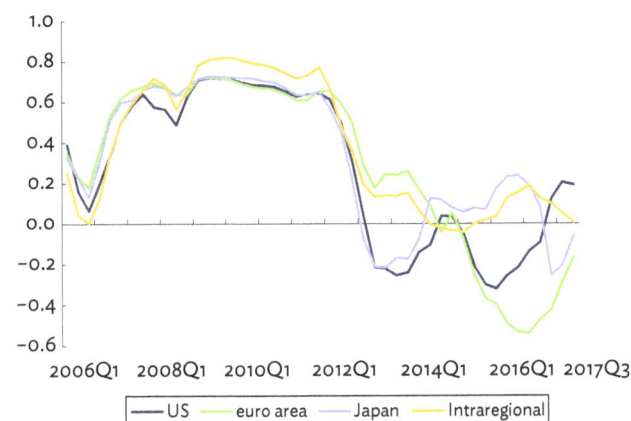

US = United States.
Notes: Developing Asia includes ASEAN4 (Indonesia, Malaysia, the Philippines, and Thailand), NIE4 (Hong Kong, China; the Republic of Korea; Singapore; and Taipei,China), India, and the People's Republic of China. Three-year moving correlations based on cyclical Hodrick-Prescott filtered seasonally-adjusted gross domestic product at constant prices.
Source: ADB calculations using data from Oxford Economics. Global Economic Databank. http://www.oxfordeconomics.com/ (accessed September 2017).

Figure 1.2: Change in GDP Growth During US and EU Recessions—Developing Asia (percentage point change relative to the US)

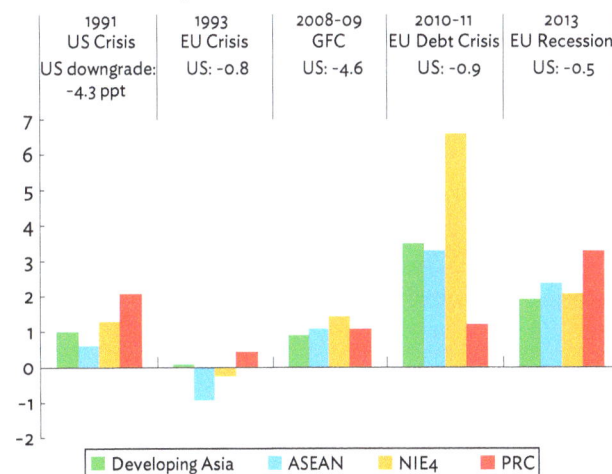

ASEAN = Association of Southeast Asian Nations (Brunei Darussalam, Cambodia, Indonesia, the Lao People's Democratic Republic, Malaysia, Myanmar, the Philippines, Singapore, Thailand, and Viet Nam); EU = European Union; GDP = gross domestic product; GFC = global financial crisis; NIE4 = newly industrialized economies (Hong Kong, China; the Republic of Korea; Singapore; and Taipei,China); PRC = People's Republic of China; ppt = percentage point; and US = United States.
Notes: Change in GDP growth is computed as the difference between peak and trough before and during the US and EU recessions. Aggregates are weighted using gross national income (Atlas method, current $). Developing Asia includes ASEAN, NIE4, India, and the PRC.
Sources: ADB calculations using data from CEIC; and World Bank. World Development Indicators. http://databank.worldbank.org/ (both accessed August 2017).

Figure 1.3: Financial Stress Index—Developing Asia

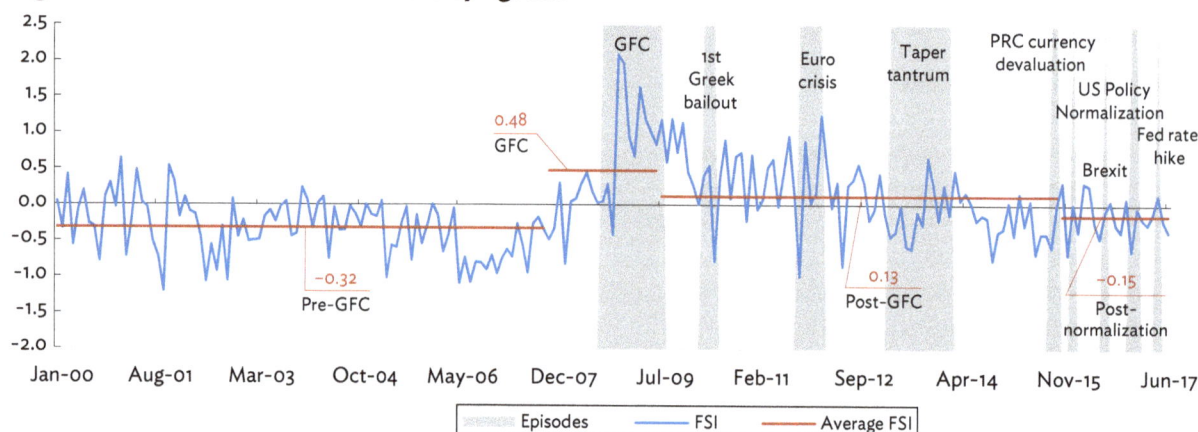

FSI = Financial Stress Index, GFC = global financial crisis, PRC = People's Republic of China, US = United States.
Pre-GFC = January 2000–September 2007, GFC = October 2007–June 2009, Post-GFC = July 2009–September 2015, Post-normalization = October 2015–June 2017.
Notes: Based on principal components analysis. Includes the PRC; Hong Kong, China; India; Indonesia; the Republic of Korea; Malaysia; the Philippines; Singapore; Thailand; and Viet Nam.
Sources: ADB staff calculations using data from Bloomberg, CEIC, and Haver Analytics (all accessed September 2017).

economies. Similarly, as its exports grew, the PRC economy became more sensitive to the US and euro area recessions. Its growth moderation also continues to affect the region's growth cycle and prospects.

While Asia has endured several economic and financial crises—strengthening its financial resilience in response—global shocks can still affect the region's financial markets and economies.

The current Financial Stress Index (FSI) for developing Asia is quite benign (Figure 1.3). The stress level for the region has subsided since the spikes during the 2008/09 global financial crisis (GFC), reflecting improved resilience in the region's financial systems. Nonetheless, the FSI shows financial systems remain prone to increased volatility from potential global shocks—as seen from the spikes during the taper tantrum, the PRC currency devaluation, and Brexit.

Transmission Mechanism

The GFC severely affected the region's credit, equity, and currency markets—as risk aversion triggered capital outflows from the region. In turn, tighter credit conditions and weak external demand affected the real sector, as seen from the large declines in trade volume and GDP growth. However, adequately capitalized banks

and appropriate monetary and fiscal responses from policy makers provided an effective firewall that allowed the region to recover quickly and rekindle robust growth. Nonetheless, it is important to revisit how external shocks from the rest of the world could transmitted to the region.

Given Asia's strong trade orientation and openness, trade remains a key transmission channel for global shocks to affect the region.

Over time, the region has strengthened its capacity to cope with cyclical downturns in external demand by expanding domestic and regional demand. This can be seen from the higher share of intraregional trade, which increased from 53.9% in 2008 to about 57.3% in 2016. At the same time, Asia's trade share with the EU and the US (G2) declined from 25.1% to 24.2% over the same period. Still, a large portion of Asia's intraregional trade appears to be linked to external demand. For instance, a decomposition of Asia's value-added exports show that its own final demand accounts only for 36.8% of its total value-added exports, while 63.2% accrues to external final demand, of which 26.9% is accounted for by final demand from G2 markets. Once the cascading effect of "intermediate goods exports" are accounted for, the region's dependence on external demand grows—particularly with the US. This is consistent with an ADB study that finds the US economy remains an important source of external demand shock for the region although the impact of the PRC has also increased sharply, more recently (Park 2017).

Furthermore, the relationship between the region's exports and growth in US non-oil imports continues to be tight, although loosening somewhat in recent years—from 0.91% in 2000–2010 to 0.84% in 2010–2016 (Figure 1.4). Due in part to improving US domestic demand, most export-oriented economies in the region have seen consistent recovery in export growth since the last quarter of 2016 (see *Trade and the Global Value Chain,* page 14). This recovery is expected to continue as global demand improves in the near future (Box 1.1).

External shocks could also affect Asia through the financial channel via capital outflows and liquidation of foreign asset holdings.

As the region's financial markets deepen and continue to open up, foreign holdings of portfolio assets have grown, making emerging Asia more susceptible to sudden

Figure 1.4: Correlation between US Non-oil Imports and Developing Asia's Exports

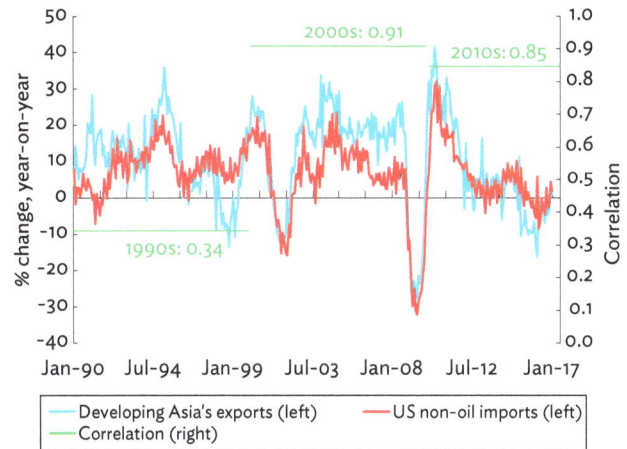

US = United States.
Notes: Non-oil imports is computed by subtracting crude oil imports from total goods imports. Developing Asia includes ASEAN4 (Indonesia, Malaysia, the Philippines, and Thailand), NIE4 (Hong Kong, China; the Republic of Korea; Singapore; and Taipei,China), India, and the People's Republic of China.
Sources: ADB calculations using data from CEIC; International Monetary Fund. International Financial Statistics. https://www.imf.org/en/Data; and United States Census Bureau. https://www.census.gov/ (all accessed August 2017).

Box 1.1: Trade Volume Outlook for Asia

The strengthening global economy is expected to give a boost to the near-term outlook for global trade; trade volume is expected to grow 3.4% in 2017. In turn, steady growth in advanced economies—especially in the United States and euro area—will buoy external demand across Asia; trade volume growth will likely accelerate from 1.8% in 2016 to 4.4% in 2017, 1 percentage point above forecast global trade growth.

The People's Republic of China and middle-income ASEAN (Indonesia, Malaysia, the Philippines, and Thailand) will continue to drive the region's trade, while Asia's more export-reliant emerging economies (Hong Kong, China; the Republic of Korea; Singapore; and Taipei,China) will also receive a needed boost. In these economies, export will benefit from weakening local currencies and a mild rebound in commodity prices. Buoyant domestic demand—especially from resilient private consumption and sustained public and private investment—will also support import growth.

Trade Volume Growth (%, year-on-year)

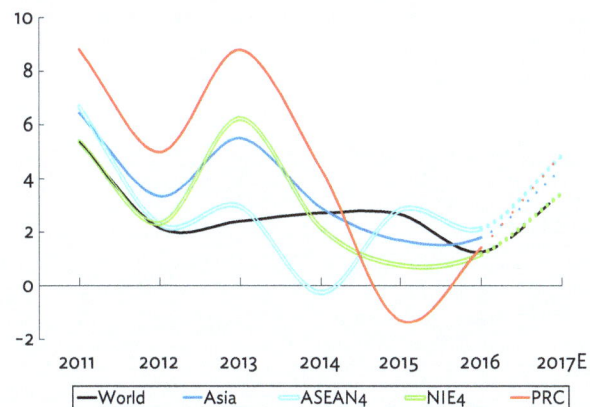

ASEAN = Association of Southeast Asian Nations, E = estimate, NIE4 = newly industrialized economies, PRC = People's Republic of China.
Notes: ASEAN4 includes Indonesia, Malaysia, the Philippines, and Thailand. The NIE4 include Hong Kong, China; the Republic of Korea; Singapore; and Taipei,China. Asia covers ADB's 45 developing member economies plus Australia, Japan, and New Zealand. Trade volume growth estimates are calculated using estimated trade volume growth of all Asian economies, which were generated using each economy's elasticities-to-real gross domestic product (GDP) (for imports) and elasticities-to-real GDP of top trading partners (for exports).
Sources: ADB calculations using data from International Monetary Fund. World Economic Outlook April 2017 database. https://www.imf.org/external/pubs/ft/weo/2017/01/weodata/index.aspx (accessed October 2017); International Monetary Fund. Direction of Trade Database. https://www.imf.org/en/Data (accessed July 2017); and World Trade Organization Statistics database. http://stat.wto.org (accessed May 2017).

Figure 1.5: Foreign Holdings of Equity and Bonds, as of end 2016—Developing Asia (% of GDP)

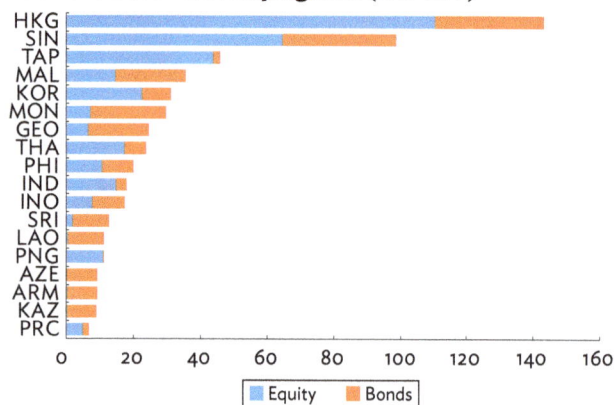

ARM = Armenia; AZE = Azerbaijan; GEO = Georgia; GDP = gross domestic product; HKG = Hong Kong, China; IND = India; INO = Indonesia; KAZ = Kazakhstan; KOR = Republic of Korea; LAO = Lao People's Democratic Republic; MAL = Malaysia; MON = Mongolia; PHI = Philippines; PNG = Papua New Guinea; PRC = People's Republic of China; SIN = Singapore; SRI = Sri Lanka; THA = Thailand; VIE = Viet Nam; TAP = Taipei,China.
Source: ADB calculations using data from International Monetary Fund. Coordinated Portfolio Investment Survey. http://cpis.imf.org (accessed September 2017).

capital outflows (Figure 1.5). Many economies in the region continue to rely on foreign borrowing and foreign investment in their financial assets. This reflects the increasing integration of regional financial markets with global markets—increasing the impact and influence of global investor sentiment and asset price movements on the region's financial markets.

There are also other transmission channels, such as commodity prices—which could transmit terms-of-trade shocks to Asia's resource-dependent economies. Similarly, changes in the US monetary policy and exchange rate movements could also transmit some second-round price and wealth effects on trade and global financial asset positions.

Emerging Vulnerabilities

Despite strong resilience against a weak external environment, vulnerabilities in Asia's financial systems should not be underestimated. Generally, the region's policy makers have remained prudent in managing their economies—as seen in much-improved financial and external vulnerability indicators since 2006. However, some financial vulnerabilities linger and policy space could contract further should external conditions worsen.

While banking systems in the region remain healthy, high leverage and credit growth could increase some economies' vulnerability to tightening global financial conditions.

Certain financial vulnerability indicators suggest that loose global monetary policy has fueled excessive credit growth in Asia over the past 10 years. This is evident from high and rising bank loan-to-deposit ratios and foreign liabilities-to-foreign assets ratios in several Asian economies (Figures 1.6 and 1.7). In particular, loan-to-deposit ratios in Cambodia, the Republic of Korea, Indonesia, the PRC, Malaysia, Singapore, Thailand, and Viet Nam remain above 80% with loan-to-deposit ratios rising for most economies (colored red) since 2006. Similarly, foreign liabilities-to-foreign assets ratios in Cambodia, Indonesia, the Republic of Korea, Malaysia, Singapore, and Thailand are also above 80%. The loan-to-deposit ratio is a measure of liquidity, and the concern is that a high ratio could imply that a country could run out of liquidity to cover unforeseen funding requirements. On the other hand, Asia's experience tends to suggest that financial crises are often preceded by a buildup of foreign liabilities in the banking sector—used to fund domestic lending—thereby contributing to currency and maturity mismatches.

Figure 1.6: Loan-to-Deposit Ratio—Developing Asia (%)

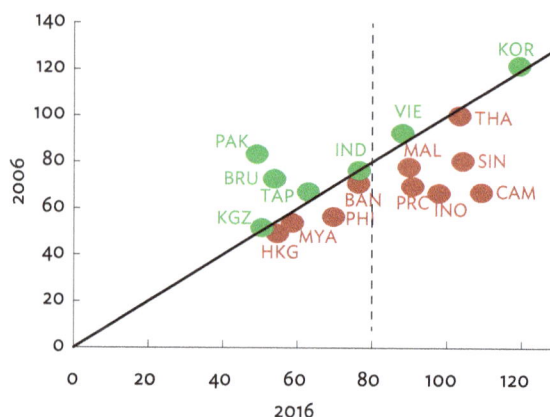

BAN = Bangladesh; BRU = Brunei Darussalam; CAM = Cambodia; HKG = Hong Kong, China; IND = India; INO = Indonesia; KOR = Republic of Korea; KGZ = Kyrgyz Republic; MAL = Malaysia; MYA = Myanmar; PAK = Pakistan; PHI = Philippines; PRC = People's Republic of China; SIN = Singapore; TAP = Taipei,China; THA = Thailand; VIE = Viet Nam.
Sources: ADB calculations using data from CEIC; and International Monetary Fund. International Financial Statistics. http://www.imf.org/en/Data (both accessed August 2017).

Figure 1.7: Foreign Liabilities-to-Foreign Assets Ratio —Developing Asia (%)

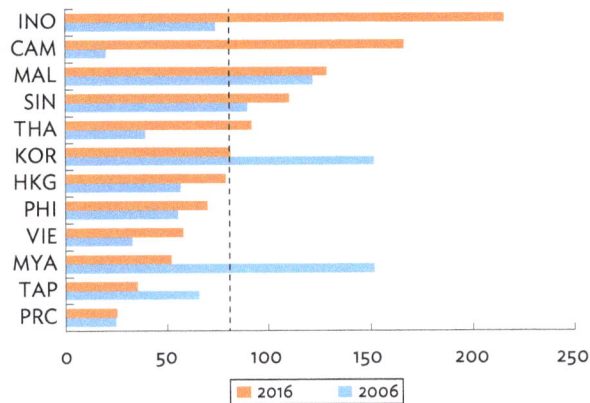

CAM = Cambodia; HKG = Hong Kong, China; INO = Indonesia; KOR = Republic of Korea; MAL = Malaysia; MYA = Myanmar; PHI = Philippines; PRC = People's Republic of China; SIN = Singapore; TAP = Taipei,China; THA = Thailand; VIE = Viet Nam.
Source: ADB calculations using data from CEIC; and International Monetary Fund. International Financial Statistics. http://www.imf.org/en/Data (both accessed August 2017).

The growing share of credit to private nonfinancial institutions and the proliferation of new risk instruments are potential risks.

In many economies, lending to private nonfinancial institutions has been increasing (Figure 1.8). Lending to private nonfinancial institutions have increased since the GFC, particularly in the PRC; Hong Kong, China; the Republic of Korea; Singapore; and the ASEAN4. More so, comparing credit extended to private nonfinancial institutions with historical trends, shows that recent credit-to-GDP ratios exceeded their long-term trend by about 10–30 percentage points, with credit to the private nonfinancial sector at 300% of GDP in Hong Kong, China; more than 200% in the PRC; and close to 190% in the Republic of Korea and Singapore.

Dependence on external funding is also a concern for the region.

External funding conditions remain broadly stable. However, with the expected increase in the US Federal Funds rate, external funding costs will likely increase and lead to heightened financial volatility. Depending on the pace of the hikes, this could affect domestic credit conditions and ultimately slow economic growth if domestic borrowing costs rise, bank lending volumes fall and asset prices drop.

Figure 1.8: Credit to Private Nonfinancial Sector— Selected Developing Asian Economies

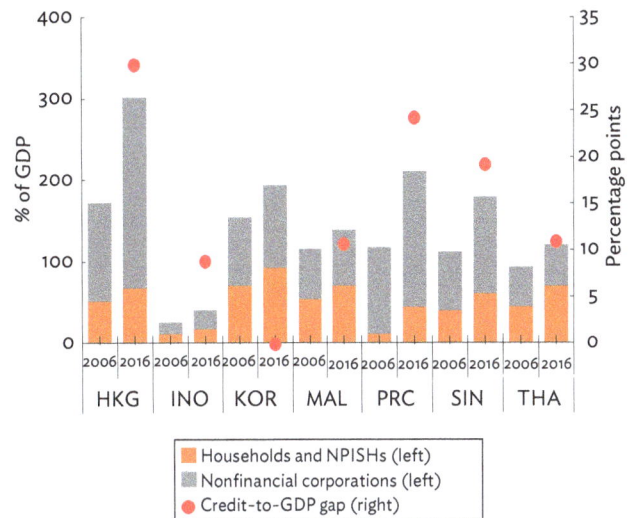

HKG = Hong Kong, China; GDP = gross domestic product; INO = Indonesia; KOR = Republic of Korea; MAL = Malaysia; NPISHs = nonprofit institutions serving households; PRC = People's Republic of China; SIN = Singapore; THA = Thailand.
Notes: Data is based on market values and refer to the total outstanding credit provided by domestic banks, other economic sectors, and nonresidents. The credit-to-GDP gap is defined as the difference between the credit-to-GDP ratio and its long-run trend.
Source: Bank for International Settlements. https://www.bis.org/ (accessed September 2017).

The concern is over the degree of an economy's dependence on short-term flows of external funds placed through stocks, bonds, overseas borrowing, and its current account deficit. Generally, an economy's exposure to short-term external funding could affect its ability to meet external obligations—through either liquidity or solvency problems—in turn affecting its exchange rates and introducing further uncertainty and financial volatility. This can be seen by plotting a country's external vulnerability—measured by the sum of its current account deficit, short-term external debt, and foreign holdings of equity and bond securities as a percent of gross international reserves—against 2016 currency movements (Figure 1.9). It is clear that economies with higher dependence on short-term external funds tend to experience larger currency depreciations. However, other idiosyncratic country-specific factors can also contribute to a country's currency fluctuations.

Another concern involves capital flows, which have started to reverse as the US begins to normalize its monetary policy stance.

Studies have shown that monetary policy in advanced economies influence financial flows to Asia. For instance,

Figure 1.9: External Vulnerability versus Currency Movement, 2016—Selected Developing Asian Economies

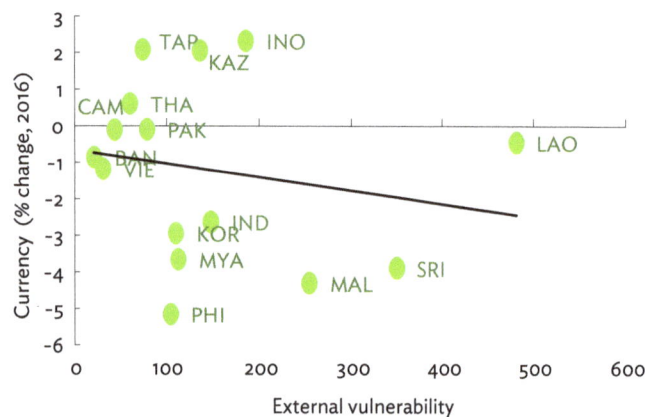

BAN = Bangladesh; CAM = Cambodia; IND = India; INO = Indonesia; KAZ = Kazakhstan; KOR = Republic of Korea; LAO = Lao People's Democratic Republic; MAL = Malaysia; MYA = Myanmar; PAK = Pakistan; PHI = Philippines; SRI = Sri Lanka; TAP = Taipei,China; THA = Thailand; VIE = Viet Nam.
Notes: External vulnerability ratio is derived by dividing the sum of current account deficit, short-term debt, and foreign holdings of stocks and bonds by gross international reserves (excluding gold). Currency movement is the percentage change in the $ value of local currency. Negative values indicate depreciation of local currency, and positive values indicate appreciation.
Sources: ADB calculations using data from Bloomberg; International Monetary Fund. Coordinated Portfolio Investment Survey. http//cpis.imf.org; and World Bank. World Development Indicators. http://databank.worldbank.org/ (all accessed July 2017).

Figure 1.10: Net Financial Flows—Developing Asia ($ billion)

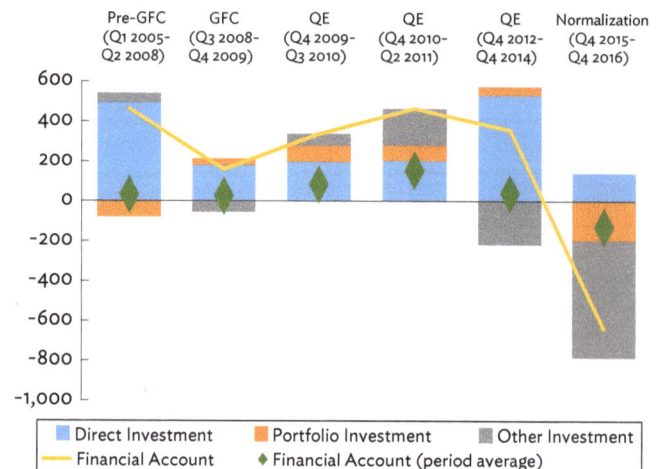

GFC = global financial crisis, QE = quantitative easing, Q = quarter.
Notes:
(i) There was a break in data comparability for the Philippines (2005), India (2009), Brunei Darussalam (2010), and Malaysia (2010). For Malaysia, "other investment" was discounted in the assets and liabilities breakdown.
(ii) For consistency, net of "other investment" corresponds to resident inflows for Malaysia starting 2010.
(iii) In the Lao People's Democratic Republic, net of direct, portfolio, and other investments correspond to "nonresident inflows" direct, portfolio, and other investments starting 2014.
(iv) Developing Asia includes ASEAN (Brunei Darussalam, Cambodia, Indonesia, the Lao People's Democratic Republic, Malaysia, Myanmar, the Philippines, Singapore, Thailand, and Viet Nam), NIE4 (Hong Kong, China; the Republic of Korea; Singapore; and Taipei,China), India, and the People's Republic of China. Excludes Cambodia starting Q1 2015; Brunei Darussalam, Myanmar, and Viet Nam for Q1 2016.
Source: ADB calculations using data from International Monetary Fund. Balance of Payments Statistics. http://www.imf.org/external/datamapper/datasets/BOP (accessed July 2017).

an ADB study by Park et al. (2014) observed that the US quantitative easing (QE) had a significant impact on capital flows to Asian developing economies. Examining flows before and after periods of QE in the US found that while total flows were comparable, their composition changed—direct financing through capital markets partly replaced bank financing. When the individual impact of the three rounds of QE were examined, only the impact of the first was significant. Global risk variables and emerging stock market returns were also significant drivers (Cho and Rhee 2013, Koepke 2016, Morgan 2011, Park et al. 2014, and Sarno et al. 2016).

In step with these findings, the region's cumulative and average net financial flows were compared pre-GFC, post-GFC, and during the normalization period (Figure 1.10). There are indications that changes in global monetary policy—as captured by expected movement in the US Federal Funds rate—affect financial inflows in the region. While developing Asia received average net financial inflows of $33 billion per quarter during the pre-GFC period, they fell to $27 billion per quarter during the GFC, suggesting only modest GFC impact on the region. However, net financial inflows to the region increased significantly during QE—peaking at $155 billion per quarter during the second QE period. As expected,

net financial flows reversed, averaging $128 billion in outflows per quarter during normalization. It is also notable that the primary source of financial outflows in the region was from other investment, which includes bank lending.

Coping Mechanisms

Countercyclical macroeconomic policies can help support domestic demand in times of economic crisis.

At the height of the GFC, many governments in the region used countercyclical policy measures—such as expansionary monetary policy and fiscal stimulus—to support domestic demand and counter weakening external demand from advanced economies. These fiscal and monetary interventions helped the region weather

**Figure 1.11: Policy Rate, 2016 versus 2006—
Developing Asia** (% per annum)

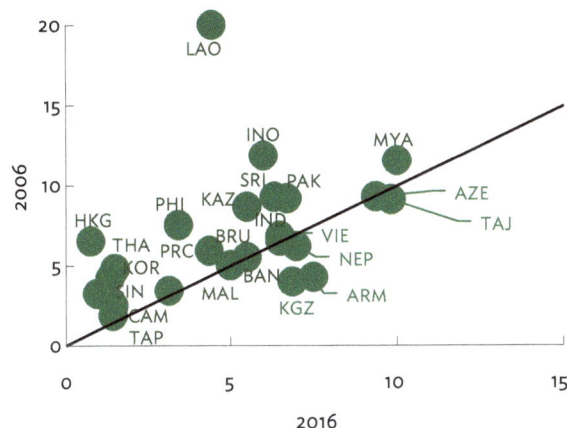

ARM = Armenia; AZE = Azerbaijan; BAN = Bangladesh; BRU = Brunei
Darussalam; CAM = Cambodia; HKG = Hong Kong, China; IND = India;
INO = Indonesia; KAZ = Kazakhstan; KOR = Republic of Korea;
KGZ = Kyrgyz Republic; LAO = Lao People's Democratic Republic;
MAL = Malaysia; MYA = Myanmar; NEP = Nepal; PAK = Pakistan;
PHI = Philippines; PRC = People's Republic of China; SIN = Singapore;
SRI = Sri Lanka; TAJ = Tajikistan; TAP = Taipei,China; THA = Thailand;
VIE = Viet Nam.
Sources: Bloomberg and CEIC (both accessed July 2017).

the GFC largely unscathed. Therefore, it is important to have adequate policy space in preparing for future crises.

Easy monetary policy provided important support to domestic demand and economic growth during the post-GFC recovery. However, against rising US interest rates, is not easy to maintain low interest rates—as widening interest rate differentials between the US and domestic markets would set off further capital outflows. Higher US interest rates could also transmit across the region, thereby increasing capital costs, raising debt servicing, and weakening investment and growth prospects. Trend analysis suggests that—except for Cambodia; Hong Kong, China; the Republic of Korea; Singapore; Taipei,China; and Thailand (where rates are already very low)—Asia's economies have ample room to maintain accommodative monetary policy and/or cut rates if global shocks affect domestic demand (Figure 1.11). However, economies in the region should also weigh the benefit of domestic policy rate

adjustments—based on the US Federal Fund rate movements—to support their growth prospects.

Building sufficient fiscal space is central to maintaining macroeconomic stability and coping with potential external shocks.

Maintaining fiscal soundness and intensifying fiscal consolidation efforts could help create fiscal buffers against future shocks. However, fiscal balances in 25 out of 40 developing Asian economies—mostly coming from the Pacific and Central Asia—have deteriorated compared with pre-crisis levels (Figure 1.12a). Some Central Asian economies, Malaysia, the PRC, Singapore, and Viet Nam have also accumulated additional public debt (ranging from 15%-20% of GDP) over the past decade to 2016 (Figure 1.12b). This means that the region has more limited fiscal space to maneuver should another demand shock emerge in the future.

Adequate reserves can also provide an economy a much-needed cushion in case of sharp swings in external demand and financial conditions.

The region's large holdings of international reserves provided effective cushion against the financial turmoil during the GFC. Ample international reserves raise confidence that an economy can cover imports and debt service even during periods of dollar illiquidity. Reserves are also useful when financial volatility triggers regional contagion through sharp currency devaluations. Asian economies have accumulated foreign exchange reserves well beyond the levels required for precautionary or self-protection reasons since the Asian financial crisis. The trend continues and the region has secured adequate levels of reserves relative to GDP and imports requirements (Figures 1.13a and 1.13b).

Figure 1.12: Change in Fiscal Indicators, 2016 versus 2006—Developing Asia (percentage point)

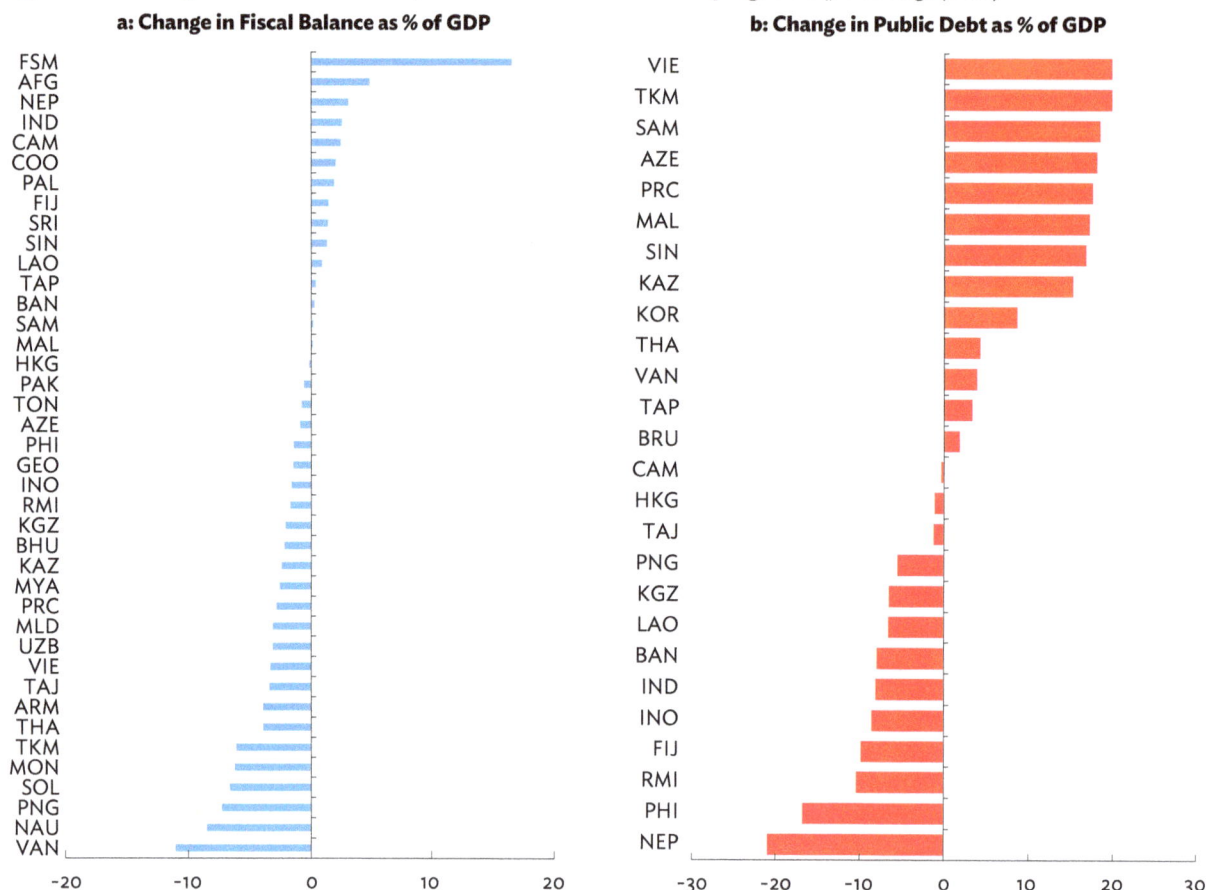

a: Change in Fiscal Balance as % of GDP

b: Change in Public Debt as % of GDP

AFG = Afghanistan; ARM = Armenia; AZE = Azerbaijan; BAN = Bangladesh; BHU = Bhutan; BRU = Brunei Darussalam; CAM = Cambodia; COO = Cook Islands; FIJ = Fiji; FSM = Federated States of Micronesia; GDP = gross domestic product; GEO = Georgia; HKG = Hong Kong, China; IND = India; INO = Indonesia; KAZ = Kazakhstan; KOR = Republic of Korea; KGZ = Kyrgyz Republic; LAO = Lao People's Democratic Republic; MAL = Malaysia; MLD = Maldives; MON = Mongolia; MYA = Myanmar; NAU = Nauru; NEP = Nepal; PAK = Pakistan; PAL = Palau, PHI = Philippines; PNG = Papua New Guinea; PRC = People's Republic of China; RMI = Marshall Islands; SAM = Samoa; SIN = Singapore; SOL = Solomon Islands; SRI = Sri Lanka; TAJ = Tajikistan; TAP = Taipei,China; THA = Thailand; TKM = Turkmenistan; UZB = Uzbekistan; VAN = Vanuatu; VIE = Viet Nam.
Sources: ADB calculations using data from CEIC; and International Monetary Fund. International Financial Statistics. www.imf.org/en/Data (both accessed August 2017).

Figure 1.13: Gross International Reserves—Developing Asia

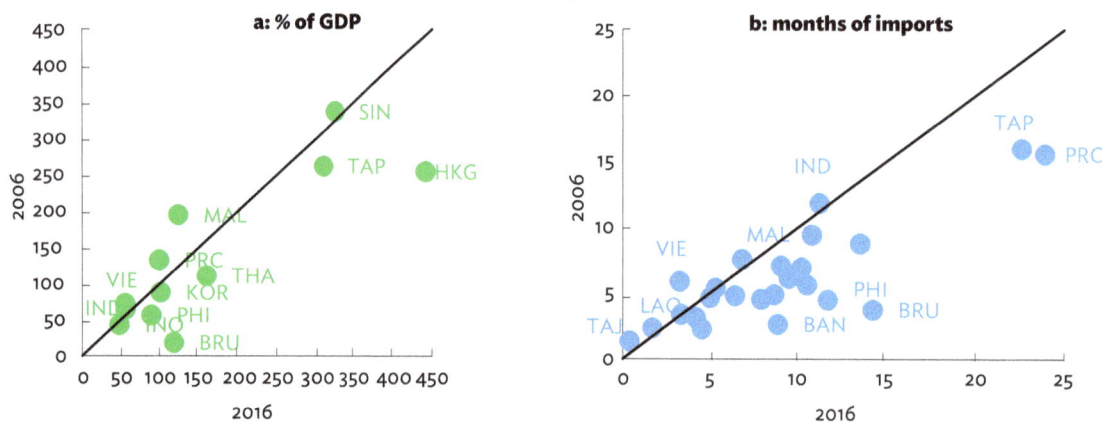

a: % of GDP

b: months of imports

BAN =Bangladesh; BRU = Brunei Darussalam; GDP = gross domestic product; HKG = Hong Kong, China; IND = India; INO = Indonesia; KOR = Republic of Korea; LAO = Lao People's Democratic Republic; MAL = Malaysia; PHI = Philippines; PRC = People's Republic of China; SIN = Singapore; TAJ = Tajikistan; TAP = Taipei,China; THA = Thailand; VIE = Viet Nam.
Sources: ADB calculations using data from CEIC; and International Monetary Fund. International Financial Statistics. www.imf.org/en/Data (both accessed August 2017).

Concluding Remarks

While the economic outlook for developing Asia has improved and risks have become more balanced, policy makers must still address some important and lingering concerns.

The region remains vulnerable to global economic shocks as its business cycles have become increasingly synchronized with cycles in advanced economies. The regional economy has also become more sensitive to output shocks in the US, reflecting the significant role that final demand from this economy still plays in regional trade. High leverage and credit growth—particularly to private nonfinancial institutions—with a dependence on external funding, and potential capital flow reversals related to widening interest rate differentials are among the most pressing concerns.

Since the GFC, developing Asia has accumulated additional external borrowing equivalent to $3.4 trillion.[1] The fiscal space—measured as the sum of combined fiscal surpluses and deficits in the region—has also shrunk by $0.5 trillion. And while many regional economies still have ample room to follow accommodative monetary policies, ongoing US monetary policy normalization will make it more challenging for them to keep interest rates low without further undermining foreign capital inflows.

Asia's policy makers should continue to strengthen macroeconomic fundamentals and prepare for a prolonged weak recovery.

Against the backdrop of monetary policy normalization in advanced economies, maintaining sufficient international reserves and policy space should help cushion against potential shocks. Monetary policy must remain flexible to allow timely responses, while keeping inflationary expectations firmly anchored.

Macroeconomic policy support may need to be maintained and only gradually unwound in the face of the prolonged weak post-crisis recovery. In particular,

and wherever possible, fiscal buffers could be built up and stand ready for use to mitigate the impact of external shocks. While extreme financial volatility requires careful monitoring of capital flows, excessive exchange rate intervention could lead to drawdowns in foreign reserves, which would further weaken investor confidence.

The region must also monitor any buildup of economic imbalances, while pursuing necessary long-term reforms.

Short-term responses can help stabilize financial volatility and lift market confidence. But the region's policy makers need to deepen reforms to strengthen economic and financial resilience and upgrade regulatory and supervisory frameworks to ensure vulnerabilities are addressed.

Broader and deeper structural reforms will be needed to raise productivity, competitiveness, and economic growth. Asian economies can also explore ways to spur new growth drivers by improving policies that support trade, such as the promotion of foreign direct investment and innovation. An ADB study has noted the importance of policies that offer competitive labor costs, an efficient and reliable business environment, and strong linkages of global value chain with the domestic market through foreign direct investment. Linkages with domestic markets in particular can be better served by helping small and medium enterprises gain greater access to finance, and through supportive institutional mechanisms (ADB 2016).

References

ADB. 2016. *Asian Economic Integration Report 2016: What Drives Foreign Direct Investment in Asia and the Pacific?* Manila.

_____. 2017. *Asian Development Outlook 2017 Update: Sustaining Development Through Public-Private Partnership.* Manila.

Bank for International Settlements. https://www.bis.org/ (accessed September 2017).

D. Cho and C. Rhee. 2013. Effects of Quantitative Easing on Asia: Capital Flows and Financial Markets. *ADB Economics Working Papers.* No. 350. Manila: Asian Development Bank.

---

[1] Based on available data for developing Asian economies: Bangladesh; Fiji; Hong Kong, China; India; Indonesia; Kazakhstan; Malaysia; Pakistan; Papua New Guinea; the Philippines; the PRC; the Republic of Korea; Singapore; Sri Lanka; Taipei,China; and Thailand.

International Monetary Fund. Balance of Payments Statistics. http://www.imf.org/external/datamapper/datasets/BOP (accessed July 2017).

R. Koepke. 2016. Fed Policy Expectations and Portfolio Flows to Emerging Markets. *IIF Working Paper.* Washington, DC: Institute of International Finance.

P. Morgan. 2011. Impact of US Quantitative Easing Policy on Emerging Asia. *ADBI Working Paper.* No. 321. Tokyo: Asian Development Bank Institute.

D. Park, A. Ramayandi, and K. Shin. 2014. Capital Flows During Quantitative Easing and Aftermath: Experiences of Asian Countries. *ADB Economics Working Papers.* No. 409. Manila: Asian Development Bank.

C.Y. Park. 2017. Decoupling Asia Revisited. *ADB Economics Working Paper Series.* No. 506. Manila: Asian Development Bank.

L. Sarno, I. Tsiakas, and B. Ulloa. 2016. What Drives International Portfolio Flows? *Journal of International Money and Finance.* 60(C). pp. 53–72.

02

Trade and the Global Value Chain

Trade and the Global Value Chain

Recent Trends in Asia's Trade

In 2016, Asia's trade volume grew faster than global trade, but remained below growth in gross domestic product.

By volume, Asia was the only region in the world that saw trade grow faster in 2016 than 2015. Asia's trade volume grew 1.7% in 2016, up from 1.4% in 2015—as growth globally fell to 1.3% from 2.6% in 2015. Trade volume contracted in the Middle East (–6.4%), Latin America (–4.4%), and Africa (–3.7%), while it grew more slowly than 2015 in the European Union (EU) and North America. Asia's exports rose 1.5% in 2016 (1.0% in 2015), while imports increased slightly to 2.0% (from 1.9%). Since 2012, growth in merchandise trade volume has been below growth in gross domestic product (GDP) (Figures 2.1a, 2.1b).

Asia's trade volume growth in 2016 was largely driven by exports from Japan; Taipei,China; and Hong Kong, China; and a rebound in imports in the People's Republic of China.

Excluding the People's Republic of China (PRC), Asia's export volume growth rose to 2.3% in 2016 from 1.9% in 2015—covering almost half of Asia's overall trade growth by volume (Figure 2.2). Japan; Taipei,China; and

Figure 2.2: Sources of Asia's Trade Volume Growth

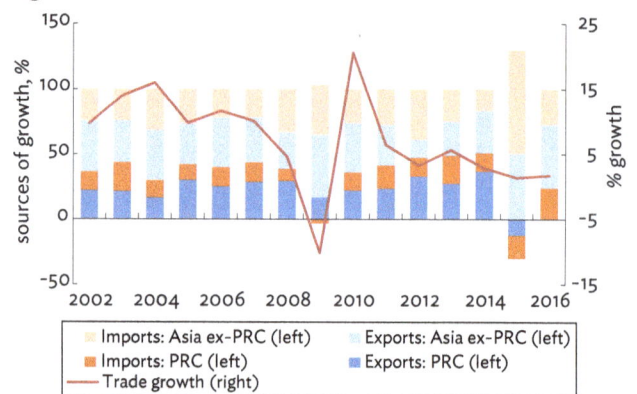

PRC = People's Republic of China.
Source: ADB calculations using data from World Trade Organization Statistics. http://stat.wto.org (accessed May 2017).

Figure 2.1: Merchandise Trade Volume and Real GDP Growth—Asia and World (%, year-on-year)

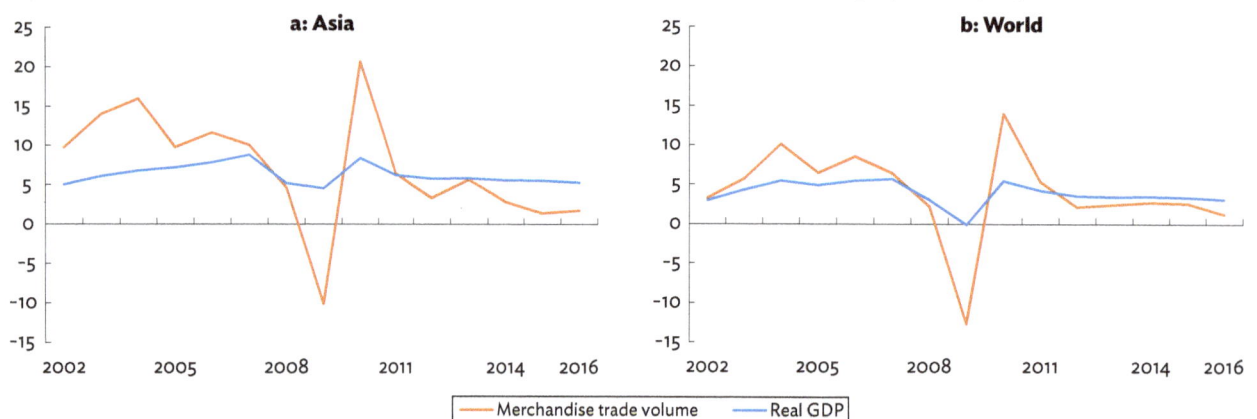

GDP = gross domestic product.
Note: Real GDP growth is weighted using nominal GDP in purchasing power parity.
Sources: ADB calculations using data from International Monetary Fund. World Economic Outlook April 2017 Database. https://www.imf.org/external/pubs/ft/weo/2017/01/weodata/index.aspx; World Trade Organization Statistics. http://stat.wto.org (both accessed May 2017).

Hong Kong, China accounted for much of the increase. While PRC export volume was flat in 2016, growth in import volume rebounded to 3.1%, following a 1.8% drop in 2015—PRC imports accounted for about 24% of Asia's total trade volume growth.

By value, Asia's overall trade continued to shrink in 2016, but at a slower pace than 2015.

Asia's trade by value fell 3.4% in 2016, much less than the sharp 10.2% decline in 2015 (Figure 2.3). Exports contracted 4% in 2016, above the 2.7% drop in imports. World trade growth showed similar trends.

Figure 2.3: Trade Value—Asia and World

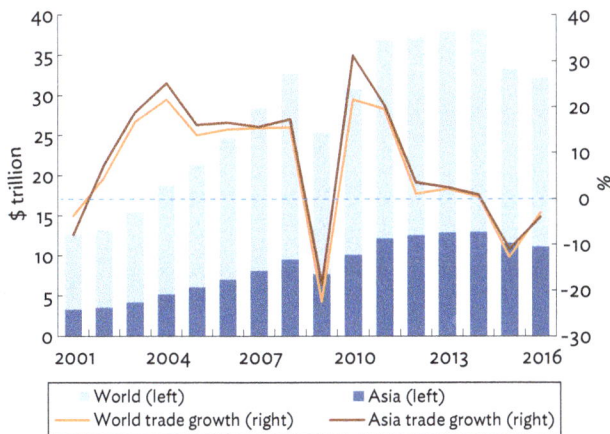

Source: ADB calculations using data from World Trade Organization Statistics. http://stat.wto.org (accessed May 2017).

More recent data point to a continued recovery in Asia's trade.

Gradually increasing global economic growth has allowed Asia's trade to continue its recent growth momentum. For most of 2015 and into 2016, Asia's trade volume growth stagnated or declined, falling below global trade growth (Figure 2.4). Beginning March 2016, growth returned and has been rising steadily. The ongoing global economic recovery lifted demand for the region's exports, particularly in Hong Kong, China; Japan; Taipei,China; and Viet Nam. The region's import growth has also accelerated recently due to robust demand from the PRC and India, among others. The region's trade recovery accelerated further in 2017—with average trade volume growth reaching 7.5% in the first 7 months. Asia's imports grew 9.3% in the same period, helping propel regional and global trade. Exports rose 5.7%.

As global commodity prices began to rebound, Asia's trade growth by value has also been rising, surpassing trade volume growth beginning December 2016. Along with the recovery of external demand and strong domestic demand, growth rose to a record 17.1% in February 2017—it has remained at 13% on average since. Asia's trade growth will likely continue to gain momentum as global (and regional) economic growth gathers pace. However, potential bilateral trade friction and policy uncertainties among the world's major trading partners remain downside risks.

Figure 2.4: Asia's Monthly Trade by Value and Volume

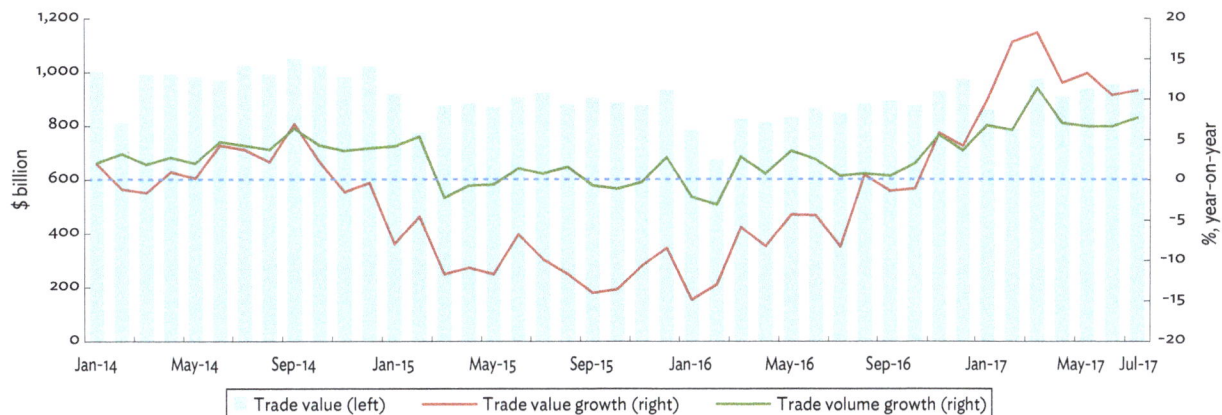

Notes: Trade volume growth rates were computed using volume indexes. For every period and trade flow type (i.e. imports and exports), the available data includes only an index for Japan and an aggregate index for selected Asian economies, which include the People's Republic of China; Hong Kong, China; India; Indonesia; the Republic of Korea; Malaysia; Pakistan; the Philippines; Singapore; Taipei,China; Thailand; and Viet Nam. To come up with an index for Asia, trade values were used as weights for the computations. On the other hand, trade value levels and growth rates were computed by aggregating import and export values of the same Asian economies.
Sources: ADB calculations using data from CEIC; and CPB Netherlands Bureau for Economic Policy Analysis. World Trade Monitor. https://www.cpb.nl/en/data (both accessed September 2017).

Asia's Intraregional Trade

Asia's intraregional trade share continued to grow in 2016.

Measured by value, Asia's intraregional trade share rose to 57.3% in 2016 from 56.9% in 2015, above the 55.9% average during 2010–2015 (Figure 2.5). By comparison, intraregional trade shares in the EU and North America is 64% and 41%, respectively. The increase in Asia's intraregional trade share points to the resilience of the intraregional trade linkage amidst falling global trade (extraregional trade fell 4.2% in 2016 against a 2.8% intraregional contraction) (Figure 2.6). Asia's strong intraregional trade should provide a buffer against potential headwinds emanating from global policy uncertainties and a worsening global trade environment.

Intra-subregional trade remains strong, while trade across different subregions weakened— evidenced by gravity model estimations based on bilateral trade data.

Intraregional trade relations are analyzed for Asia and other subregional groupings therein. For subregions of Central Asia, East Asia, South Asia, and the Pacific and Oceania, intra-subregional trade rose in 2016 from 2015, Southeast Asia's fell (Figure 2.7).[2] Intra-subregional trade share in Southeast Asia is second highest in the region,

Figure 2.5: Intraregional Trade Share—Asia, European Union, North America (%)

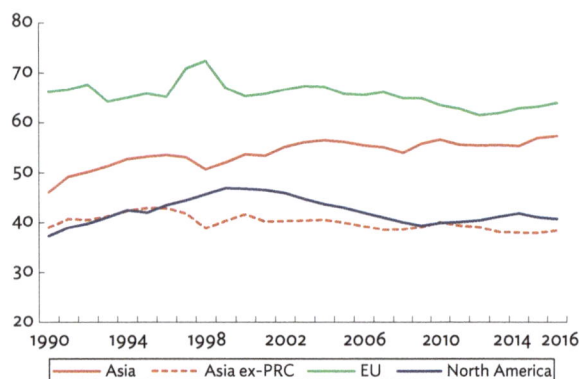

EU= European Union, PRC= People's Republic of China.
Notes: EU refers to aggregate of 28 EU members. North America covers Canada, Mexico, and the United States.
Source: ADB calculations using data from International Monetary Fund. Direction of Trade Statistics. https://www.imf.org/en/Data (accessed July 2017).

---

2   The Pacific and Oceania includes ADB Pacific developing member countries plus Australia and New Zealand.

Figure 2.6: Asia Trade Value Growth, Intraregional and Extraregional (%)

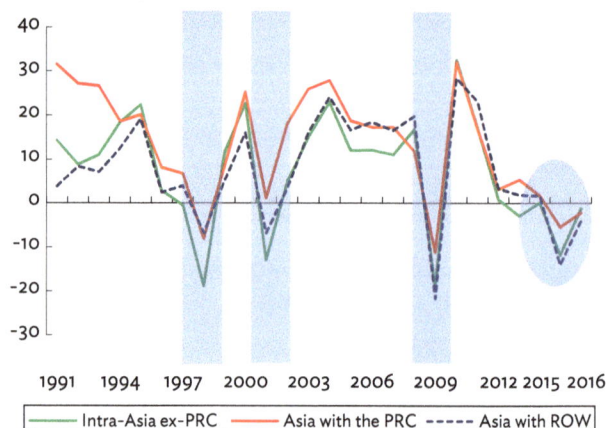

PRC = People's Republic of China, ROW = rest of the world.
Note: Shaded areas indicate 1997/98 Asian financial crisis, 2000/01 "dot.com" recession, 2008/09 global financial crisis, and ongoing global trade growth slowdown.
Source: ADB calculations using data from International Monetary Fund. Direction of Trade Statistics. https://www.imf.org/en/Data (accessed July 2017).

Figure 2.7: Asia Intra- and Inter-subregional Trade Shares (%)

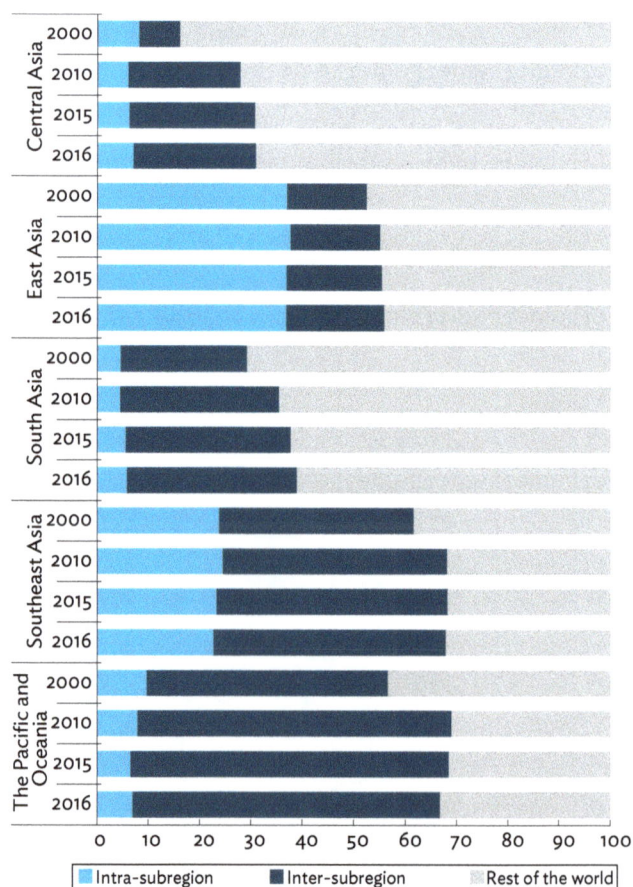

Source: ADB calculations using data from International Monetary Fund. Direction of Trade Statistics. https://www.imf.org/en/Data (accessed July 2017).

next to East Asia. The slight decline in Southeast Asia's intra-subregional trade share (from 23.3% to 22.8%) was mainly due to the rise in the share of the PRC and the Republic of Korea in the subregion's trade. The share of the United States (US) and EU also increased slightly. South Asia continued to have the lowest share, but not far behind Central Asia.

Inter-subregional trade shares—trade across subregions within Asia—increased in East Asia, South Asia, and Southeast Asia, but declined in Central Asia, and the

Pacific and Oceania. Nevertheless, the Pacific and Oceania continues to trade significantly more with other subregions in Asia than within itself—it has the highest inter-subregional trade share among Asian subregions (see Figure 2.7).

Gravity model estimation results based on data for 2012–2016 (the most recent period) show intraregional trade bias declined to 0.42 from 0.95 in 2011–2015 and became insignificant (Box 2.1).[3] The periods covered coincide with those when Asia and global trade growth

Box 2.1: Gravity Model Estimation of Bilateral Exports

Results of a gravity model estimation using annual data covering 2012–2016 and 2011–2015 are shown in box table 1. The 5-year rolling regression, updated annually, provides a snapshot of progress in regional trade integration. The coefficient of "both in Asia" dummy can be viewed as a trade integration index.

In terms of intra-subregional trade bias, East Asia continues to stand out, followed by Southeast Asia and Central Asia. South Asia continues to trade significantly more with other subregions within Asia, although its inter-subregional bias weakened slightly (box table 2). While Asia's intra-subregional

1: Gravity Model Estimation Results, 2012–2016
Dependent Variable: Log(Bilateral Exports)

Variables	All Goods	Capital Goods	Consumption Goods	Intermediate Goods
Log(distance)	-1.65***	-1.65***	-1.72***	-1.70***
	(0.02)	(0.02)	(0.02)	(0.02)
Colonial relationship dummy	0.85***	0.90***	0.94***	0.89***
	(0.09)	(0.09)	(0.10)	(0.10)
Common language dummy	0.98***	0.93***	1.06***	0.90***
	(0.04)	(0.04)	(0.04)	(0.04)
Contiguity dummy	1.04***	1.18***	1.27***	1.13***
	(0.10)	(0.10)	(0.10)	(0.11)
Regional dummies (base: Asia to ROW)				
Both in Asia dummy	0.42 [0.95***]	0.31 [0.43]	0.40 [0.72***]	-0.34* [0.11]
	(0.34)	(0.33)	(0.35)	(0.33)
Importer in Asia dummy	1.09*	-1.41**	1.44**	0.55
	(0.56)	(0.68)	(0.62)	(0.65)
Both in ROW dummy	0.32	-2.16***	0.50	0.50
	(0.41)	(0.54)	(0.46)	(0.53)
Rho (sample selection term)	0.10***	0.29***	0.18***	0.16***
Sample size	172,492	172,492	172,492	172,492
Censored observations	21,546	66,817	43,577	40,067
Uncensored observations	150,946	105,675	128,915	132,425

*** = significant at 1%, ** = significant at 5%, * = significant at 10%, ROW = rest of the world. Estimates for 2011–2015 are in brackets. Robust standard errors in parentheses.
Notes: Time-varying economy dummies are included but not shown for brevity. Heckman sample selection estimation was used to account for missing economy-pair data. Data cover 173 economies, of which 43 are from Asia. Trade data based on Broad Economic Categories.
Sources: ADB calculations using data from Institute for Research on the International Economy. http://www.cepii.fr/CEPII/en/cepii/cepii.asp (accessed May 2017); and United Nations. Commodity Trade Database. https://comtrade.un.org (accessed July 2017).

---

[3]   Intraregional trade bias refers to the coefficient of the intra-Asia dummy in the gravity model of bilateral export flows. A positive and significant coefficient means that Asia's trade with itself is higher than its trade with non-Asian economies.

Box 2.1 continued

bias remained high for both estimation periods (2012–2016 and 2011–2015) in all goods across most subregions, inter-subregional bias weakened. While this is partly due to the recent global trade growth slowdown—of which Asia has been

no exception—more work is called for to improve connectivity and trade facilitation across subregions, given the much weaker inter-subregional trade linkages compared with intra-subregional ones.

2: Gravity Model Estimation Results, 2012-2016: Intra- and Inter-subregional Trade (All Goods)

Variables	Central Asia	East Asia	South Asia	Southeast Asia	The Pacific and Oceania
Intra-subregional Trade Dummy	3.77***	6.37***	0.48	4.45***	1.02
	[3.65***]	[6.27***]	[1.01**]	[4.66***]	[0.43]
Inter-subregional Trade Dummy	-0.18	0.30	3.75***	0.40	-0.58
	[0.53]	[0.78***]	[3.92***]	[0.87***]	[-0.75]

*** = significant at 1%, ** = significant at 5%, * = significant at 10%. Estimates for 2011–2015 are in brackets.
Notes: Base category (benchmark) is the subregion's trade with economies outside Asia. The usual gravity model variables and time-varying economy dummies are included but not shown for brevity. Heckman sample selection estimation was used to account for missing bilateral economy-pair data. Data cover 173 economies, of which 43 are from Asia. Trade data based on Broad Economic Categories.
Sources: ADB calculations using data from Institute for Research on the International Economy. http://www.cepii.fr/CEPII/en/cepii/cepii.asp (accessed May 2017); and United Nations. Commodity Trade Database. https://comtrade.un.org (accessed July 2017).

slumped, falling below GDP growth. The overall trade growth slump could have led to no conspicuous regional trade bias after controlling for bilateral and time-variant economy-specific fixed effects.

Progress of Global and Regional Value Chains

Asia's value chain linkage with the global economy continued to slow in 2016.

The *Asian Economic Integration Report 2016* discussed how global and regional value chain expansion has been slowing. Asia's integration into global value chain (GVC) intensified early 2000s but stagnated after the 2008/09 global financial crisis. Asia's GVC participation—as measured by the share of value-added contents of gross exports used for further processing through cross-border production networks—indicated that Asia's GVC participation deepened early 2000s, rose further by 2011 but declined in 2015. The latest ADB Multi-Regional Input-Output Table data gives a sense of how

this trend is evolving recently.[4] As shown in Figure 2.8a, the domestic value-added portion of gross exports decreased from 2014 and 2015, while other components' shares grew—indicating some slight progress in deepening the GVC. This trend reversed in 2016, with the domestic value-added portion increasing and the shares of other components falling.

As a major contributor to international trade and the deepening GVC, Asia is no exception. Value-added decomposition of Asia's gross exports shows deepening integration into the GVC from 2014 to 2015, but reversed the direction between 2015 and 2016 (Figure 2.8b). Asia's GVC participation rate—hints at Asia's overall declining GVC participation in recent years. The GVC participation ratio decreased from 61.7% in 2014 to 61.3% in 2015 and 61.1% in 2016.[5]

---

[4] The 2014-2016 ADB Multi-Regional Input-Output Table covers 60 economies, with 24 from Asia (Australia; Bangladesh; Bhutan; Brunei Darussalam; Cambodia; Fiji; India; Indonesia; Japan; Kazakhstan; the Kyrgyz Republic; the Republic of Korea; the Lao People's Democratic Republic; Malaysia; Maldives; Mongolia; Nepal; Pakistan; the Philippines; the PRC; Sri Lanka; Taipei,China; Thailand; and Viet Nam).

[5] The GVC participation rate is measured by the share of value-added contents of gross exports used for further processing through cross-border production networks. It is computed as the ratio of GVC components of exports (gross exports less the sum of domestic value added in final goods exports and purely double-counted terms) to gross exports.

Figure 2.8: Components of Gross Exports (%)

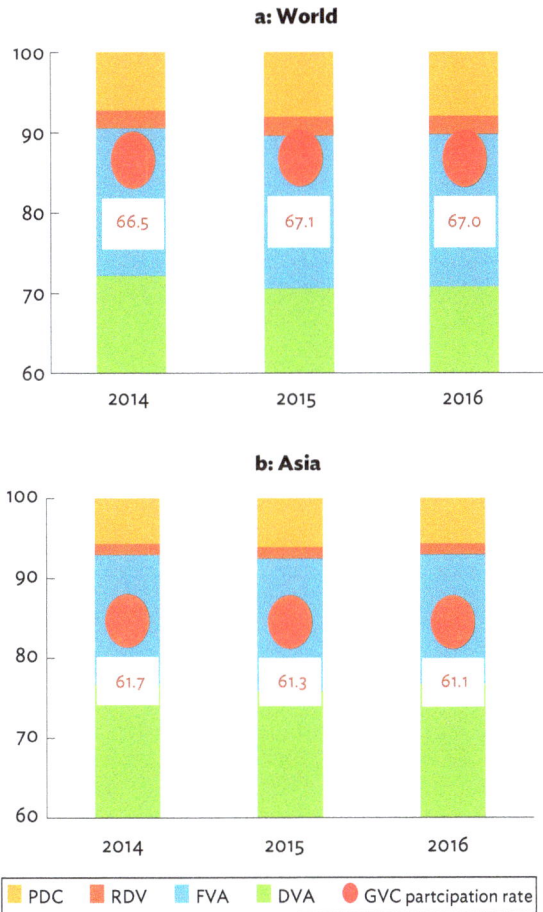

a: World

b: Asia

DVA = domestic value added, FVA = foreign value added, GVC = global value chain, PDC = purely double-counted terms, RDV = returned value added.
Sources: ADB calculations using 2014–2016 ADB Multi-Regional Input-Output Tables, and methodology by Wang, Wei, and Zhu (2014).

Updates on Regional Trade Policy

While the number of Asia's free trade agreements appears to be stagnating, Asia's FTAs with non-Asian partners are expected to increase. Efforts to deepen and upgrade existing FTAs are also actively under way.

Recently, the number of free trade agreements (FTAs) worldwide taking effect continued to decline (Figure 2.9). In 2016, 12 new FTAs entered into force. This year, four new FTAs entered into force (as of September). Three of last year's FTAs involved Asian economies: the Japan–Mongolia Economic Partnership

Figure 2.9: Number of Newly Effective FTAs— Asia and World

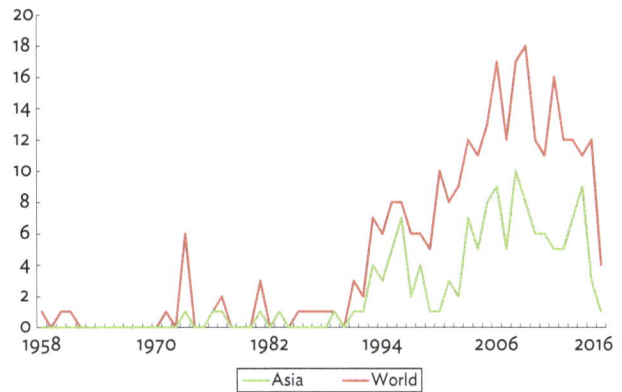

FTA = free trade agreement.
Source: World Trade Organization. Regional Trade Agreement Information System. http://rtias.wto.org (accessed September 2017).

Figure 2.10: Number of FTAs Proposed and Signed by Year—Asia

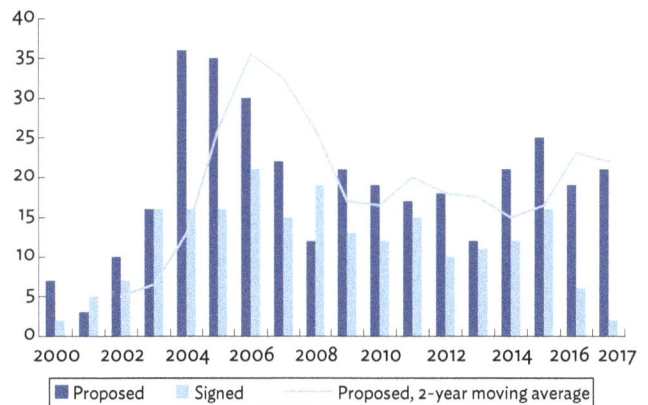

FTA = free trade agreement.
Notes: Includes bilateral and plurilateral FTAs with at least one of ADB's 48 regional members as signatory. 2017 covers FTAs that came into effect from January to July. "Signed" includes FTAs that are signed but not yet in effect, and those signed and in effect. "Proposed" includes FTAs that are: (i) proposed (the parties consider an FTA, governments or ministries issue a joint statement on the FTA's desirability, or establish a joint study group and joint task force to conduct feasibility studies); (ii) framework agreements signed and under negotiation (the parties, through ministries, negotiate the contents of a framework agreement that serves as a framework for future negotiations); and (iii) under negotiation (the parties, through ministries, declare the official launch of negotiations, or start the first round of negotiations).
Source: ADB. Asia Regional Integration Center FTA Database. https://aric.adb.org/fta (accessed August 2017).

Agreement (EPA), Korea–Colombia FTA, and the Eurasian Economic Union–Viet Nam FTA.

The number of signed FTAs has been declining since 2015 (Figure 2.10). In 2016, six were signed—down from 16 in 2015. Through July 2017, two FTAs were signed—the PRC–Georgia FTA on 13 May 2017 and the Pacific

Figure 2.11: Number of Signed FTAs— Asia
(cumulative since 1975)

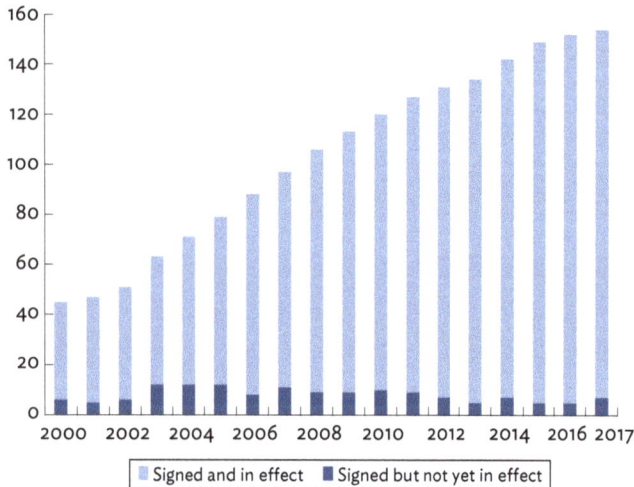

FTA = free trade agreement.
Notes: Includes bilateral and plurilateral FTAs with at least one of ADB's 48 regional members as signatory. 2017 covers FTAs that came into effect from January to July.
Source: ADB. Asia Regional Integration Center FTA Database. https://aric.adb.org/fta (accessed August 2017).

Figure 2.12: Number of Signed FTAs, Intraregional and Extraregional (cumulative since 2000)

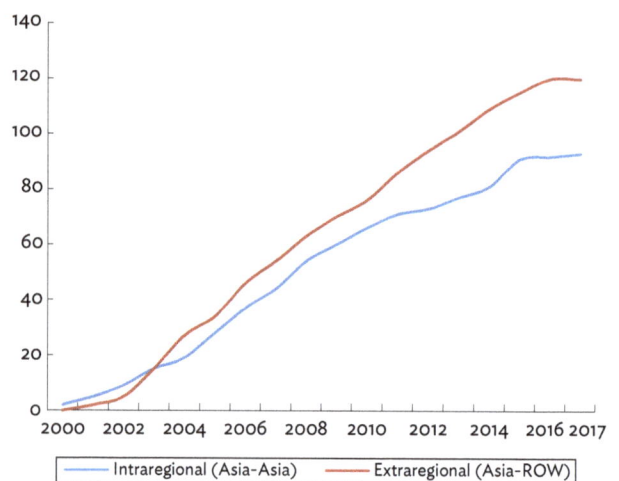

FTA = free trade agreement, ROW = rest of the world.
Notes: Includes bilateral and plurilateral FTAs with at least one of ADB's 48 regional members as signatory. 2017 covers FTAs that came into effect from January to July.
Source: ADB. Asia Regional Integration Center FTA Database. https://aric.adb.org/fta (accessed August 2017).

Agreement on Closer Economic Relations (PACER) Plus 10 on 14 June 2017.[6] Pakistan–Turkey FTA is expected to be signed on 14 August 2017. This brings the cumulative number of signed and in effect FTAs in Asia to 148 as of July 2017 (Figure 2.11).

Several other FTA negotiations in the region have moved forward. The Korea–Central America FTA concluded negotiations in November 2016. The Korea–Central America FTA concluded negotiations in November 2016. A significant milestone for the Association of Southeast Asian Nations (ASEAN) is the conclusion of trade talks with Hong Kong, China in July 2017 after 3 years of negotiations. The ASEAN–Hong Kong, China FTA is expected to be signed in November, which will be the first ASEAN FTA to be signed in nearly a decade. The PRC and Maldives launched FTA negotiations in December 2016, while the Australia–Hong Kong, China FTA; the Korea–Mercosur FTA; and Australia–New Zealand-Pacific Alliance FTA are some of the trade pacts

that launched negotiations this year.[7] A total of 17 new FTAs have been proposed from January to July 2017.

Two recent developments could affect Asia's FTA future landscape: (i) the rise in the number of FTAs with non-Asian partners and (ii) the upgrading or deepening of provisions of existing FTAs in Asia (Figure 2.12). FTAs with non-Asian partners underscore Asia's strong trade openness and its close links to GVCs. The trend is expected to continue—the majority of Asian FTAs starting negotiations in the last 5 years involve non-Asian partners (Ramizo 2017).

Several FTAs are being upgraded. The expanded India-Chile Preferential Trade Agreements with wider coverage of tariff lines under concession entered into force 16 May 2017. And the PRC is currently negotiating an upgraded FTA with four existing FTA partners—Pakistan, Singapore, New Zealand, and Chile. The PRC is also conducting feasibility studies on upgrading existing FTAs with Switzerland and Peru.

[6] PACER plus 10 includes Australia, the Cook Islands, the Federated States of Micronesia, Kiribati, Nauru, New Zealand, Niue, the Marshall Islands, Palau, Samoa, Solomon Islands, Tonga, Tuvalu, and Vanuatu.

[7] The Pacific Alliance FTA is composed of Chile, Colombia, Mexico, and Peru. Mercosur or *Mercado Comun del Sur* (Southern Common Market) is a subregional bloc composed of Argentina, Brazil, Paraguay, and Uruguay.

Trans-Pacific Partnership

The future of Trans-Pacific Partnership remains uncertain after the US' withdrawal.

While the US withdrew from the Trans-Pacific Partnership (TPP), Japan and New Zealand have ratified the Agreement.[8] Ministers of TPP member economies have released a statement 21 May 2017 expressing their agreement to "launch a process to assess options to bring the comprehensive, high quality agreement into force expeditiously, including how to facilitate membership for the original signatories."[9] It remains uncertain if the option of a TPP without the US will push through given the lack of unity among the remaining countries involved.

The US says it will now pursue trade growth through bilateral rather than multilateral arrangements (The White House Office of Press Secretary 2017). The renegotiation of the North American Free Trade Agreement began 16 August 2017. The US recently called for a special session of the joint committee for the Korea–US FTA.

Regional Cooperation Economic Partnership

Another "mega" trade deal, the Regional Cooperation Economic Partnership, is under negotiation.

The Regional Cooperation Economic Partnership (RCEP) would bind the 10 ASEAN members and the six economies that have existing FTAs with ASEAN. The Joint Media Statement released after the 5th RCEP Ministerial Meeting (held 10 September 2017 in the Philippines) further emphasized the importance of RCEP's conclusion, having been identified as a key

output for ASEAN's 50th anniversary this year. The ministers lauded the preparation of "RCEP Key Elements for Significant Outcomes by End of 2017" as agreed by the RCEP Trade Negotiating Committee. The document, which aims to move trade negotiations one step closer to conclusion, specifically identifies a set of "clear key elements" or negotiating areas that can be realistically achieved and lead to RCEP's substantial conclusion by year-end.[10]

Japan-European Union Economic Partnership Agreement

Japan-EU EPA negotiations are being finalized.

After 18 rounds of negotiations (which began in 2013), Japan and the EU reached a political agreement in principle 6 July 2017 on an EPA.[11] Japan and the EU together account for a third of global GDP. The EPA sends a strong signal to the rest of the world that the two remain committed to trade openness. The deal is known to substantially liberalize trade in goods. The EPA also covers key provisions on nontariff measures (like technical barriers to trade and sanitary and phytosanitary measures), trade remedies, trade in services, customs and trade facilitation, state-owned enterprises, government procurement, investment, data protection, intellectual property rights, competition, and small and medium enterprises. Although the agreement in principle includes key EPA provisions, some areas—such as investment protection, regulatory cooperation, and general and institutional chapters—will require further work. Negotiators say they plan to conclude the final text of the agreement by the end of 2017. Both sides will then proceed to legal verification and translation, with the final text submitted to their respective legislatures for approval.

---

[8]   For the TPP to come into force, it must be passed by members' legislatures and ratified within 2 years of the date of TPP signing (4 February 2016). If one or more members miss the ratification deadline, the TPP can survive if at least six original signatories—accounting for 85% of the region's 2013 GDP—complete ratification, preferably but not necessarily within 2 years. Failure by either Japan or the US to ratify the agreement, constituting slightly less than 80% of total GDP of all TPP members, would effectively block the agreement.

[9]   See TPP Ministerial Statement issued on 21 May 2017 (Australian Government, Department of Foreign Affairs and Trade 2017).

---

[10]   See *Xinhua* (2017) for details.

[11]   While the EPA agreement in principle does not conclude the negotiation process, it means both parties have agreed on generally everything of significance. As the final text of the EPA has not been released, the discussion of provisions should not be considered final (European Commission 2017).

Figure 2.13: Trade-related Measures in Asia

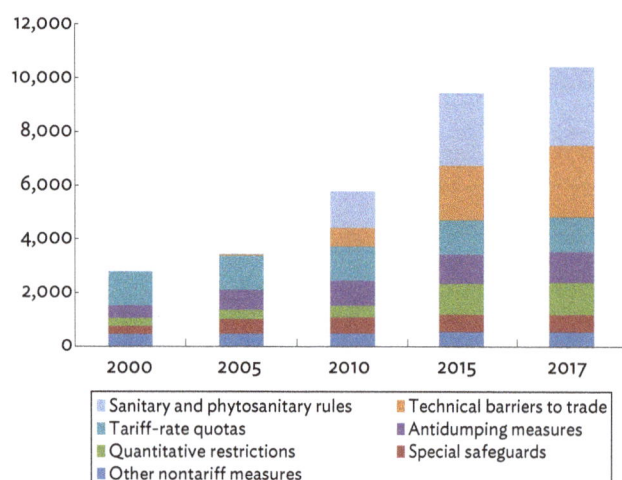

Note: Based on cumulative number of measures in force as of end of each year.
Source: ADB calculations using data from World Trade Organization. Integrated Trade Intelligence Portal. https://www.wto.org/english/res_e/statis_e/itip_e.htm (accessed September 2017).

Trade Remedies

While traditional tariff barriers have been significantly lowered, other types of tariff and nontariff measures are on the rise.

The trend of rapidly growing tariff and nontariff measures amid tepid international trade growth continued during 2017 (Figure 2.13). While increasing in number, not all nontariff measures are protectionist—some have valid socio-economic objectives. For example, the sanitary and phytosanitary measures aim to protect the safety of food for consumers and prevent or limit the spread of pests and outbreak of diseases among plants and animals.

Antidumping duties remain the most prevalent trade remedy used against Asia's exporters (Table 2.1).

Table 2.1: Trade Remedy Measures[a] and WTO Cases[b], 2010–2017

Measures	World Total	Asia[c] Total	Asia (Affected/Complainant)-ROW (Imposing/Respondent)	ROW (Affected/Complainant)-Asia (Imposing/Respondent)	Asia (Affected/Complainant)-Asia (Imposing/ Respondent)
Antidumping (Article VI of GATT 1994)					
Number of measures implemented	1,074	856	408	122	326
Number of cases	38 (3.5%)	28 (3.3%)	16	7	5
Countervailing Measures					
Number of measures implemented	104	87	70	7	10
Number of cases[d]	32 (30.8%)	21 (24.1%)	10	10	1
Safeguards[e]					
Number of measures implemented	78	49	29	49	49
Number of cases	13 (16.7%)	6 (12.2%)	3	0	3
Total					
Number of measures implemented	1,256	992	507	178	385
Number of cases	83 (6.6%)	55 (5.5%)	29	17	9

GATT = General Agreement on Tariffs and Trade, ROW = rest of the world, WTO = World Trade Organization.
Note: Numbers in parentheses are percentage share of cases to total measures implemented.
[a] Trade remedy measures are trade rules or policies implemented by an economy. In the table, trade remedies include measures which are in force.
[b] WTO cases are disputes on trade measures among WTO members that are brought before the WTO Dispute Settlement Body.
[c] Asia as implementing/affected region equals the number of global trade remedy measures minus ROW-ROW measures (not shown in table).
[d] Includes cases involving complaints on the grant of subsidies and countervailing measures.
[e] Safeguard measures are imposed on all WTO members; no bilateral data available.
Sources: ADB calculations using data from WTO. Integrated Trade Intelligence Portal. https://www.wto.org/english/res_e/statis_e/itip_e.htm; and WTO. Disputes by agreement. https://www.wto.org/english/tratop_e/dispu_e/dispu_agreements_index_e.htm (both accessed September 2017).

Table 2.2: Number of New Trade Remedy Measures Involving Asia

Year	a: Asia as Imposing Party				b: Asia as Affected Party			
	AD	CV	SG	Total	AD	CV	SG	Total
2010	59	3	1	63	99	13	5	117
2011	57	3	9	69	76	6	10	92
2012	62	2	3	67	79	10	6	95
2013	69	3	3	75	133	13	6	152
2014	61	2	11	74	104	7	18	129
2015	70	2	12	84	128	11	18	157
2016	70	2	4	76	115	20	6	141

AD = antidumping, CV = countervailing measures, SG = safeguards, WTO = World Trade Organization.
Notes: Trade remedy measures include measures which are in force. Safeguard measures are applied to all WTO members, hence the number of measures implemented include measures that are applied to all WTO members.
Source: ADB calculations using data from WTO. Integrated Trade Intelligence Portal. https://www.wto.org/english/res_e/statis_e/itip_e.htm (accessed September 2017).

Table 2.3: Number of Trade Remedy Measures Affecting Asia, 2010–2017—Top Affected Sectors

HS Product Description	Total	Antidumping Duties	Countervailing Duties	Safeguards
Base metals and articles	362	291	45	26
Products of the chemical and allied industries	161	143	10	8
Resins, plastics, and articles; rubber and articles	96	87	7	2
Machinery and electrical equipment	89	75	8	6

HS = harmonized system, WTO = World Trade Organization.
Notes: Trade remedy measures include measures which are in force. Safeguard measures are applied to all WTO members, hence the number of measures implemented include measures that are applied to all WTO members.
Source: ADB calculations using data from WTO. Integrated Trade Intelligence Portal. https://www.wto.org/english/res_e/statis_e/itip_e.htm (accessed September 2017).

The key objective of antidumping duty is to protect importing economies against predatory practices of exporting firms and uphold fair trade. The Agreement on Implementation of Article VI of World Trade Organization (WTO) General Agreement on Tariffs and Trade 1994 specifies that a WTO member may not impose an anti-dumping duty unless an investigation proves that dumping exists, which causes material injury to a domestic industry. Under the agreement, the basic requirement in establishing injury is an objective examination built on positive evidence of the volume and price effects of dumping and their subsequent impact on the domestic industry.

The number of antidumping measures imposed on Asia has steadily increased during 2010–2016 (Table 2.2). Base metals and chemicals are most targeted in the region (Table 2.3). The PRC; the Republic of Korea; and Taipei,China are most affected by trade remedies (Table 2.4).

Table 2.4: Number of Implemented Trade Remedy Measures, 2010–2017—Top Affected Asian Economies

Economy Affected	Number of Measures Implemented		
	ROW	Asia	Total
People's Republic of China	290	171	461
Republic of Korea	70	89	159
Taipei,China	66	85	151

ROW = rest of the world, WTO = World Trade Organization.
Note: Trade remedies include measures which are in force.
Source: ADB calculations using data from WTO. Integrated Trade Intelligence Portal. https://www.wto.org/english/res_e/statis_e/itip_e.htm (accessed September 2017).

References

ADB. Asia Regional Integration Center FTA Database. https://aric.adb.org/fta (accessed August 2017).

_____. 2014-2016 Multi-Regional Input-Output Tables.

_____. 2016 Asian Economic Integration Report 2016: What Drives Foreign Direct Investment in Asia and the Pacific? Manila.

Association of Southeast Asian Nations. 2017. *Fifth Regional Comprehensive Economic Partnership (RCEP) Ministerial Meeting Joint Media Statement.* 10 September. http://asean.org/storage/2017/09/RCEP-5MM-Final-JMS1.pdf

Australian Government, Department of Foreign Affairs and Trade. 2017. Trans-Pacific Partnership (TPP) Agreement Ministerial Statement. News Release. 21 May.

CPB Netherlands Bureau for Economic Policy Analysis. World Trade Monitor. https://www.cpb.nl/en/data (accessed September 2017).

European Commission. 2017. EU–Japan EPA: The Agreement in Principle. 6 July. http://trade.ec.europa.eu/doclib/docs/2017/july/tradoc_155693.doc.pdf

Institute for Research on the International Economy. http://www.cepii.fr/CEPII/en/cepii/cepii.asp (accessed May 2017)

International Monetary Fund. Direction of Trade Database. https://www.imf.org/en/Data (accessed July 2017).

———. World Economic Outlook April 2017 Database. https://www.imf.org/external/pubs/ft/weo/2017/01/weodata/index.aspx (accessed May 2017).

D. M. Ramizo. 2017. The Resurgence of Bilateralism and Asia's Evolving FTA Landscape. *Asian Regional Integration Center Blog.* https://aric.adb.org/blog/the-resurgence-of-bilateralism-and-asias-evolving-fta-landscape

The US White House Office of the Press Secretary. 2017. *Memorandum for the United States Trade Representative. Subject: Withdrawal of the United States from the Trans-Pacific Partnership Negotiations and Agreement.* https://aric.adb.org/pdf/Withdrawal%20of%20the%20United%20States%20from%20the%20TPP%20Negotiations.pdf

United Nations. Commodity Trade Database. https://comtrade.un.org (accessed July 2017).

Z. Wang, S.J. Wei, and K. Zhu. 2014. Quantifying International Production Sharing at the Bilateral and Sector Levels. *NBER Working Paper.* No. 19677. Cambridge, MA: National Bureau of Economic Research.

World Trade Organization. 1994. *General Agreement on Tariffs and Trade 1994.* https://www.wto.org/English/Docs_E/legal_e/06-gatt_e.htm

———. Disputes by Agreement. https://www.wto.org/english/tratop_e/dispu_e/dispu_agreements_index_e.htm (accessed September 2017).

———. Integrated Trade Intelligence Portal (I-TIP). http://i-tip.wto.org/goods/default.aspx?language=en (accessed September 2017).

———. Regional Trade Agreement Information System. http://rtias.wto.org (accessed September 2017).

———. WTO Statistics. http://stat.wto.org (accessed May 2017).

Xinhua. 2017. RCEP Ministers Agree on "Key Elements" to Speed Up Talks on "Mega Trade Pact". 11 September.

03

Cross-border Investment

Cross-border Investment

Trends and Patterns of FDI in Asia

Asia is increasingly a magnet for foreign direct investment and a prominent global investor.

Over the past two decades, the benefits of increased trade and investment rewarded many Asian economies with strong economic growth and rising incomes. The proliferation of cross-border production networks created opportunities for even lower-income countries in the region to attract export-oriented multinationals.

Asia's share of global inward foreign direct investment (FDI) has been rising.[12] In 2016, almost 30% of global FDI went to Asia, up from less than 20% in 2000–2005. At the same time, better finance and structural changes to production created opportunities for major Asian firms to invest abroad, particularly within the region. In 2000–2005, Asia's share of global outward FDI ranged from 10% to 15%. In 2016, Asia's share rose to more than 30%—with more than a third originating from the People's Republic of China (PRC). Outward FDI from Asia have been growing since 2010, slightly interrupted in 2012 and 2015, but regaining strong momentum in 2016.

Updates on Global Inward FDI to Asia

Global inward FDI fell slightly in 2016, with inward FDI to Asia falling 6.4% to $492 billion.

Based on standard balance of payments (BOP) data, global inward FDI totaled $1.75 trillion in 2016,

Figure 3.1: Total Inward FDI ($ trillion)

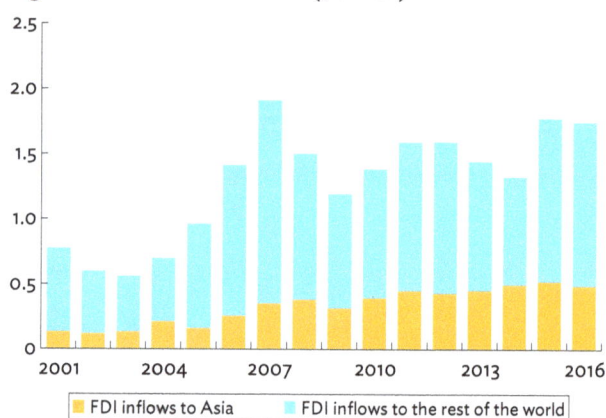

FDI = foreign direct investment.
Source: ADB calculations using data from United Nations Conference on Trade and Development. Bilateral FDI Statistics. http://unctad.org/en/Pages/DIAE/FDI%20Statistics/FDI-Statistics-Bilateral.aspx (accessed July 2017).

down slightly from $1.77 trillion in 2015 (Figure 3.1). The uncertain global economic environment and geopolitical shocks may have helped dampen the 2015 growth rebound.

Inward FDI to Europe and developing Asia fell, while North America, transition economies and other advanced economies attracted more FDI. In Asia, the PRC; Hong Kong, China; Australia; Singapore; and India remained the main recipients (Table 3.1). Although Asia attracted 28% of global inward FDI, they were $34 billion below the 2015 level.

A steep decline in cross-border mergers and acquisitions—especially in services—was largely behind the overall drop in Asia's inward FDI in 2016.

Based on firms' investment activity data—which provides information on mode of entry[13] and ultimate

---

[12]   Unless otherwise specified, FDI is a flow.

[13]   Investments can either be greenfield (building new assets) or merger and acquisition (acquiring existing ones).

Table 3.1: Top 10 Destinations of Global and Asian FDI ($ billion)

Global	2016	2015	2010	Asia	2016	2015	2010
United States	391.1	348.4	198.0	PRC	133.7	174.4	114.7
United Kingdom	253.8	33.0	58.2	Hong Kong, China	108.1	135.6	70.5
PRC	133.7	135.6	114.7	Singapore	61.6	70.6	55.1
Hong Kong, China	108.1	174.4	70.5	Australia	48.2	19.5	36.4
Netherlands	92.0	68.8	-7.2	India	44.5	44.1	27.4
Singapore	61.6	70.6	55.1	Viet Nam	12.6	11.8	8.0
British Virgin Islands	59.1	28.9	50.5	Japan	11.4	-2.3	-1.3
Brazil	58.7	64.3	83.7	Republic of Korea	10.8	4.1	9.5
Australia	48.2	19.5	36.4	Malaysia	9.9	11.1	9.1
Cayman Islands	45.0	63.4	9.4	Kazakhstan	9.1	4.0	11.6

FDI = foreign direct investment, PRC = People's Republic of China.
Source: ADB calculations using data from United Nations Conference on Trade and Development. Bilateral FDI Statistics. http://unctad.org/en/Pages/DIAE/FDI%20 Statistics/FDI-Statistics-Bilateral.aspx (accessed July 2017).

Figure 3.2: FDI by Mode of Entry—Asia

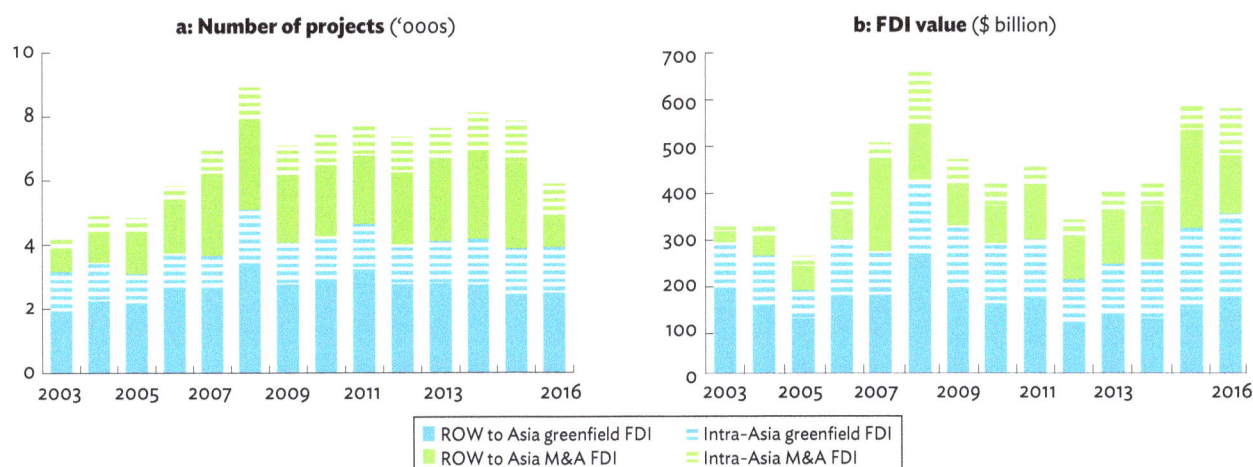

FDI = foreign direct investment, M&As = merger and acquisition, ROW = rest of the world.
Note: Asia refers to the 48 regional members of ADB.
Sources: ADB calculations using data from Financial Times. fDi Markets; and Bureau van Dijk. Zephyr M&A Database (both accessed May 2017).

investment ownership globally—mergers and acquisitions (M&As) have increased steadily since the GFC, driven mainly by M&As in Asia from the rest of the world (ROW) (Figure 3.2). This changed in 2016 as the number of M&As fell 51%—mostly in India and the PRC—as investments from outside Asia dropped. Similarly, the value of M&A deals fell by $42 billion, 15% below the 2015 peak of $272 billion. Services was particularly hard hit with M&As falling by more than

half its 2015 level (Figure 3.3), of which FDI from ROW fell to just one-fifth of the 2015 total, or $50 billion (Figure 3.4).

However, greenfield investments continued to grow after having plateaued in 2012–2014 reaching $348.4 billion in 2016. New greenfield investments in India, Viet Nam and the Republic of Korea surpassed the number of M&As in 2016.

Figure 3.3: Total Inward FDI to Asia by Sector ($ billion)

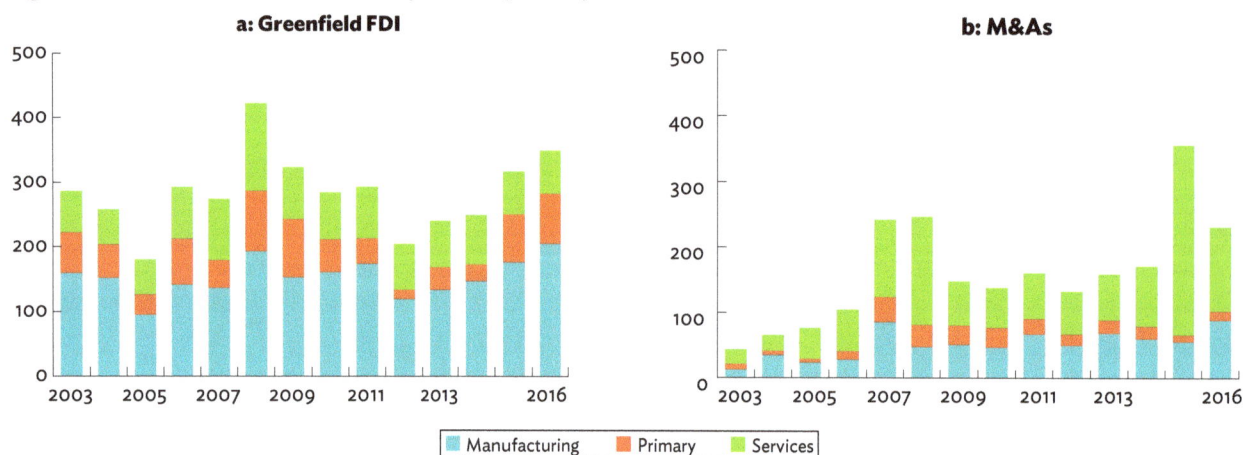

a: Greenfield FDI

b: M&As

FDI = foreign direct investment, M&As = mergers and acquisitions.
Note: Asia refers to the 48 regional members of ADB.
Sources: ADB calculations using data from Financial Times. fDi Markets; and Bureau van Dijk. Zephyr M&A Database (both accessed May 2017).

Figure 3.4: Rest of the World FDI to Asia by Sector ($ billion)

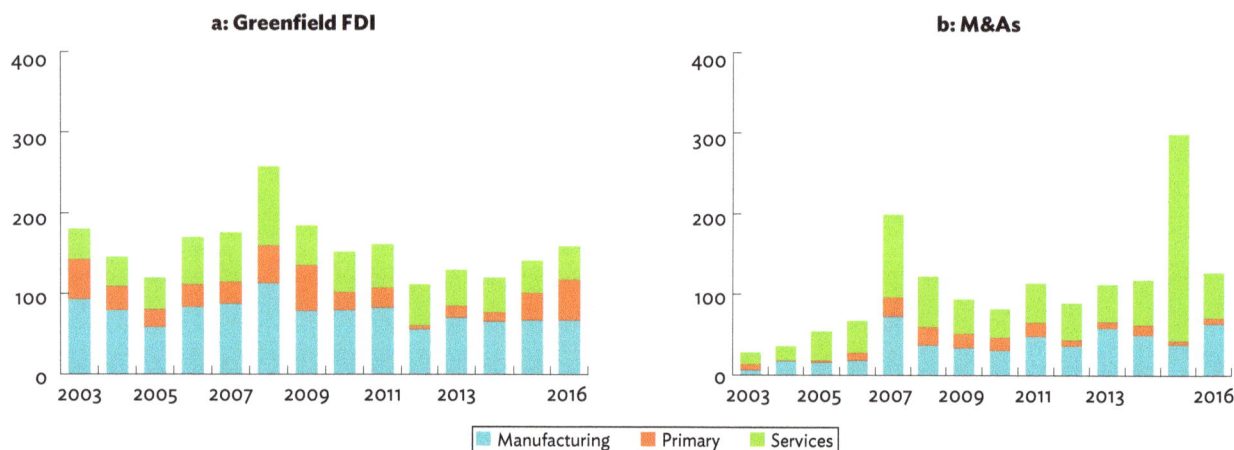

a: Greenfield FDI

b: M&As

FDI = foreign direct investment, M&As = mergers and acquisitions.
Note: Asia refers to the 48 regional members of ADB.
Sources: ADB calculations using data from Financial Times. fDi Markets; and Bureau van Dijk. Zephyr M&A Database (both accessed May 2017).

Update on Regional Trends

Inward FDI to major subregions in Asia generally fell as global investments favored more advanced economies; East Asia and Southeast Asia were most affected.

BOP data show inward FDI to Asia dipped both in absolute and relative terms—to $492 billion in 2016 from $525.4 billion in 2015. The region's share of global FDI fell to 28% from 30% in 2015. Inward FDI to East Asia and Southeast Asia dropped by 14% and 20%, respectively (Figure 3.5). The downturn in East Asia was due to a $66-billion drop in inward FDI to Hong Kong,

China—more than the combined increase in inward FDI to Japan; the Republic of Korea; and Taipei,China. East Asia still attracts more than half of FDI inflows to the region.

In 2016, Southeast Asia received $101 billion in FDI, down from $127 billion in 2015. Its share, 20% of Asia's total, was below its average 25% share during 2010–2015 and the lowest since 2010. A drop in M&As from North America, Latin America, and ROW, especially in the primary sector was behind the slowdown. Singapore, Indonesia, and Malaysia accounted for the largest shares of FDI into Southeast Asia from 2010 to 2015—averaging 53%, 16% and 9%, respectively—but this

Figure 3.5: Global Inward FDI to Asia by Subregion ($ billion)

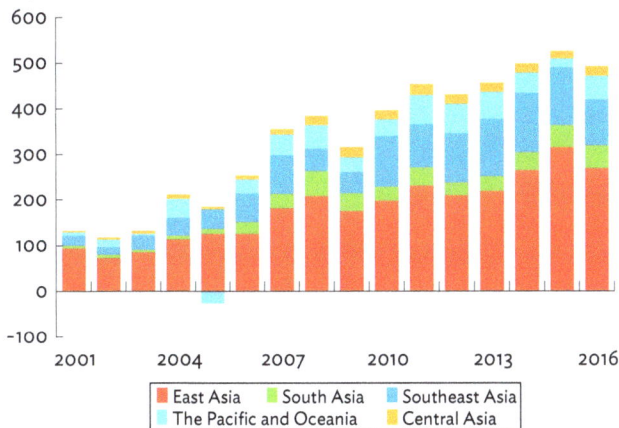

FDI = foreign direct investment.
Source: ADB calculations using data from United Nations Conference on Trade and Development. Bilateral FDI Statistics. http://unctad.org/en/Pages/DIAE/FDI%20Statistics/FDI-Statistics-Bilateral.aspx (accessed July 2017).

changed in 2016. Indonesia's share fell 10 percentage points—inward FDI dropped to $2.7 billion in 2016 from a high of $16.6 billion in 2015. Among other Southeast Asian economies, inward FDI to the Philippines jumped to $7.9 billion (up 60% from 2015). M&As—such as the $802-million deal between Mitsubishi UFJ Financial Group and Security Bank—were behind the increase.

South Asia saw a marginal increase (3%) in inward FDI to $50.4 billion—with all economies above 2015 levels except Afghanistan and Bhutan. Mauritius, Singapore, and Japan were the top three sources accounting for 90% of FDI in India. Inward FDI to Pakistan, Sri Lanka, and Bangladesh grew 56%, 32%, and 4%, respectively.

Central Asia attracted $5.1 billion more FDI in 2016. Around 40% went to Kazakhstan ($9.1 billion), Turkmenistan ($4.5 billion), and Azerbaijan ($4.5 billion). Among top sources of FDI to Central Asia were the Netherlands, Switzerland, the PRC, and the United States (US) (around 60%). Inward FDI to Australia grew 147% in 2016, to $48 billion, ranking ninth worldwide. In the Pacific, only Kiribati and Vanuatu attracted investment flows, keeping the subregion's share at less than 1% of Asia-bound FDI.

Despite the slowdown in inward FDI worldwide, intraregional investment continues to strengthen—the intraregional share of inward FDI to Asia increased from 32% in 2007 to 55% in 2016 (from $112 billion to $272 billion).

Buying into Asia-based enterprises has been notable among emerging Asian investors. The PRC, Japan, and Singapore continue to diversify their international portfolios in developing Asian economies (such as in Indonesia and India, and from others into the PRC) to gain competitive advantage in broadening manufacturing networks, securing export markets and driving innovation.

During 2010–2015, about half of inward FDI to Asia based on BOP data were intraregional (Figure 3.6a). In 2016, despite the drop in inward FDI worldwide, intraregional inflows in Asia increased by 9 percentage points. FDI from Hong Kong, China accounted for the lion's share of intra-Asian FDI (nearly 37%), followed by Singapore (16%), Japan (16%), and the PRC (16%).

Using firm-level data to trace ultimate investment ownership—BOP data do not—the increase in intraregional FDI was even more substantial, from $232 billion in 2015 to $292 billion in 2016 (Figure 3.6b). The share of intraregional FDI to East Asia was lower than indicated by BOP data, and Southeast Asia ranked highest based on the firm-level data. This suggests that BOP may inflate intraregional inward FDI to East Asia, possibly due to transshipments and round-tripping. Except for East Asia, all subregions showed higher intraregional inward FDI based on firm-level data, indicating that a portion of intra-Asian flows were routed from outside the region, which BOP fails to record.

From both BOP data and firm level activity, FDI links both within and across subregions are strengthening, although integration levels vary by subregion (Figure 3.7). Over 2001–2016, BOP data show the share of inter-subregional investment to total inward FDI gradually grew from 9% to 20%, mainly at the expense of FDI from the ROW. This trend accompanied the strengthening of trade linkages between subregions, highlighting the complementarity of trade and investment in the context of cross-border production networks between subregions. However, most intraregional FDI occurs

Figure 3.6: Intraregional FDI Inflows—Asia

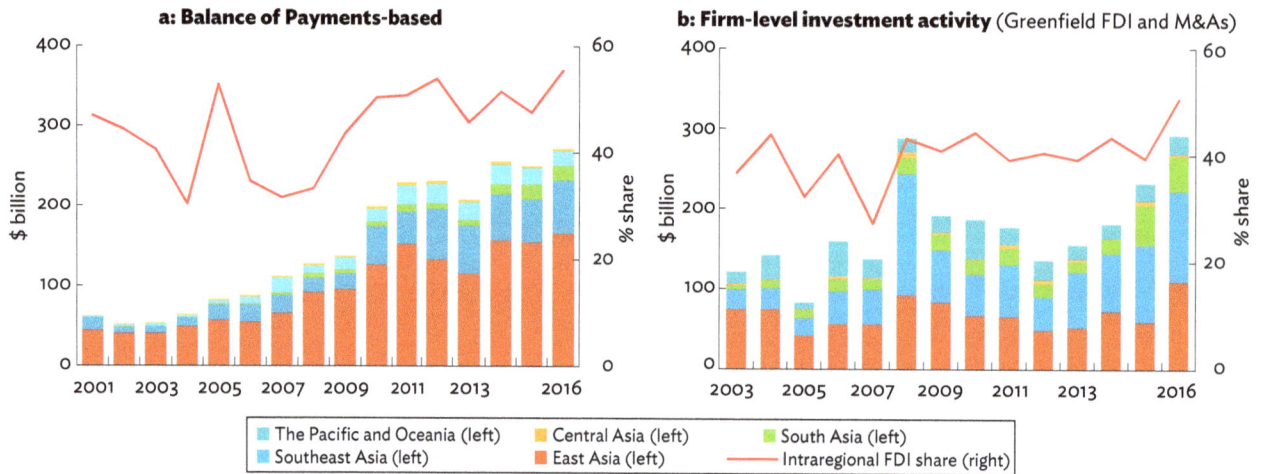

a: Balance of Payments-based

b: Firm-level investment activity (Greenfield FDI and M&As)

The Pacific and Oceania (left)   Central Asia (left)   South Asia (left)
Southeast Asia (left)   East Asia (left)   Intraregional FDI share (right)

FDI = foreign direct investment, M&As = mergers and acquisitions.
Notes: For the right panel chart, values and shares are based on the sum of greenfield FDI and M&A deal values. Asia refers to the 48 regional members of ADB.
Sources: ADB calculations using data from Association of Southeast Nations Secretariat; CEIC; Eurostat. Balance of Payments. http://ec.europa.eu/eurostat/web/balance-of-payments/data/database (accessed July 2017); Korean Statistical Information Service. Balance of Payments. http://kosis.kr/statHtml/statHtml.do?orgId=301&tblId=DT_022Y016&language=en&conn_path=I3 (accessed August 2017); Rep. of Korea Ministry of Trade, Industry, and Energy. http://www.motie.go.kr/www/main.do (accessed August 2017); United Nations Conference on Trade and Development. Bilateral FDI Statistics. http://unctad.org/en/Pages/DIAE/FDI%20Statistics/FDI-Statistics-Bilateral.aspx (accessed July 2017); Financial Times. fDi Markets (accessed May 2017); and Bureau van Dijk. Zephyr M&A Database (accessed May 2017).

Figure 3.7. Regional FDI Share—Asia (%)

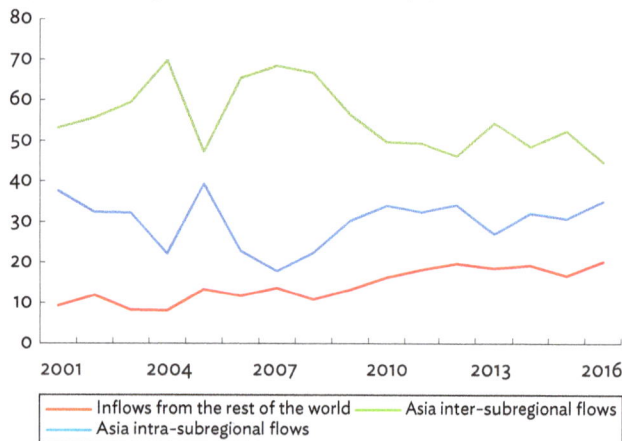

Inflows from the rest of the world   Asia inter-subregional flows
Asia intra-subregional flows

FDI = foreign direct investment.
Sources: ADB calculations using data from Association of Southeast Nations Secretariat; CEIC; Eurostat. Balance of Payments. http://ec.europa.eu/eurostat/web/balance-of-payments/data/database (accessed July 2017); Korean Statistical Information Service. Balance of Payments. http://kosis.kr/statHtml/statHtml.do?orgId=301&tblId=DT_022Y016&language=en&conn_path=I3 (accessed August 2017); Rep. of Korea Ministry of Trade, Industry, and Energy. http://www.motie.go.kr/www/main.do (accessed August 2017); and United Nations Conference on Trade and Development. Bilateral FDI Statistics. http://unctad.org/en/Pages/DIAE/FDI%20Statistics/FDI-Statistics-Bilateral.aspx (accessed July 2017).

within subregions—the share of intra-subregional investment has stayed around 40% since 2001.

Intra-Asian FDI supports global value chains more than FDI from outside the region. And given the uncertain

global economic environment, geopolitical changes and the uncertain prognosis for future FDI flows, developing Asia must continue to foster intraregional trade and investment linkages to strengthen resilience to external shocks.

Outward FDI

Lower outward investment from advanced economies reduced global outward FDI in 2016.

Based on BOP data, global outward FDI in 2016 were 9% below 2015 levels (Figure 3.8). Outward investment from advanced economies fell 11% to $1 trillion in 2016. The largest drop was in Ireland, Switzerland and Germany—together investing $254 billion less than in 2015.

Despite weakening outward FDI worldwide, Asia's outward FDI increased 11% in 2016.

BOP-based outward FDI from Asia reached $482 billion in 2016, up 11% from 2015—91% by value came from East Asia (Figure 3.9). The PRC was the second-largest global investor in 2016, up from fifth in 2015. It is also the largest Asian investor, with $183.1 billion invested globally and over 75% outside Asia. Japan's outward FDI surged 13% to $145 billion in 2016, its largest expansion since 2010 (around 70% directed outside the region). In Southeast Asia, Thailand increased investments eightfold in 2016 to $13.2 billion (its largest investment overseas since 2000). The most significant drop was in Indonesia—outward investment fell $18.4 billion.

Figure 3.8: Global Outward FDI by Source ($ trillion)

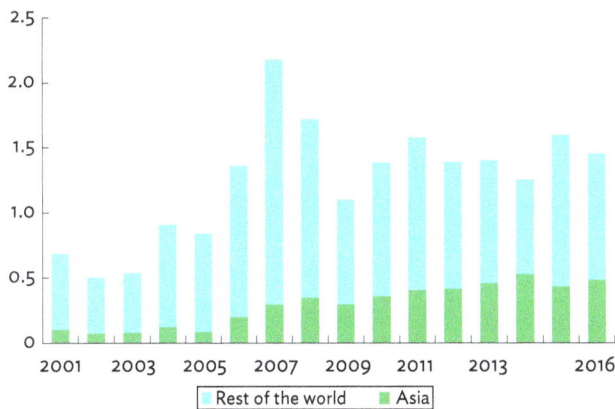

FDI = foreign direct investment.
Source: ADB calculations using data from United Nations Conference on Trade and Development. Bilateral FDI Statistics. http://unctad.org/en/Pages/DIAE/FDI%20Statistics/FDI-Statistics-Bilateral.aspx (accessed July 2017).

Figure 3.9: Asian Outward FDI by Source ($ billion)

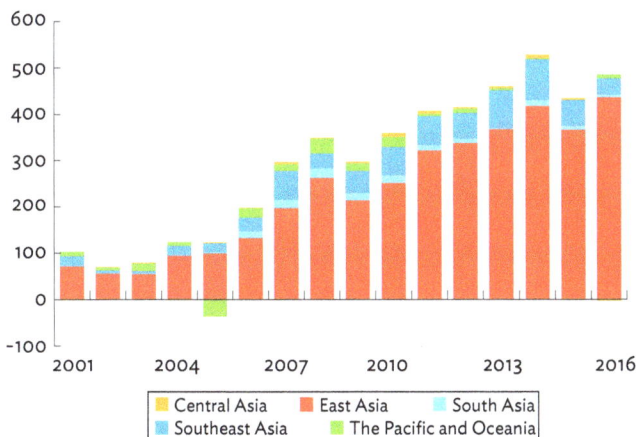

FDI = foreign direct investment.
Sources: ADB calculations using data from Association of Southeast Nations Secretariat; CEIC; Eurostat. Balance of Payments. http://ec.europa.eu/eurostat/web/balance-of-payments/data/database (accessed July 2017); Korean Statistical Information Service. Balance of Payments. http://kosis.kr/statHtml/statHtml.do?orgId=301&tblId=DT_022Y016&language=en&conn_path=I3 (accessed August 2017); Republic of Korea Ministry of Trade, Industry, and Energy. http://www.motie.go.kr/www/main.do (accessed August 2017); and United Nations Conference on Trade and Development. http://unctad.org/en/Pages/DIAE/FDI%20Statistics/FDI-Statistics-Bilateral.aspx (accessed July 2017).

Firms in Asia are bolstering their status as global investors.

Outward FDI from the region began to exceed inward FDI in 2013, when economies such as Hong Kong, China and the PRC increased outward investments, while investments from the US and Europe slowed (Figure 3.10).

At the firm-level, the value of combined outward greenfield and M&A FDI exceeded inward FDI by $90.6 billion in 2016 (Figure 3.11). The increase in intra-Asian FDI narrowed the gap between inward and outward FDI, especially in 2016. But a large part

Figure 3.10: Total FDI Flows—Asia ($ billion)

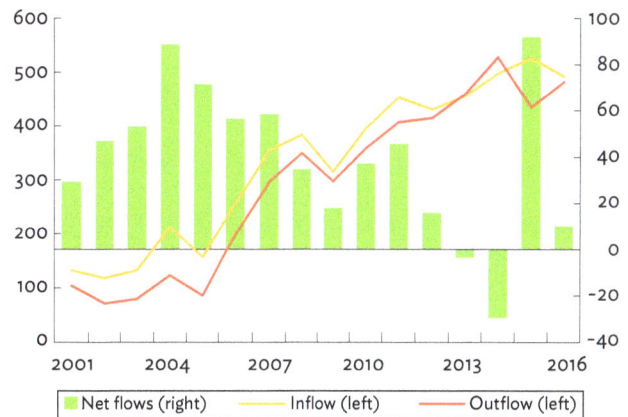

FDI = foreign direct investment.
Source: ADB calculations using data from United Nations Conference on Trade and Development. Bilateral FDI Statistics. http://unctad.org/en/Pages/DIAE/FDI%20Statistics/FDI-Statistics-Bilateral.aspx (accessed July 2017).

Figure 3.11: Greenfield FDI and M&A in Asia ($ billion)

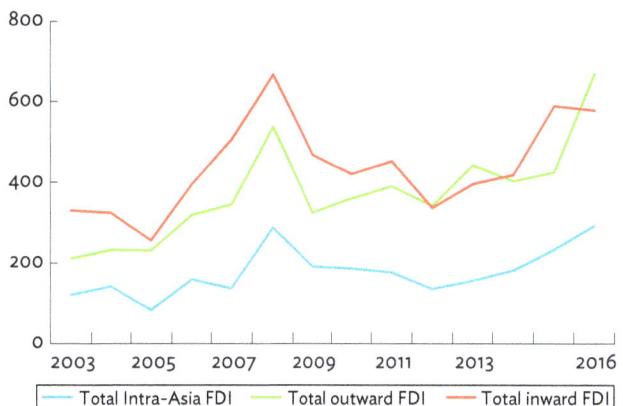

FDI = foreign direct investment, M&A = merger and acquisition.
Note: Asia refers to the 48 regional members of ADB.
Sources: ADB calculations using data from Financial Times. fDi Markets; and Bureau van Dijk. Zephyr M&A Database (both accessed May 2017).

of greenfield investments and M&A deals still are targeted outside Asia. In particular, Asian investors are increasingly investing outside the region through M&As—$250 billion in 2016 compared with just over $100 billion in 2015. For instance, PRC investments in the US (both greenfield and M&As) reached $46 billion in 2003–2015 (36% in real estate and financial services).

A large part of intraregional FDI is greenfield investment, mainly in manufacturing, while M&As are more dominant for FDI going outside the region.

Aggregating greenfield investments and M&As show almost 50% of Asia's investments are intraregional, followed by the European Union (EU)-28 (19%) and North America (15%). Intra-Asian greenfield investments ($189 billion) are almost twice as large as M&As (Figure 3.12). This is expected as a substantial amount of intra-Asian FDI is linked to global value chains, which generally take the greenfield mode of entry. Most intraregional greenfield investments are in manufacturing, which rapidly increased since 2012 to reach $139 billion (73% of the total) in 2016. In contrast, intraregional M&As are mostly in services—$72 billion (or 70% of total) in 2016. There was a jump in intra-Asia M&As in manufacturing between 2015 and 2016, due to an influx of manufacturing M&As in Thailand; Viet Nam; and Hong Kong, China.

In contrast, Asian investments outside the region were mostly in M&As, far exceeding greenfield investments—$254 billion in M&As versus $127 billion in greenfield investments. This suggests extraregional FDI remains mostly market-seeking (Figure 3.13). Manufacturing accounted for almost two-third ($81 billion) of the total greenfield investment. While Asia's investments in services comprise a much larger share of M&As outside the region, manufacturing M&As more than tripled to reach $135 billion in 2016.

Asia's emerging role as a global investor could further increase the intraregional share of inward FDI, and allow the region to leverage its own trade and investment linkages to achieve more inclusive and sustainable growth.

Asia has been and will continue to be a major driver of world growth—Asia accounted for more than half of global growth in gross domestic product and has been steadily increasing its share since at least 2012. Its stable share of global inward FDI (at least 25% since 2008) underscores the region's reliability as an investment platform. In addition, the recent growth in outward investment from emerging Asian investors highlights the growing internationalization of Asia's multinationals, which are increasing their global presence especially within the region. This is an encouraging sign for the region's capacity to create jobs, promote small and medium enterprises and innovation, and advance income opportunities toward more inclusive and sustainable growth regardless of the external economic environment.

Figure 3.12: Intra-Asia FDI by Sector ($ billion)

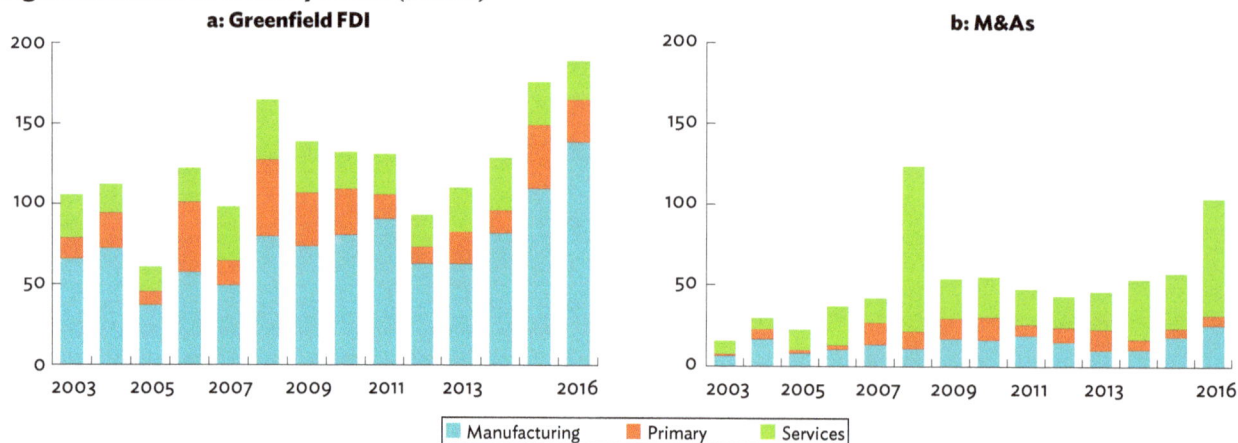

FDI = foreign direct investment, M&As = mergers and acquisitions.
Note: Asia refers to the 48 regional members of ADB.
Sources: ADB calculations using data from Financial Times. fDi Markets; and Bureau van Dijk. Zephyr M&A Database (both accessed May 2017).

Figure 3.13: Extra-Asia FDI by Sector ($ billion)

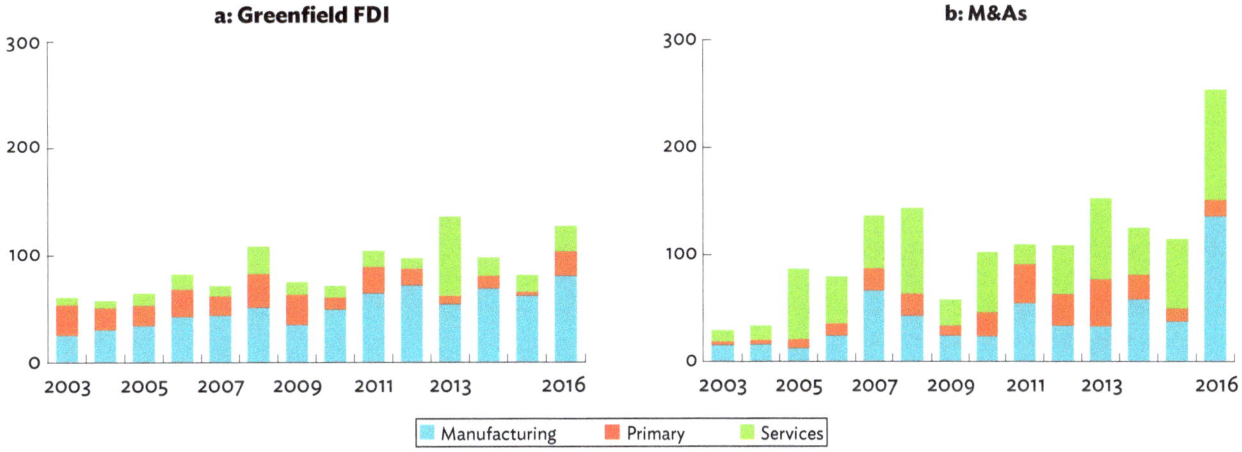

a: Greenfield FDI

b: M&As

Manufacturing | Primary | Services

FDI = foreign direct investment, M&As = mergers and acquisitions.
Note: Asia refers to the 48 regional members of ADB.
Sources: ADB calculations using data from Financial Times. fDi Markets; and Bureau van Dijk. Zephyr M&A Database (both accessed May 2017)

Box 3.1: Outward Investments from Selected Asian Economies[a]

Despite the downturn in foreign direct investment (FDI) globally, Asia bolstered its role as dominant global investor in 2016. Based on balance of payments (BOP) data—which do not trace ultimate investment ownership—outward FDI (OFDI) from the region increased 11%. In 2016, the region's share of global FDI was 33%, up from 27% in 2015.

Characterized by deeper financial markets and the growing internalization of its multinationals, East Asian economies were the largest investors from the region. The People's Republic of China (PRC); Japan; and Hong Kong, China have consistently been among the world's top 10 investors.[a] In 2016, these three economies invested $391 billion—27% of global investments and 81% of total outward investments from Asia.

Based on firms' investment activity data—which does trace ultimate investment ownership—the increase in OFDI from Asia was even starker. M&As and greenfield investments grew 57% to $669 billion in 2016, accounting for 32% of the global total (up from 20% in 2015). Viewed against the 6.5% contraction in global M&As and greenfield investments, the brisk pace of FDI outflows from Asia illustrates the region's growing integration, both intraregionally and even more so elsewhere. Intraregional

investments have increased since 2013, reaching $291 billion in 2016 ($232 billion in 2015). But its share in Asia's total OFDI declined 11 percentage points (to 43%).

OFDI from the region increasingly enters markets through M&As—Asia's share of global M&As more than doubled to 26% in 2016 (up 109%) to reach $354 billion. Greenfield investments from the region also expanded faster than the global average (at 23%) to reach $316 billion in 2016, or 41% of the world total. While greenfield investments are primarily concentrated in manufacturing (69% of total greenfield Asian outflows from the region)—and even more so intraregionally (73%)—M&As are mostly targeted at services (49%) especially within the region (70%). Manufacturing OFDI expanded most (67%), accounting for the majority (56%) of the region's total 2016 investment, followed by services (33%). OFDI in the primary sector continued to grow in 2016 despite a global contraction.

The largest recipient industry for Asian investments is real estate (19% of total OFDI)—a mix of both manufacturing and services—primarily through greenfield investment. The second largest was financial services (13%), predominantly through M&As.[b] Semiconductors followed third (11%),

---

[a]   For more details on the investment profile of the top 10 Asian investors, see http://aric.adb.org/aeir2017_onlineannex1.pdf

[b]   In fact, intraregional OFDI in financial services grew 260% against an 8% extraregional contraction.

Continued on next page

Box 3.1 continued

with the vast majority also via M&As. Asian investments in real estate and financial services were mostly intraregional (24% and 20% of total intra-Asian FDI, respectively). Semiconductors were the fastest growing, with Asian investments increasing more than eight times to $76 billion, almost entirely through M&As outside the region.

The PRC emerged as the largest Asian investor in 2016. Prior to the global financial crisis (GFC), Japan's OFDI was, on average, five times the size of PRC investments. Since then, the PRC has grown to become dominant investor in all sectors, but particularly in services, accounting for 45% of total Asian OFDI. As the PRC moves away from export-oriented manufacturing toward more domestic consumption demand, the character of PRC investment has changed as well. In 2016, services accounted for 67% of M&As by the PRC, and more than tripled in value ($88 billion)—with intraregional M&As spiking tenfold (to $50 billion)—mainly in real estate and financial services in the United States (US) and Hong Kong, China. In contrast, most Japanese investments are in manufacturing, with semiconductors the largest recipient industry. Most of Japan's OFDI (73%) is targeted outside the region, while its most popular destination in Asia is the PRC.

Hong Kong, China is the third-largest Asian investor based on BOP data, but firm-level data show investment activity is $20 billion lower than indicated by BOP.[c] This suggests the economy is a conduit for investments originating elsewhere. Hong Kong, China's investments abroad reached $40.2 billion in 2016, based on firm-level data, mainly directed to non-Asian countries. The top recipients within Asia, Thailand and the PRC, each accounted for about 14% of its total outbound FDI. Its investment portfolio favors business and real estate services, mainly through cross-border M&As, while the majority of its manufacturing investments are in consumer products.

Most of the increase in the Republic of Korea's foreign investments in 2016 was in the primary sector—especially coal, oil and natural gas (almost a quarter of OFDI)—but greenfield investments in manufacturing continued to make up the lion's share. In a marked reversal from 2015, only 50% of OFDI from the Republic of Korea was intraregional (74% in 2015), with Viet Nam and Islamic Republic of Iran as first

and third largest destination, respectively. Multinationals from the Republic of Korea also invested considerably in alternative and renewable energy, mainly in the US.

In sharp contrast with other East Asian economies, investments from Taipei,China were mostly intraregional (83% in 2016)—the highest in the region. M&As in developing Asia drove much of its OFDI, which quadrupled from $3.7 billion in 2010 to $14.8 billion in 2016. Taipei,China's investments are primarily concentrated in labor-intensive manufacturing such as electronic components and consumer electronics, as well as services such as financial services. Partner firms in the PRC accounted for almost half (46.1%) of Taipei,China's OFDI, followed by Viet Nam (13.1%). Low labor costs, among other factors, attract export-oriented multinationals from Taipei,China.

Outside East Asia, Singapore is the dominant investor, with its OFDI mostly heading to the US (56.1%), followed by the PRC (7.8%) and India (7.4%). Since 2003, Singapore's outward investments have been mostly in services. But recently it has shifted into manufacturing, with semiconductors accounting for almost half of all Singaporean investments in 2016.

In addition to Taipei,China; Thailand; Malaysia; and India were among source economies with an intraregional share of OFDI above 50%. Since 2000, Malaysia and India have emerged as prominent Asian investors. While interrupted by the GFC, Malaysia's OFDI returned to growth in 2011, increasing 6% during 2010–2016 to $28.7 billion. In 2016, Malaysian OFDI grew fastest among Asian economies (164%). Traditionally, Malaysian investments have been in the primary sector (especially coal, oil and natural gas), but shifted markedly toward services, particularly financial services, in 2016.

By contrast, India's OFDI slowed from the GFC to 2015, before recovering 17.0% in 2016 to $21.1 billion—still less than half its 2007 peak. While India's emergence as a notable investor was driven by services—software, information technology and financial services to the United Kingdom (UK) and the US—the 2016 recovery was largely from greenfield investments in coal, oil and natural gas (Australia attracted about 20% of the total). India's multinationals also invested in pharmaceuticals in Bangladesh.

Unlike Malaysia and India, Thailand's OFDI have been consistently increasing despite the GFC, expanding from $2.3 billion in 2007 to $17.2 in 2016 (84% intraregional). The spike since 2011 has been driven mainly by greenfield real-

---

[c] Hong Kong, China is the only top-10 source economy with outflows overestimated, rather than underestimated, by BOP data.

estate investments in the manufacturing sectors of neighboring economies, with Viet Nam attracting almost a third of the total in 2016.

Among the top Asian investors, Australia's investment fell 30% in 2016. A majority were greenfield investments in manufacturing and services, and mainly in non-Asian and advanced economies, primarily the UK.

A regression analysis based on gravity modeling sheds more light on the drivers of Asian OFDI in comparison with a global sample.[d] The analysis also examines the drivers of intra-Asian FDI. The host economy's business environment (as measured by World Bank's Ease of Doing Business indicators) and quality of governance (from the Worldwide Governance Indicators) are the most important policy determinants of FDI, particularly from Asia's source economies (box table). For Asia's investors, the quality of governance is even more important when investing within the region, most crucial in services. With all else equal, an improvement of the governance score from median to the top quartile[e] is associated with a 28% increase in Asian

Effects of Governance and Business Environment on FDI

Dependent variable: Total number of FDI projects	Overall			Primary			Manufacturing			Services		
	All sample	Source: Asia	Intra-Asia	All sample	Source: Asia	Intra-Asia	All sample	Source: Asia	Intra-Asia	All sample	Source: Asia	Intra-Asia
Overall Ease of Doing Business Index - host (expected sign = plus)	0.022*** (0.004)	0.028*** (0.009)	0.021 (0.015)	0.013 (0.009)	-0.005 (0.012)	-0.060*** (0.016)	0.022*** (0.005)	0.036*** (0.012)	0.058*** (0.020)	0.024*** (0.005)	0.030*** (0.010)	-0.003 (0.010)
Overall World Governance Index - host (expected sign = plus)	0.012*** (0.004)	0.016*** (0.005)	0.024** (0.010)	0.000 (0.012)	0.027** (0.011)	0.052*** (0.014)	0.010** (0.004)	0.012* (0.007)	0.005 (0.013)	0.015*** (0.005)	0.020*** (0.005)	0.048*** (0.009)
log(Population - host)	0.669*** (0.020)	0.595 (0.038)	0.439*** (0.036)	0.345*** (0.031)	0.306*** (0.074)	0.201*** (0.068)	0.776*** (0.017)	0.731*** (0.037)	0.600*** (0.050)	0.686*** (0.026)	0.569*** (0.050)	0.372*** (0.037)
log(PCGDP - host)	0.263*** (0.046)	0.078 (0.078)	-0.143 (0.120)	0.386*** (0.120)	0.238** (0.115)	0.409** (0.159)	0.277*** (0.047)	0.039 (0.116)	-0.308** (0.154)	0.270*** (0.053)	0.111 (0.073)	-0.117 (0.120)
Growth Rate - host	2.158** (0.902)	2.703** (1.105)	5.392*** (1.469)	1.638 (1.625)	1.656 (3.532)	0.863 (1.931)	1.526* (0.863)	2.296 (1.439)	5.224** (2.073)	2.613*** (0.983)	5.143*** (1.086)	8.087*** (1.301)
Inflation Rate - host	0.000 (0.001)	-0.010 (0.018)	-0.051*** (0.017)	0.001*** (0.000)	-0.002 (0.015)	-0.048** (0.024)	-0.001 (0.004)	-0.017 (0.027)	-0.054** (0.022)	0.000 (0.002)	-0.010 (0.015)	-0.062*** (0.017)
log(Distance between source and host)	-0.449*** (0.039)	-0.489*** (0.086)	-0.415*** (0.116)	-0.023 (0.115)	-0.009 (0.221)	0.016 (0.167)	-0.473*** (0.033)	-0.432*** (0.100)	-0.379*** (0.142)	-0.522*** (0.049)	-0.572*** (0.097)	-0.561*** (0.117)
Common language (=1 if yes)	0.724*** (0.113)	0.870*** (0.116)	0.824*** (0.129)	1.036*** (0.202)	1.104*** (0.422)	-0.152 (0.335)	0.463*** (0.100)	0.727*** (0.121)	0.855*** (0.161)	0.921*** (0.122)	1.034*** (0.118)	0.933*** (0.140)
Contiguity (=1 if yes)	-0.062 (0.137)	0.301* (0.177)	0.382** (0.164)	0.292 (0.337)	0.291 (0.415)	0.017 (0.294)	0.086 (0.110)	0.350 (0.239)	0.510*** (0.177)	-0.208 (0.182)	0.371* (0.204)	0.442** (0.213)
Constant	-16.758*** (0.629)	-10.981*** (1.210)	-8.009*** (1.172)	-10.317*** (1.352)	-10.727*** (3.519)	-4.975** (2.309)	-12.642*** (0.524)	-13.141*** (1.388)	-8.859*** (2.049)	-13.960*** (0.551)	-7.949*** (1.461)	-6.892*** (1.348)
Number of observations	19015	4485	1653	2994	717	275	7645	1884	649	8357	1878	725
R-squared	0.509	0.437	0.453	0.352	0.221	0.603	0.792	0.770	0.845	0.779	0.667	0.726

*** = significant at 1%, ** = significant at 5%, * = significant at 10%, FDI = foreign direct investment, PCGDP = per capita gross domestic product.
Notes: Estimates are obtained with Poisson Pseudo-Maximum Likelihood estimator. Source country-period fixed effects and period fixed effects are included but not shown for brevity. Standard errors in parenthesis are based on clustering by country-pair. Data cover 172 host economies and 159 home economies, for 2003–2015. Asia refers to the 48 regional members of ADB.
Sources: ADB calculations using data from Financial Times. fDi Markets (accessed May 2017); and Bureau van Dijk. Zephyr M&A Database; World Bank. Ease of Doing Business Index, World Governance Index, and World Development Indicators, http://worldbank.org (all accessed May 2017).

[d]   The analysis is based on an estimation of a semi-structural gravity model using the Poisson Pseudo-Maximum Likelihood methodology. More details on data sources and coverage, and methodology, can be found in the AEIR 2016 Special Theme Chapter, pages 151-155.

[e]   The overall governance at the median is 56.5 and 74.2 at the top quartile.

Continued on next page

Box 3.1 continued

investment projects, and 42% when the host economy is also Asian. In the services sector, the corresponding marginal impact is 35% and 85%, respectively. The growth rate of the host economy also matters significantly more for attracting intra-Asian OFDI in both manufacturing and services.

There are some interesting differences between the global and Asian sample. Results suggest that Asia's multinationals are motivated by efficiency-seeking considerations (such as lower labor costs) when investing in manufacturing within the region. This reinforces the view that intra-Asian investments are tied to regional value chains (more so for greenfield investments). This contrasts with the global sample where per capita gross domestic product of the host economy is positively associated with the number of FDI projects. Asia's investors are even more likely to invest in manufacturing in economies sharing a border, pointing to a high level of intra-subregional investment integration. Asian manufacturing investments in economies sharing a border are 67% higher, whereas there is no similar positive association between contiguity and FDI in the global sample.

Despite the increasingly inward-oriented policies in certain advanced economies, recent trends in Asia's OFDI and the findings of the regression analysis are encouraging for the region's developing economies. Improving governance will help these economies to continue attracting export-oriented multinationals from the region, despite the uncertain global economic environment.

References

ADB. 2016. *Asian Economic Integration Report 2016: What Drives Foreign Direct Investments in Asia and the Pacific.* Manila

Association of Southeast Nations Secretariat. ASEANstats Database. https://data.aseanstats.org/ (accessed July 2017).

Eurostat. Balance of Payments. http://ec.europa.eu/eurostat/web/balance-of-payments/data/database (accessed July 2017).

Korean Statistical Information Service. Balance of Payments. http://kosis.kr/statHtml/statHtml.do?orgId=301&tblId=DT_022Y016&language=en&conn_path=I3 (accessed August 2017).

Government of the Republic of Korea. Ministry of Trade, Industry, and Energy. FDI Arrival. http://www.motie.go.kr/www/main.do (accessed August 2017).

World Bank. 2017. Doing Business 2017: Equal Opportunity for All. http://www.doingbusiness.org/ (accessed September 2017).

_____. World Development Indicators. http://databank.worldbank.org/data/reports.aspx?source=world-development-indicators (accessed September 2017).

_____. Worldwide Governance Indicators. http://info.worldbank.org/governance/wgi/#home (accessed September 2017).

United Nations Conference on Trade and Development. Bilateral FDI Statistics. http://unctad.org/en/Pages/DIAE/FDI%20Statistics/FDI-Statistics-Bilateral.aspx (accessed July 2017).

04

Financial Integration

Financial Integration

Progress in Cross-border Financial Transactions

From 2010 to 2015, Asia's intraregional cross-border asset holdings grew faster than total holdings.

Asia's total cross-border asset holdings between 2010 and 2015 rose from $11.5 trillion to $14.6 trillion—a compounded annual growth rate (CAGR) of 4.9%. Intraregional holdings increased 8.8% CAGR (Figure 4.1).[14] Foreign direct investment (FDI) increased from $2.5 trillion to $3.6 trillion. It accounted for the largest share (39.4%) of intraregional holdings to total holdings in 2015. Still, given its much larger holdings of non-Asian assets, Asia remains more financially linked to the rest of the world (ROW) than to itself.

During this period of uneven global economic recovery and diverging monetary policies in advanced economies, Asia's intraregional share of total cross-border asset holdings increased over all asset classes—except for portfolio equities, which declined from 24.2% to 20.0%. The intraregional share of Asia's cross-border debt asset holdings increased from 11.9% to 16.7%, but remained the smallest component. The share of intraregional bank claims increased to 22.1% in 2015 from 16.3% in 2010.

Growth in Asia's cross-border liabilities outpaced growth in cross-border assets, underscoring the region's continued investment attraction; the largest increase in share during 2010–2015 was in intraregional cross-border bank liabilities.

Asia's total cross-border liability holdings increased from $11.5 trillion in 2010 to $15.1 trillion in 2015—a 5.6% CAGR (Figure 4.2). Intraregional holdings increased

Figure 4.1: Asia's Cross-border Assets

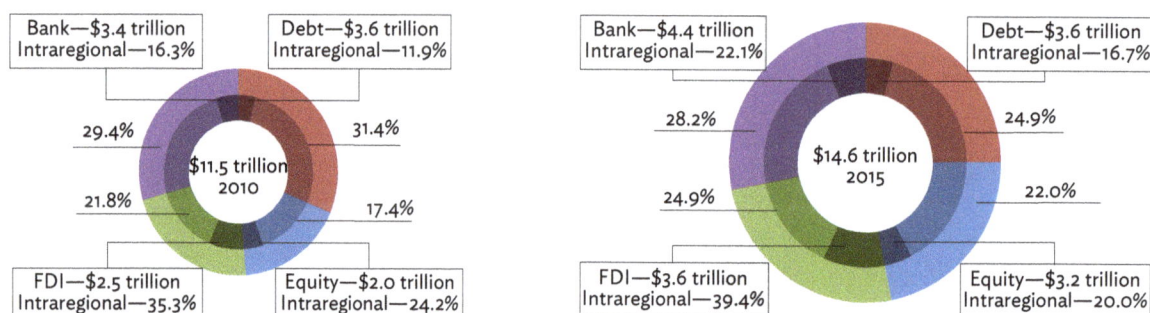

Bank—$3.4 trillion Intraregional—16.3%
Debt—$3.6 trillion Intraregional—11.9%
29.4%
31.4%
$11.5 trillion 2010
21.8%
17.4%
FDI—$2.5 trillion Intraregional—35.3%
Equity—$2.0 trillion Intraregional—24.2%

Bank—$4.4 trillion Intraregional—22.1%
Debt—$3.6 trillion Intraregional—16.7%
28.2%
24.9%
$14.6 trillion 2015
24.9%
22.0%
FDI—$3.6 trillion Intraregional—39.4%
Equity—$3.2 trillion Intraregional—20.0%

FDI = foreign direct investment.
Notes: FDI assets refer to outward FDI holdings. Bank assets refer to bank claims of Asian economies. Asia includes all 48 ADB regional members for which data are available as of December 2015.
Sources: ADB calculations using data from International Monetary Fund. Coordinated Portfolio Investment Survey. http://cpis.imf.org (accessed September 2017); International Monetary Fund. Coordinated Direct Investment Survey. http://cdis.imf.org (accessed February 2017); and Bank for International Settlements. Locational Banking Statistics. https://www.bis.org/statistics/bankstats.htm (accessed May 2017).

---

[14] Throughout this section, Asia's cross-border asset holdings refer to the stock of outbound portfolio debt, portfolio equity, and foreign direct investment (FDI), as well as cross-border bank claims. FDI stock data available only for 2009–2015.

Figure 4.2: Asia's Cross-border Liabilities

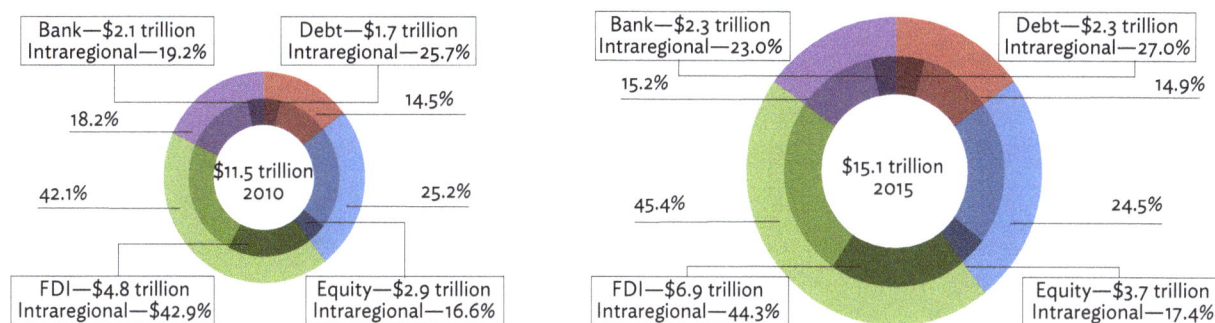

Bank—$2.1 trillion
Intraregional—19.2%

Debt—$1.7 trillion
Intraregional—25.7%

14.5%

18.2%

$11.5 trillion
2010

42.1%

25.2%

FDI—$4.8 trillion
Intraregional—$42.9%

Equity—$2.9 trillion
Intraregional—16.6%

Bank—$2.3 trillion
Intraregional—23.0%

Debt—$2.3 trillion
Intraregional—27.0%

15.2%

14.9%

$15.1 trillion
2015

45.4%

24.5%

FDI—$6.9 trillion
Intraregional—44.3%

Equity—$3.7 trillion
Intraregional—17.4%

FDI = foreign direct investment.
Notes: FDI liabilities refer to inward FDI holdings. Asia includes all 48 ADB regional members for which data are available as of December 2015.
Sources: ADB calculations using data from International Monetary Fund. Coordinated Portfolio Investment Survey. http://cpis.imf.org (accessed September 2017); IMF. Coordinated Direct Investment Survey. http://cdis.imf.org (accessed February 2017); and Bank for International Settlements. Locational Banking Statistics. https://www.bis.org/statistics/bankstats.htm (accessed May 2017).

7.3% CAGR, reaching $4.8 trillion in 2015. The larger rise in liabilities shows Asia continues to be an attractive destination for investors. The proportion of Asia's FDI liabilities also increased. The intraregional share for inward FDI rose to 44.3%, followed by debt liabilities (27.0%), bank liabilities (23.0%) and equity liabilities (17.4%). In particular, the intraregional share of Asia's cross-border intraregional bank liabilities had the largest increase in share among asset classes.

Portfolio Debt Holdings

The intraregional share of portfolio debt declined in 2016 as the steady recovery in advanced economies attracted more investors, both from the region and elsewhere.

Asia's outward portfolio debt investments rose from $1.3 trillion in 2001 to $4.0 trillion in 2016 (Figure 4.3).[15] Between 2001 and 2014, growth in intraregional investment (15.8% annually) outpaced ROW investment (7.1%). The intraregional share grew by 7.1% to 18.9% during the period.

Figure 4.3: Outward Portfolio Debt Investment—Asia

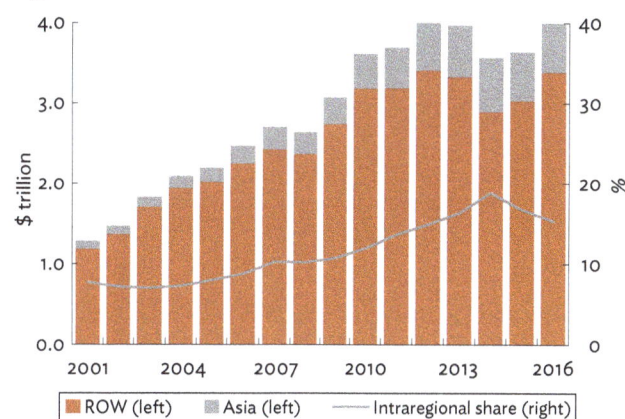

ROW = rest of the world.
Note: Asia includes 48 ADB regional members for which data are available as of December 2016.
Source: ADB calculations using data from International Monetary Fund. Coordinated Portfolio Investment Survey. http://cpis.imf.org (accessed September 2017).

However, between 2014 and 2016, after the 2013 taper tantrum, Asia's outward ROW investments grew by 8.2% CAGR, while intraregional outward investments declined 4.5%—the intraregional share fell from 18.9% to 15.3%. Regional investors increased their portfolio debt investment in the United States (US) and the European Union (EU), attracted by rising interest rates, in line with the global trend.

Asia's outward debt investments increased as higher yields attracted investors.

In 2016, Asia's outward portfolio debt investment increased $360 billion, well above the $73.4 billion increase during 2015 (Figure 4.4). The significant rise

---

[15]   For outward portfolio investment, several economies included in AEIR 2016 are excluded due to unavailable or lack of comparable data. They include Aruba, the Bahamas, Kingdom of Bahrain, Barbados, Chile, Curacao and Sint Maarten, Ireland, Netherlands Antilles, and Uruguay. Data on outward portfolio investment from the People's Republic of China are also excluded due to lack of comparable data for 2001–2014.

Figure 4.4: Change in Outward Portfolio Debt Investment—Asia ($ billion)

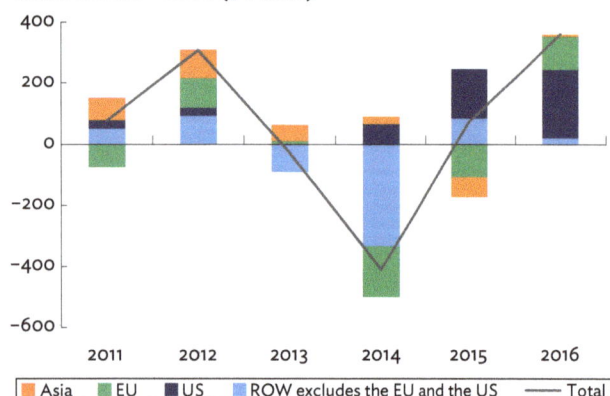

EU = European Union, ROW = rest of the world, US = United States.
Note: Asia includes 48 ADB regional members for which data are available as of December 2016.
Source: ADB calculations using data from International Monetary Fund. Coordinated Portfolio Investment Survey. http://cpis.imf.org (accessed September 2017).

derived from a trend reversal in outward investment with the EU and within Asia. Intraregional outward investment increased $5.8 billion—after decreasing $64.6 billion during 2015. Outward investment to the EU increased $109.6 billion—a sharp reversal from its $107.1 billion decrease in 2015.

In 2016, investors from Japan flocked to the region seeking higher-yielding bonds—particularly in Australia, New Zealand, Singapore, and Indonesia. Japan, together with Australia, was also a primary contributor to the

increase in Asia's outward debt investment to the EU—Japan's EU investments increased $41.3 billion in 2016 after declining $74.0 billion in 2015. EU bonds, especially French bonds, are higher yielding than Japanese bonds (Reuters 2016).

While investors across the region contributed to the $233.8 billion rise in Asia's outward investment to the US, Japan contributed most—$168.5 billion.

The US remains top destination for Asia's outward portfolio debt investment and is increasing its share coinciding with US monetary policy normalization—the US share rose from 31.0% in 2011 to 40.6% in 2016 (Table 4.1).

In Asia, while Australia, the People's Republic of China (PRC), and Japan remain top destinations for outward portfolio debt investment, other Asian economies are seeing their share rise as well—from 5.1% in 2011 to 5.7% in 2016. Singapore; Hong Kong, China; and Indonesia were among the fastest growing destinations for Asia's outward portfolio debt investment.

The increase in the proportion of Asia's total outward portfolio debt investment to the PRC and Japan drove East Asia's share up from 42.2% in 2011 to 48.1% in 2016 (Figure 4.5). Southeast Asia's share rose from 12.5% in 2011 to 16.7% in 2016 as Singapore (as a financial hub) continued to grow along with investment to Indonesia

Table 4.1: Destinations for Asia's Outward Portfolio Debt Investment ($ billion)

	2016		2011		**
Asia					
Australia	171	(4.3%)	188	(5.1%)	▼
People's Republic of China	148	(3.7%)	89	(2.4%)	▲
Japan	68	(1.7%)	38	(1.0%)	▲
Other Asia	226	(5.7%)	189	(5.1%)	▲
Asia's outward portfolio debt investment to Asia	613	(15.3%)	503	(13.6%)	▲
Non-Asia					
United States	1,621	(40.6%)	1,144	(31.0%)	▲
European Union	1,034	(25.9%)	1,089	(29.5%)	▼
Cayman Islands	205	(5.1%)	476	(12.9%)	▼
Other non-Asia	521	(13.0%)	477	(12.9%)	▼
Asia's outward portfolio debt investment to non-Asia	3,381	(84.7%)	3,185	(86.4%)	▼
Asia's total outward portfolio debt investment	**3,994**	**(100.0%)**	**3,688**	**(100.0%)**	

** = direction of change in the shares to total, ▼ = decrease, ▲ = increase.
Source: ADB calculations using data from International Monetary Fund. Coordinated Portfolio Investment Survey. http://cpis.imf.org (accessed September 2017).

Figure 4.5: Asia's Intraregional Portfolio Debt Investment by Subregion (%)

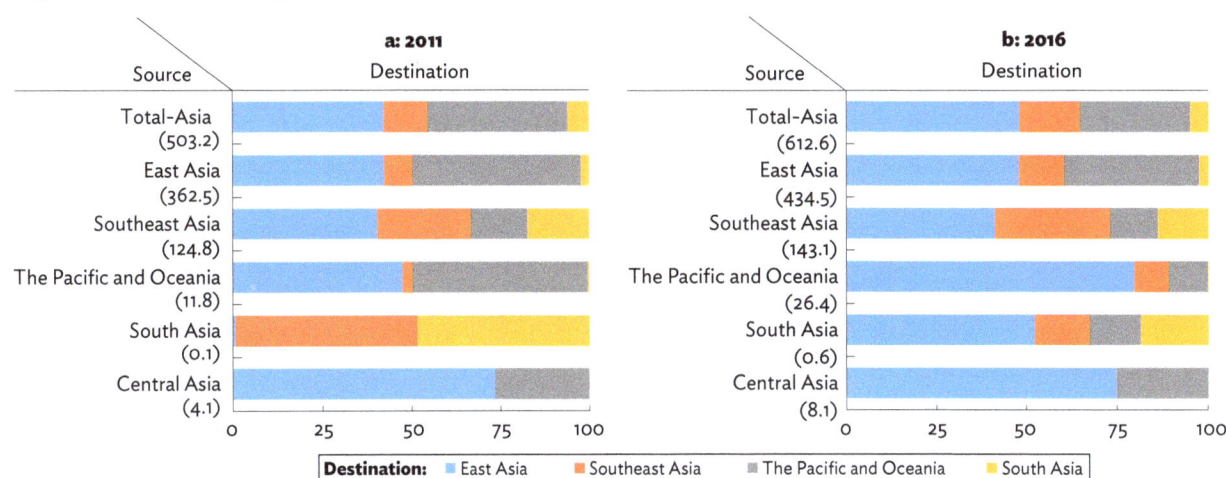

Note: Numbers in parentheses are total investments (in $ billion) from the respective subregions.
Source: ADB calculation using data from International Monetary Fund. Coordinated Portfolio Investment Survey. http://cpis.imf.org (accessed September 2017).

Table 4.2: Sources of Asia's Inward Portfolio Debt Investment ($ billion)

	2016		2011		**
Asia					
Hong Kong, China	226	(10.1%)	181	(9.5%)	▲
Japan	187	(8.4%)	178	(9.3%)	▼
Singapore	111	(5.0%)	104	(5.5%)	▼
Other Asia	89	(4.0%)	40	(2.1%)	▲
Asia's inward portfolio debt investment from Asia	613	(27.4%)	503	(26.4%)	▲
Non-Asia					
European Union	645	(28.9%)	555	(29.1%)	▼
United States	438	(19.6%)	416	(21.8%)	▼
International Organizations	260	(11.6%)	322	(16.9%)	▼
Other non-Asia	277	(12.4%)	110	(5.8%)	▲
Asia's inward portfolio debt investment from non-Asia	1,619	(72.6%)	1,403	(73.6%)	▼
Asia's total inward portfolio debt investment	**2,232**	**(100.0%)**	**1,906**	**(100.0%)**	

** = direction of change in the share to total, ▼ = decrease, ▲ = increase.
Source: ADB calculations using data from International Monetary Fund. Coordinated Portfolio Investment Survey. http://cpis.imf.org (accessed September 2017).

and Malaysia. East Asia remained the top source of Asia's intraregional portfolio debt investment in 2016 (70.9%), despite dropping from 2011 (72.0%). Southeast Asia, the second top investment source, saw its share decrease from 24.8% in 2011 to 23.4% in 2016.

By economy, the top sources of Asia's intraregional portfolio debt investment in 2016 were the ASEAN+3 financial centers—Hong Kong, China; Japan; and Singapore (Table 4.2). However, the share of Hong Kong, China's portfolio debt investments to the PRC fell dramatically—from 80.4% in 2011 to 54.8% in 2016. Outside Asia, the EU, the US, and international

organizations remained top sources for inward portfolio debt investment to Asia. Despite a drop in non-Asia's relative share of inward portfolio debt investment—from 73.6% in 2011 to 72.6% in 2016—non-Asian economies remained the primary source of Asia's inward portfolio debt investment.

Asia's inward portfolio debt investment increased dramatically, from $410.5 billion in 2001 to $2.2 trillion in 2015 (Figure 4.6). In 2015, low-yielding debt securities in the EU and the US drove investors from non-Asian economies toward Asia's portfolio debt markets—investment rose from $1.54 trillion in 2014 to

Figure 4.6: Asia's Inward Portfolio Debt Investment—Asia

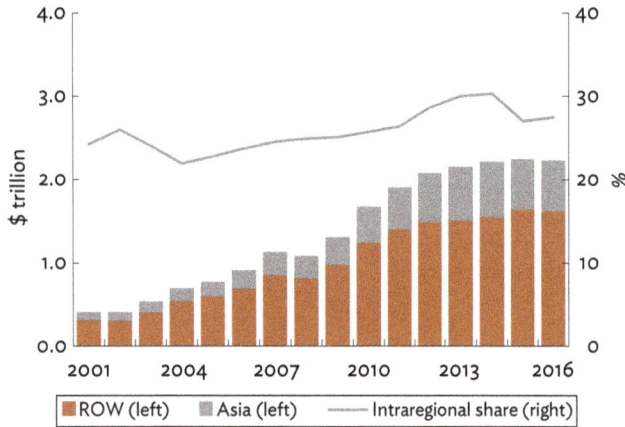

ROW = rest of the world.
Note: Asia includes 48 ADB regional members for which data are available as of December 2016.
Source: ADB calculations using data from International Monetary Fund, Coordinated Portfolio Investment Survey. http://cpis.imf.org (accessed September 2017).

Figure 4.7: Change in Inward Portfolio Debt Investment—Asia ($ billion)

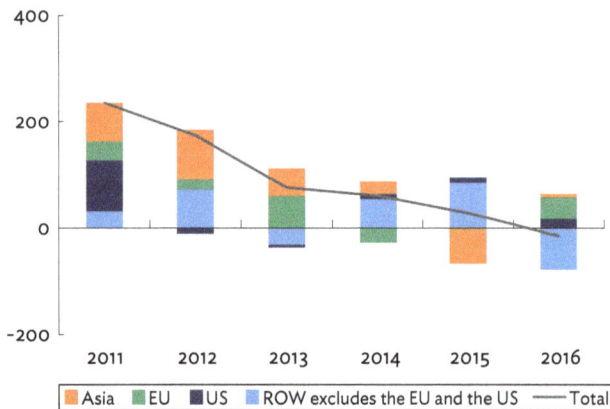

EU = European Union, ROW = rest of the world, US = United States.
Note: Asia includes 48 ADB regional members for which data are available as of December 2016.
Source: ADB calculations using data from International Monetary Fund. Coordinated Portfolio Investment Survey. http://cpis.imf.org (accessed September 2017).

$1.64 trillion in 2015. Higher US yields drove investment to Asia down slightly—from $1.64 trillion to $1.62 trillion in 2016. Intraregional investment rose to $612.6 billion as Japanese investors sought securities with higher yields than domestic debt. This increased Asia's intraregional share to 27.5%.

Asia's inward portfolio debt investment decreased $13.9 billion in 2016—a reversal from its $28.8 billion increase in 2015 (Figure 4.7)—as a result of a drastic increase in Cayman Island investment in 2015.

The United Kingdom drove much of the EU change in debt investment toward Asia, increasing its investments in Japan ($48.7 billion). The increased inward portfolio debt investment from the US in 2016 ($18.0 billion) also had much of it invested in Japan ($46.6 billion), coinciding with Japan's economic recovery. Moreover, the $77.6 billion decrease in inward portfolio debt investment into Asia, particularly the ROW excluding the EU and the US, was due to the region's relative local currency depreciation (or slowed appreciation)—triggered by the expected series of US interest rate hikes in 2016.

Portfolio Equity Holdings

In 2016, Japan's appetite for non-regional equity markets led to a decline in intraregional share of portfolio equity investments and an increase in Asia's linkage to the ROW.

Asia's outward portfolio equity investment increased from $3.2 trillion in 2015 to $3.5 trillion in 2016—its highest level since 2001 (Figure 4.8). The increase was largely to the ROW—from $2.6 trillion to $2.8 trillion. Much of the increase can be traced to Japan, which held $1.3 trillion in outward portfolio equity securities of non-Asian economies in 2016, up from $1.2 trillion in 2015. Intraregional outward portfolio equity investment rose from $644.0 billion in 2015 to $666.4 billion in

Figure 4.8: Outward Portfolio Equity Investment—Asia

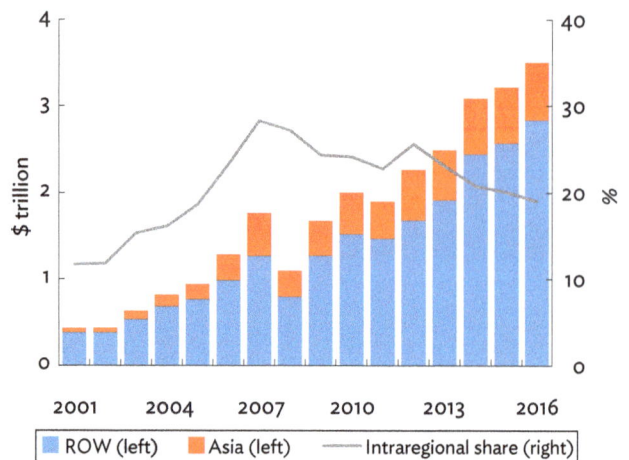

ROW = rest of the world.
Note: Asia includes 48 ADB regional members for which data are available as of December 2016.
Source: ADB calculations using data from International Monetary Fund. Coordinated Portfolio Investment Survey. http://cpis.imf.org (accessed September 2017).

2016. However, Asia's intraregional share dropped from 20.0% in 2015 to 19.0% in 2016, given its growing linkage to the ROW. By comparison, the EU's intraregional share remained significantly above Asia's (51.0%), down from 2015 (52.7%). While intraregional shares in Latin America and the Middle East both declined from 2015 to 2016, North America's intraregional share increased (from 16.9% to 19.4%).

Intraregional outward portfolio equity investment rose in 2016 due to larger investments to the PRC and Hong Kong, China.

Asia's outward portfolio equity investment in 2016 rose by $289.2 billion, well above the $128.0 billion increase in 2015 (Figure 4.9). While primarily due to Japan's higher investment in the Cayman Islands and the US— by $59.2 billion and $56.0 billion respectively—the increase in Hong Kong, China investment to the Cayman Islands ($50.3 billion) also contributed to the significant rise in Asia's outward portfolio equity investment during the year.[16] Intraregional investment likewise rose $22.4 billion in 2016, due to an increase in outward portfolio equity investment to Hong Kong, China from the PRC ($26.3 billion) and to the PRC from Hong Kong, China ($16.4 billion).

Figure 4.9: Change in Outward Portfolio Equity Investment—Asia ($ billion)

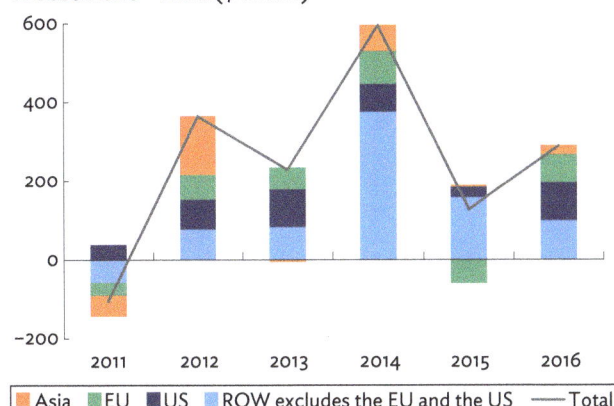

EU = European Union, ROW = rest of the world, US = United States.
Note: Asia includes 48 ADB regional members for which data are available as of December 2016.
Source: ADB calculations using data from International Monetary Fund. Coordinated Portfolio Investment Survey. http://cpis.imf.org (accessed September 2017).

16   The Cayman Islands is one of the largest offshore financial centers, acting as conduit for large international financial institutions to reduce taxes and evade onshore regulations. Investors from Asia, particularly Japan, use the Cayman Islands to indirectly access US financial markets (Fichtner 2016).

From 2011 to 2016, Asia's outward portfolio equity investment remained skewed toward the ROW than the region; unlike outward portfolio debt investment, its share of outward portfolio equity investment to non-Asian economies rose from 77.3% in 2011 to 81.0% in 2016.

The PRC remained top destination for Asia's intraregional outward portfolio equity investment (Table 4.3). The decline in intraregional share was mainly due to an increase in relative share of investment going to the Cayman Islands—from 14.6% in 2011 to 26.2% in 2016. Hong Kong, China—aside from Japan—was a major source of outward portfolio equity investment to the Cayman Islands, whose stocks are allowed to list on Hong Kong Exchanges and Clearing, Ltd. The US and the EU, along with the Cayman Islands, were the most popular destinations for Asia's outward portfolio equity investment in 2016, with much of the investment coming from Japan.

In 2016, East Asia remained top destination for intraregional portfolio equity investment (70.9%) (Figure 4.10). Southeast Asia's intraregional share inched up from 12.1% in 2011 to 12.2% in 2016. South Asia's share also rose (from 4.5% to 6.6%) due to increased investments in Pakistan and Nepal. East Asia remained the top source of intraregional portfolio equity investment, although its share slightly declined in 2016 (54.0%) from 2011 (54.2%). Southeast Asia's relative share as source of intraregional equity investments increased to 35.0% from 32.6% during the same period.

Asia continued to depend on portfolio equity investment from outside the region.

Similar to inward portfolio debt investment, the region's financial centers—Hong Kong, China; Singapore; and Japan—remained the top sources of inward portfolio equity investment (Table 4.4). Asia continues to depend on portfolio equity investment from the ROW. Despite a decline in Asia's portfolio equity investment share from the EU between 2011 and 2016 (from 26.6% to 23.6%), the EU remained ranked second behind the US—which saw its share dip slightly (from 44.4% to 44.2%).

Asia's inward portfolio equity investment increased from $653.8 billion in 2001 to $3.9 trillion in 2016 (Figure 4.11). The increase was driven by higher

Table 4.3: Destinations of Asia's Outward Portfolio Equity Investment ($ billion)

	2016		2011		**
Asia					
People's Republic of China	302	(8.6%)	188	(9.9%)	▼
Japan	72	(2.1%)	41	(2.2%)	▼
Australia	61	(1.7%)	48	(2.5%)	▼
Other Asia	231	(6.6%)	154	(8.1%)	▼
Asia's outward portfolio equity investment to Asia	666	(19.0%)	431	(22.7%)	▼
Non-Asia					
United States	924	(26.4%)	560	(29.5%)	▼
Cayman Islands	919	(26.2%)	277	(14.6%)	▲
European Union	536	(15.3%)	324	(17.1%)	▼
Other non-Asia	458	(13.1%)	304	(16.0%)	▼
Asia's outward portfolio equity investment to non-Asia	2,837	(81.0%)	1,465	(77.3%)	▲
Asia's total outward portfolio equity investment	**3,503**	**(100.0%)**	**1,896**	**(100.0%)**	

** = direction of change in the shares to total, ▼ = decrease, ▲ = increase.
Source: ADB calculations using data from International Monetary Fund. Coordinated Portfolio Investment Survey. http://cpis.imf.org (accessed September 2017).

Figure 4.10: Asia's Intraregional Portfolio Equity Investment by Subregion (%)

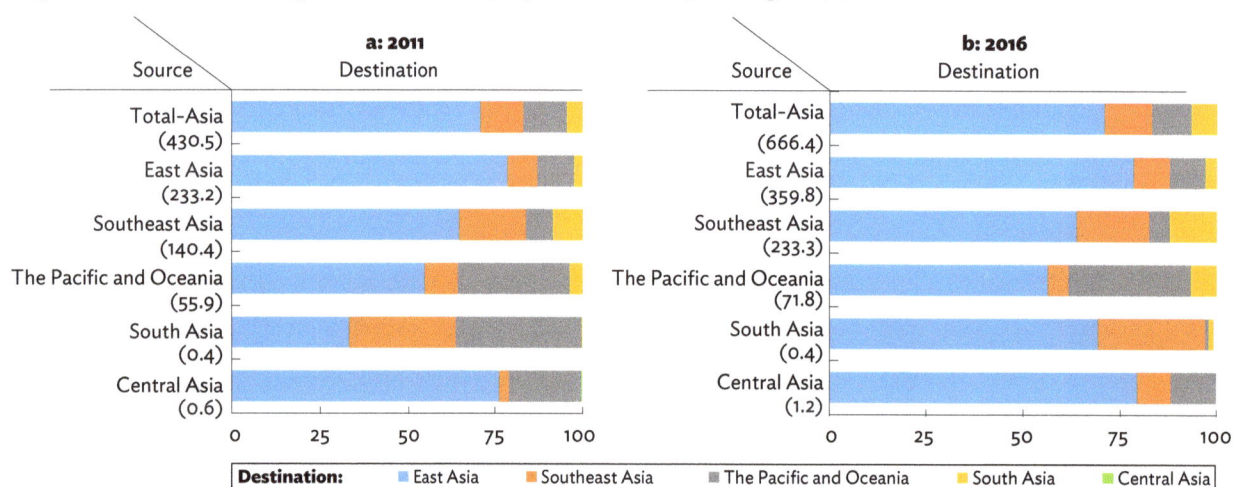

Note: Numbers in parentheses are total investments (in $ billion) from the respective subregions.
Source: ADB calculation using data from International Monetary Fund. Coordinated Portfolio Investment Survey. http://cpis.imf.org (accessed September 2017).

investments in Japan ($35.4 billion) and Singapore ($19.7 billion), along with a reversal in investments in Taipei,China (from a $14.7 billion contraction to a $34.3 billion increase), Australia (from $8.8 billion contraction to $29.7 billion increase), and the Republic of Korea (from $8.0 billion contraction to $28.1 billion increase).

Inward portfolio equity investment rose $167.6 billion in 2016, significantly above the $46.7 billion increase in 2015 (Figure 4.12). Robust equity investment inflows from countries outside Asia—such as the US ($88.7 billion), the Netherlands ($19.0 billion), Luxembourg ($9.3 billion), and the Cayman Islands ($7.7 billion)—coupled with strong intraregional equity investments from the PRC ($27.2 billion) and Hong Kong, China ($22.7 billion) contributed to the rise in 2016.

Table 4.4: Sources of Asia's Inward Portfolio Equity Investment ($ billion)

	2016		2011		**
Asia					
Hong Kong, China	236	(6.1%)	143	(5.8%)	▲
Singapore	205	(5.3%)	125	(5.1%)	▲
Japan	89	(2.3%)	68	(2.8%)	▼
Other Asia	137	(3.5%)	94	(3.8%)	▼
Asia's inward portfolio equity investment from Asia	666	(17.2%)	431	(17.5%)	▼
Non-Asia					
United States	1,713	(44.2%)	1,091	(44.4%)	▼
European Union	913	(23.6%)	653	(26.6%)	▼
Canada	133	(3.4%)	87	(3.6%)	▼
Other non-Asia	449	(11.6%)	192	(7.8%)	▲
Asia's inward portfolio equity investment from non-Asia	3,207	(82.8%)	2,023	(82.5%)	▲
Asia's total inward portfolio equity investment	**3,873**	**(100.0%)**	**2,453**	**(100.0%)**	

** = direction of change in the shares to total, ▼ = decrease, ▲ = increase.
Source: ADB calculations using data from International Monetary Fund. Coordinated Portfolio Investment Survey. http://cpis.imf.org (accessed September 2017).

Figure 4.11: Inward Portfolio Equity Investment—Asia

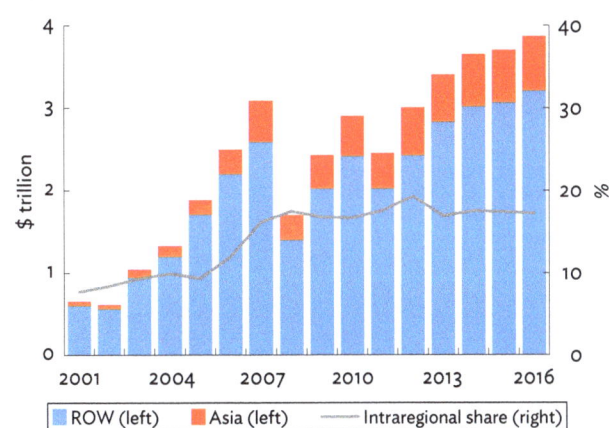

ROW = rest of the world.
Note: Asia includes 48 ADB regional members for which data are available as of December 2016.
Source: ADB calculations using data from International Monetary Fund. Coordinated Portfolio Investment Survey. http://cpis.imf.org (accessed September 2017).

Figure 4.12: Change in Inward Portfolio Equity Investment—Asia ($ billion)

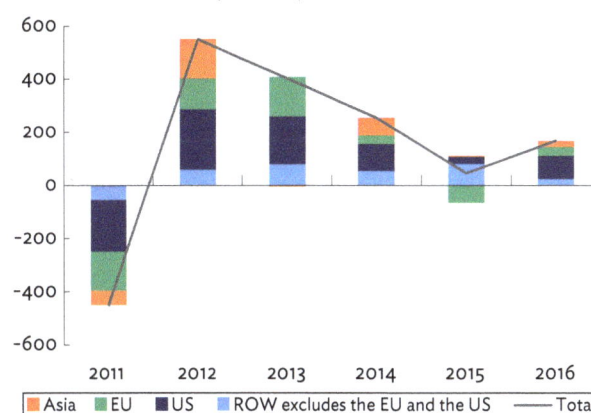

EU = European Union, ROW = rest of the world, US = United States.
Note: Asia includes 48 ADB regional members for which data are available as of December 2016.
Source: ADB calculations using data from International Monetary Fund. Coordinated Portfolio Investment Survey. http://cpis.imf.org (accessed September 2017).

Bank Holdings

While Asia's cross-border bank claims and liabilities remain largely linked outside the region—in particular the US and the EU—the intraregional shares of claims and liabilities increased during 2011–2016 (from 17.8% to 21.4% for bank claims and 18.8% to 25.7% for bank liabilities).

Asia's cross-border bank claims increased from $1.3 trillion in 2001 to $4.4 trillion in 2016 (Figure 4.13).[17] After the global financial crisis (GFC), Asia's intraregional share rapidly increased—from 14.3% in 2008 to 24.3% in 2014, before dropping to 21.4% in 2016. According to the Global Financial Stability Report (GFSR) April 2015, the EU bank retrenchment cleared the way for greater Asia bank involvement. The expansion of intraregional

[17]   Asian economies reporting locational banking statistics are Australia; Japan; the Republic of Korea; and Taipei,China.

Figure 4.13: Asia's Cross-border Bank Claims

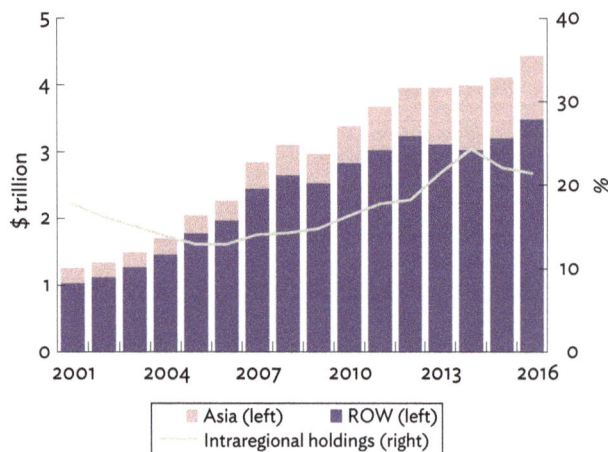

ROW = rest of the world.
Note: Asia includes all 48 ADB regional members for which data are available as of December 2016.
Source: ADB calculations using data from Bank for International Settlements. Locational Banking Statistics. https://www.bis.org/statistics/bankstats.htm (accessed May 2017).

Figure 4.14: Change in Asia's Cross-border Bank Claims ($ billion)

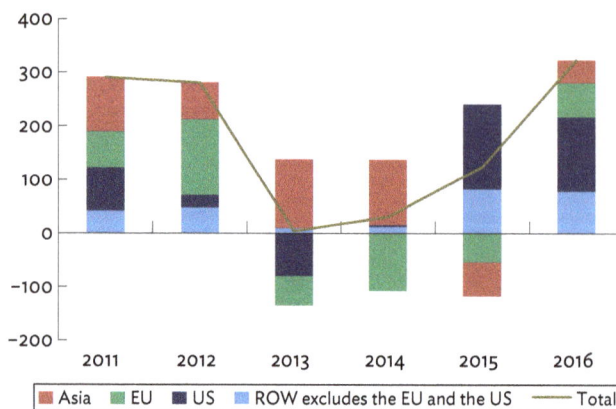

EU = European Union, ROW = rest of the world, US = United States.
Note: Asia includes all 48 ADB regional members for which data are available as of December 2016.
Source: ADB calculations using data from Bank for International Settlements. Locational Banking Statistics. https://www.bis.org/statistics/bankstats.htm (accessed May 2017).

banking could create the emergence of regional systemically important financial institutions, which requires appropriate regulation and supervision as well good risk and liquidity management (Box 4.1).

In fact, Asia's cross-border bank claims increased to $322.5 billion in 2016, above the 2015 increase of $124.1 billion (Figure 4.14). Japan contributed 88.7% of the 2016 increase against a backdrop of limited domestic credit demand and benign growth—which led Japanese banks to increase their overseas lending.

Japan's cross-border bank claims on Asia increased $19.8 billion in 2016 as it capitalized on the region's continued growth. Japan's cross-border bank claims on the EU increased $59.2 billion as it narrowed the funding gap left by retrenched EU banks (Lam 2013). Japan's cross-border bank claims on the US in 2016 also increased ($131.3 billion) due to the yen's appreciation against the US dollar. This could be due to Japan's ability to lend long-term (for project finance) and engage in syndicated loans (IMF April 2015).

Singapore; the PRC; and Hong Kong, China remained the top intraregional destinations for Asia's cross-border bank claims (Table 4.5). The increase in relative and absolute shares of cross-border bank claims in other Asian economies helped boost intraregional share from 17.8% in 2011 to 21.4% in 2016—particularly cross-border bank claims on Indonesia, Japan, and Thailand. The US,

Figure 4.15: Asia's Cross-border Bank Liabilities ($ trillion)

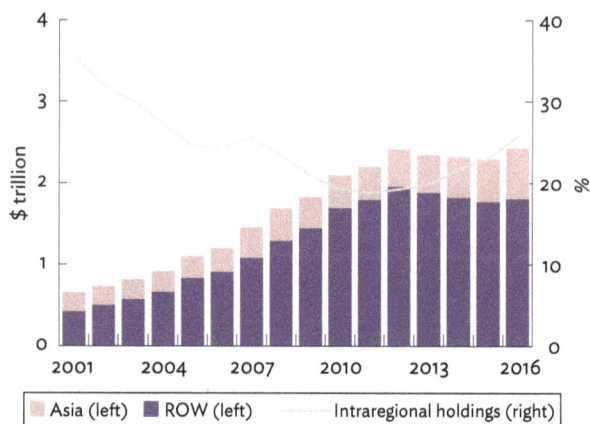

ROW = rest of the world.
Note: Asia includes all 48 ADB regional members for which data are available as of December 2016.
Source: ADB calculations using data from Bank for International Settlements. Locational Banking Statistics. https://www.bis.org/statistics/bankstats.htm (accessed May 2017).

the EU and the Cayman Islands remain top destinations for Asia's bank claims—with Japan lending heavily to these regions in 2016.

Asia's cross-border bank liabilities increased from $655.1 billion in 2001 to $2.4 trillion in 2016 (Figure 4.15). Following tighter banking restrictions and bank retrenchments during the EU crisis, Asia's intraregional bank liabilities grew 8.6% CAGR, while cross-border bank liabilities outside Asia grew a mere

Box 4.1: Asia's Cross-border Collateral Agreements

After the 2008/09 global financial crisis, intraregional cross-border banking in Asia expanded significantly. The notable increase in intraregional banking and the emergence of large regional banks creates a new concern for the region's regulators—as a financial shock create by one bank can be transmitted from its home economy to host economies or vice versa. Cross-border banking requires additional risk management because loans provided through foreign branches and subsidiaries are in foreign currencies. Banks may face difficulties in local currency funding as onshore and offshore foreign exchange and future markets are segregated.

Expanding cross-border banking must coincide with good risk and liquidity management across multiple currencies and jurisdictions. The Committee on Payment and Settlement Systems recognize that cross-border collateral arrangements (CBCAs) reduce the risk of liquidity shortfalls—which create systemic risk. Among available CBCAs, the correspondent central banking model (CCBM) used by the European Central Bank (ECB) stands out. Through the CCBM, a bank can obtain euro liquidity from its home central bank under the CCBM by pledging assets held by branches in another country (box figure).

Asia has no comparable system. But after the global financial crisis, a series of CBCAs were established and some foreign assets were included as eligible collateral. In 2009, the Bank of Japan (BOJ) expanded eligibility to

government securities of the United States (US), France, and Germany. In 2011, the BOJ and Bank of Thailand (BOT) agreed to establish a CBCA, followed by the BOJ and Monetary Authority of Singapore (MAS) in 2013, and in 2015 by the BOJ and Bank Indonesia and Bangko Sentral ng Pilipinas. MAS expanded eligibility of collateral for its standby facility under CBCAs with Bank Negara Malaysia (BNM), the Bank of England, BOT, Banque de France, De Nederlandsche Bank, Deutsche Bundesbank, the US Federal Reserve Bank and the BOJ. In 2012, the BOT and BNM signed a Memorandum of Understanding to enter into a CBCA.

For a more routinely operationalized cross-border collateral arrangement, linkages among central securities depositories (CSD) and real-time gross settlement systems (RTGS) by central banks (CSD-RTGS Linkages) were proposed in 2013 by the Cross-Border Settlement Infrastructure Forum (CSIF) (ADB 2014). CSD-RTGS Linkages enable local currency bonds to be settled by delivery versus payment via central banks and CSDs, ensuring secure settlement. CSD-RTGS Linkages are expected to free-up high quality domestic ASEAN+3 bonds for cross-border transactions and collateral, thus contributing to regional financial stability. Given different currencies, regulations, and different levels of market development, the CSIF needs to discuss various issues to make the linkages operational— such as the collateral frameworks of central banks varying across economies and private sector involvement.

Correspondent Central Banking Model

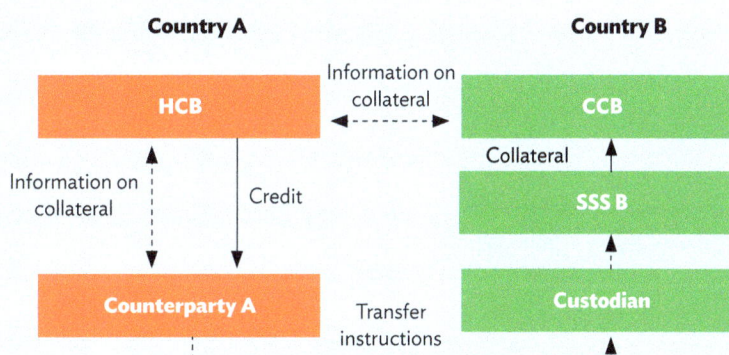

CCB = Correspondent Central Bank, HCB = Home Central Bank, SSS =Securities Settlement Systems.
Source: Bank for International Settlements (2006).

Table 4.5: Destinations of Asia's Cross-border Bank Claims ($ billion)

	2016		2011		**
Asia					
Singapore	206	(4.6%)	156	(4.3%)	▲
People's Republic of China	194	(4.4%)	74	(2.0%)	▲
Hong Kong, China	184	(4.1%)	135	(3.7%)	▲
Other Asia	365	(8.2%)	287	(7.8%)	▲
Asia's cross-border bank claims on Asia	949	(21.4%)	653	(17.8%)	▲
Non-Asia					
United States	1,348	(30.4%)	1,106	(30.1%)	▲
European Union	1,192	(26.9%)	1,201	(32.7%)	▼
Cayman Islands	617	(13.9%)	350	(9.5%)	▲
Other non-Asia	328	(7.4%)	364	(9.9%)	▼
Asia's cross-border bank claims on Non-Asia	3,486	(78.6%)	3,021	(82.2%)	▼
Asia's total cross-border bank claims	**4,435**	**(100.0%)**	**3,674**	**(100.0%)**	

** = direction of change in the shares to total, ▼ = decrease, ▲ = increase.
Source: ADB calculations using data from Bank for International Settlements. Locational Banking Statistics. https://www.bis.org/statistics/bankstats.htm (accessed May 2017).

0.1% CAGR between 2011 and 2016. This resulted in a 25.7% intraregional share.

Of the $132.4 billion increase in 2016—from a $27.8 billion drop in 2015—$95.9 billion was intraregional (Figure 4.16). Japan and Australia contributed most—$42.3 billion and $36.7 billion, respectively. Most of their intraregional bank liabilities were to Hong Kong, China; the PRC; Singapore; and Taipei,China. Asia also increased cross-border bank liabilities with the EU ($54.3 billion)—while Japan

increased its EU bank liabilities ($72.6 billion), Japan's liabilities to the US declined ($31.8 billion) along with Australia ($33.6 billion). Higher US interest rates relative to the EU were a factor in bank borrowing. Asia's cross-border bank liabilities to the ROW excluding the EU and US also increased ($13.9 billion). Japanese bank liabilities to Canada and the Cayman Islands increased $13.6 billion in 2016.

Japan and Australia relied heavily on bank lending from Hong Kong, China; Singapore; and the PRC in 2016 (Table 4.6) They emerged as the top sources of Asia's intraregional bank liabilities in 2016. Outside Asia, the EU, the US, and the Cayman Islands remained top sources—though their shares declined between 2011 and 2016 in favor of Asian and other non-Asian sources.

Figure 4.16: Change in Asia's Cross-border Bank Liabilities ($ billion)

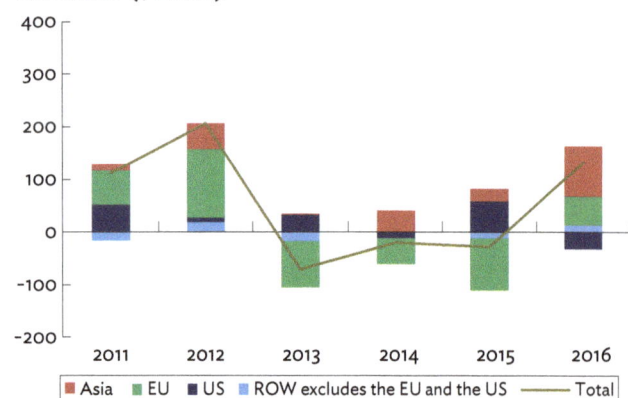

EU = European Union, ROW = rest of the world, US = United States.
Note: Asia includes all 48 ADB regional members for which data are available as of December 2016.
Source: ADB calculations using data from Bank for International Settlements. Locational Banking Statistics. https://www.bis.org/statistics/bankstats.htm (accessed May 2017).

Table 4.6: Sources of Asia's Cross-border Bank Liabilities ($ billion)

	2016		2011		**
Asia					
Hong Kong, China	241	(9.9%)	144	(6.5%)	▲
Singapore	148	(6.1%)	110	(5.0%)	▲
People's Republic of China	87	(3.6%)	21	(1.0%)	▲
Other Asia	149	(6.1%)	139	(6.3%)	▼
Asia's cross-border bank liabilities to Asia	625	(25.7%)	414	(18.8%)	▲
Non-Asia					
European Union	903	(37.2%)	953	(43.2%)	▼
United States	722	(29.8%)	665	(30.1%)	▼
Cayman Islands	53	(2.2%)	71	(3.2%)	▼
Other non-Asia	123	(5.1%)	103	(4.7%)	▲
Asia's cross-border bank liabilities to Non-Asia	1,802	(74.3%)	1,792	(81.2%)	▼
Total cross-border bank liabilities, Asia	**2,426**	**(100.0%)**	**2,206**	**(100.0%)**	

** = direction of change in the shares to total, ▼ = decrease, ▲ = increase.
Source: ADB calculations using data from Bank for International Settlements. Locational Banking Statistics. https://www.bis.org/statistics/bankstats.htm (accessed May 2017).

Analysis using Price Indicators

Asia's equity markets continue to be integrated more globally than regionally. Regional integration momentum in local bond markets weakened in the post-normalization period.

Equity

In the post-normalization period, equity market return correlations show stronger global (weaker regional) integration.

Asia's regional equity return correlation declined from 0.36 post-GFC to 0.34 in the post-normalization period (Table 4.7).[18] The declining equity return correlation can be attributed to all subregions except Oceania. However, the equity return correlation between Asia and the world remained the same at 0.42. With the exception of East Asia, which posted higher equity correlation with the world, the global equity return correlation with Asia's

subregions declined between post-GFC and post-normalization periods.

Using a dynamic conditional correlation (DCC) model—a time-varying correlation model that takes into account information on historical volatilities of equity returns—Asia's intraregional equity return DCC remained below the equity return DCC between Asia and the world, in line with the simple correlation results (Figure 4.17).[19] Consistent with theory, the equity return DCC between Asia and select economies and regions spiked during crises or stress, such as during Brexit and increased tension on the Korean peninsula. Also, large equity return DCC between Asia and the world could be attributable to the equity return DCC between Asia and the EU, as well as between Asia and the US.

---

[18] The "Asia index" of each economy is created using the weighted sum of the index of individual economies, excluding the economy considered. Current GDP in US dollars is the weight for the Asia indexes. This methodology is based on Park and Lee (2011).

[19] Estimates of the conditional correlations use the GARCH (1,1)-DCC model in which a two-step estimation procedure is applied. First, equity return residuals of individual economies are estimated using a univariate GARCH model. These residuals are subsequently used to compute the conditional correlation of each economy's equity returns with that of another economy. The correlation estimator is defined as

$$\rho_{i,j,t} = \frac{q_{i,j,t}}{\sqrt{q_{i,i,t} q_{j,j,t}}}$$

where $\rho_{i,j,t}$ is the conditional correlation between the equity asset returns of economies i and j at time t, and constitutes the off-diagonal elements of the variance-covariance matrix.

The GARCH(1,1) process followed by the qs is as follows:

$$q_{i,j,t} = \overline{\rho_{i,j}} + \alpha(\varepsilon_{i,t-1}\varepsilon_{j,t-1} - \overline{\rho_{i,j}}) + \gamma(q_{i,t-1}q_{j,t-1} - \overline{\rho_{i,j}})$$

where $\overline{\rho_{i,j}}$ is the unconditional expectation of the cross product.

Table 4.7: Average Simple Correlation of Stock Price Index Weekly Returns—Asia with Asia, and the World

Subregion	Asia				World			
	Pre-GFC Jan 1999– Sep 2007	Post-GFC Jul 2009– Dec 2015	Post-Normalization Jan 2016– Jun 2017	**	Pre-GFC Jan 1999– Sep 2007	Post-GFC Jul 2009– Dec 2015	Post-Normalization Jan 2016– Jun 2017	**
Central Asia	0.09	0.20	0.18	▼	0.02	0.24	0.19	▼
East Asia	0.35	0.47	0.46	▼	0.42	0.56	0.62	▲
Southeast Asia	0.33	0.40	0.39	▼	0.34	0.49	0.44	▼
South Asia	0.14	0.18	0.15	▼	0.15	0.18	0.17	▼
Oceania	0.38	0.52	0.54	▲	0.55	0.70	0.66	▼
Asia	**0.28**	**0.36**	**0.34**	▼	**0.36**	**0.42**	**0.42**	–

** = direction of change in simple correlation between post-GFC and post-normalization, ▼ = decrease, ▲ = increase, – = no change, GFC = global financial crisis.
Central Asia includes Georgia, Kazakhstan, and the Kyrgyz Republic. East Asia includes the People's Republic of China; Hong Kong, China; Japan; the Republic of Korea; Mongolia; and Taipei,China. Southeast Asia includes Indonesia, the Lao People's Democratic Republic, Malaysia, the Philippines, Singapore, Thailand, and Viet Nam. South Asia includes Bangladesh, India, Nepal, Pakistan, and Sri Lanka. Oceania includes Australia and New Zealand. Asia includes Central Asia, East Asia, Southeast Asia, South Asia, and Oceania.
Notes: Values refer to the average of pairwise correlations. Weekly returns are computed as the natural logarithm difference between weekly average of daily stock price index for the current week, and the weekly average of the daily stock price index from the previous week.
Sources: ADB calculations using data from Bloomberg; CEIC; and Stooq. https://stooq.com/q/?s=^sti; and World Bank. World Development Indicators http://data.worldbank.org/data-catalog/world-development-indicators (all accessed July 2017).

Figure 4.17: Conditional Correlations of Equity Markets—Asia with Select Economies and Regions

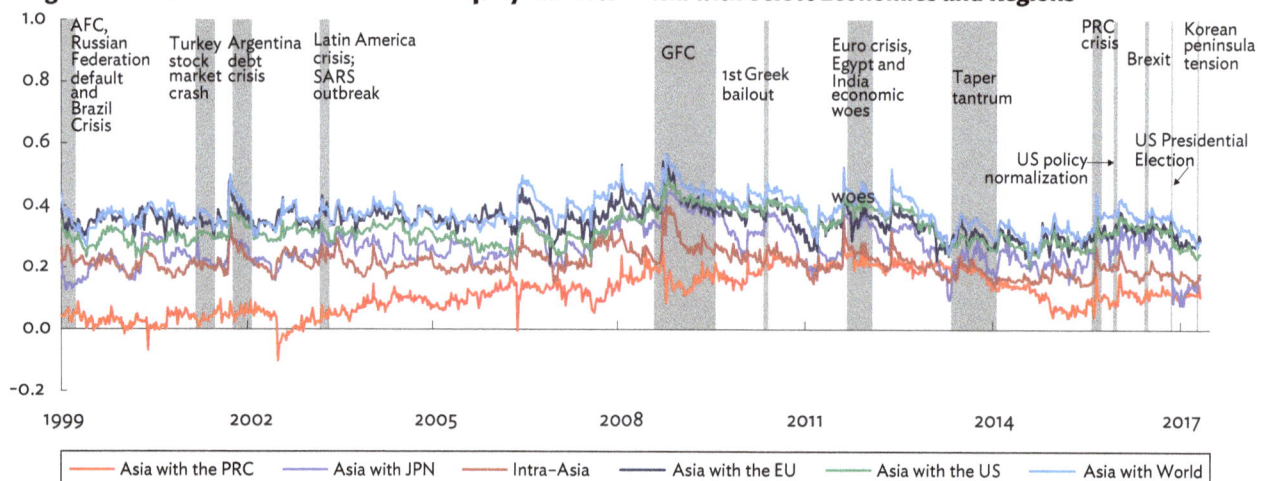

AFC = Asian financial crisis, EU = European Union, GFC = global financial crisis, JPN = Japan, PRC = People's Republic of China, US = United States, SARS = Severe Acute Respiratory Syndrome.
Note: Asia includes Australia; Bangladesh; the PRC; Georgia; Hong Kong, China; India; Indonesia; Japan; Kazakhstan; the Kyrgyz Republic; the Republic of Korea; the Lao People's Democratic Republic; Malaysia; Mongolia; Nepal; New Zealand; Pakistan; the Philippines; Singapore; Sri Lanka; Taipei,China; Thailand; and Viet Nam.
Sources: ADB calculations using Bloomberg; CEIC; and Stooq. http://stooq.com/q/d/_s=^sti (accessed July 2017); and methodology by Hinojales and Park (2010).

Debt

While Asia's bond market returns continue to show increased regional linkages, its global linkages surpassed regional linkages in the post-normalization period.

Asia's bond markets have become increasingly integrated regionally as its regional bond return correlation increased from 0.34 during post-GFC to 0.40 afterward (Table 4.8).[20] While bond return correlation between Asia and the world declined between pre- and post-GFC periods, it spiked from 0.21 during post-GFC to 0.48 during post-normalization.

---

[20]   The regional bond market is computed using the same methodology as the regional equity market.

Table 4.8: Average Simple Correlation of Weekly Bond Return Index—Asia with Asia and the World

Economy	Asia				World			
	Pre-GFC Jan 2005– Sep 2007	Post-GFC Jul 2009– Dec 2015	Post-Normalization Jan 2016– Jun 2017	**	Pre-GFC Jan 2005– Sep 2007	Post-GFC Jul 2009– Dec 2015	Post-Normalization Jan 2016– Jun 2017	**
Australia	0.38	0.46	0.49	▲	0.41	0.36	0.68	▲
PRC	0.01	0.30	0.34	▲	0.04	0.03	0.28	▲
India	0.06	0.21	0.08	▼	0.23	-0.07	-0.03	▲
Indonesia	-0.15	0.23	0.32	▲	0.02	0.25	0.52	▲
Japan	0.19	0.25	0.35	▲	0.28	0.41	0.48	▲
Republic of Korea	0.15	0.47	0.52	▲	0.37	0.23	0.66	▲
Malaysia	0.22	0.44	0.29	▼	0.13	0.15	0.44	▲
Philippines	–	0.21	0.45	▲	–	0.14	0.56	▲
Singapore	0.29	0.49	0.59	▲	0.27	0.44	0.69	▲
Thailand	0.20	0.39	0.56	▲	0.29	0.19	0.56	▲
Asia	**0.16**	**0.34**	**0.40**	▲	**0.23**	**0.21**	**0.48**	▲

** = direction of change in simple correlation between post-GFC and post-normalization, ▼ = decrease, ▲ = increase, GFC = global financial crisis, – – = no data available, PRC = People's Republic of China.
Notes: Values refer to the average of pairwise correlations. Weekly returns are computed as the natural logarithm difference between weekly average of daily bond return index for the current week, and the weekly average of the daily bond return index from the previous week. All bond return indexes are comprised by local currency government-issued bonds.
Sources: ADB calculations using data from Bloomberg; and World Bank. World Development Indicators http://data.worldbank.org/data-catalog/world-development-indicators (accessed May 2017).

Figure 4.18: Conditional Correlations of Bond Markets—Asia with Select Economies and Regions

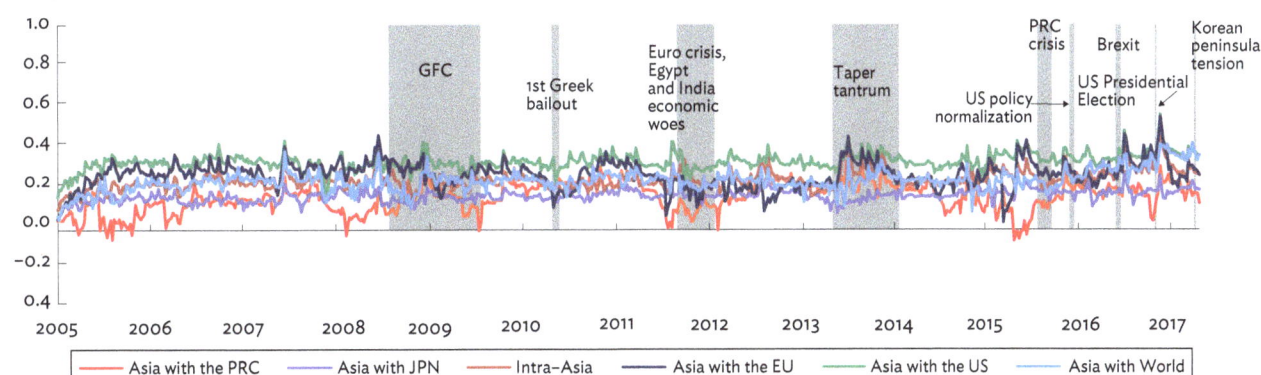

EU = European Union, GFC = global financial crisis, JPN = Japan, PRC = People's Republic of China, US = United States.
Note: Asia includes Australia, the PRC, India, Indonesia, Japan, the Republic of Korea, Malaysia, the Philippines, Singapore, and Thailand.
Sources: ADB calculations using data from Bloomberg and methodology by Hinojales and Park (2010).

The bond return DCC between Asia and the world remained consistent with the simple bond return correlation results—trending upward following the US policy normalization (Figure 4.18). While the intraregional bond return DCC spiked during the US presidential election, it suddenly declined afterward, widening the gap between the intraregional bond return DCC and the bond return DCC between Asia and the world. The increasing bond return DCC between Asia and the US buoyed the bond return DCC between Asia and the world. Meanwhile, the bond return DCC between Asia and the EU fell markedly in December 2016. These changes coincided with the US rate hike. Compared with the equity return DCC trend between Asia and Japan, Japan's ties to the region's bond markets are more evident in 2017.

Financial Spillovers

Equity

Asia's equity markets have become increasingly vulnerable to global shocks in the post-normalization period.

Increasing regional and global financial integration offers benefits such as: (i) risk sharing, (ii) improved capital allocation, and (iii) economic growth (Baele et al. 2004). However, with increasing financial integration comes the risk of greater volatility and contagion from vulnerable to stable economies. Hence, there are concerns of risk transmission channels in the post-normalization period due to increased regional and global linkages.

Asia's equity returns variance decomposition—which models risk spillovers originating from either the region or world—indicates that Asia's vulnerability to global spillovers declined between pre- and post-GFC periods (Figure 4.19).[21] Accordingly, the regional share in Asia's variance decomposition increased between pre- and post-GFC periods, indicating Asia's increased vulnerability from contagion in the region.

However, between post-GFC and post-normalization periods, the global share of Asia's variance drastically increased, perhaps reflecting Asia's more active inward/outward portfolio equity investment flows. Except for Central and South Asia, all subregions contributed

---

[21]   The formula for regional and the global variance decompositions are

$$VR_{c,t}^{EA} = \frac{(\beta_{c,t}^{EA})^2 \sigma_{EA,t}^2}{\sigma_{c,t}^2}$$

$$VR_{c,t}^{G} = \frac{(\beta_{c,t}^{G})^2 \sigma_{G,t}^2}{\sigma_{c,t}^2}$$

where , $VR_{c,t}^{EA}$ and $VR_{c,t}^{G}$ are the regional and global variance of economy c, at time t, respectively. $\beta_{c,t}^{EA}$ and $\beta_{c,t}^{G}$ are the economy-specific sensitivity to the regional and global beta at time t, respectively. These were obtained from the following equation:

$$\varepsilon_{c,t} = \alpha_{c,t} + \beta_{c,t}^{EA}\varepsilon_{EA,t} + \beta_{c,t}^{G}\varepsilon_{G,t}$$

The formula was applied on a rolling basis, with 78 weekly data points. $\sigma_{EA,t}^2$ and $\sigma_{G,t}^2$ are the regional conditional variance and global conditional variance, estimated from the equation above. They are assumed to follow a standard asymmetric GARCH (1, 1) process. $\varepsilon_{EA,t}$, $\varepsilon_{G,t}$ are the unexpected components of equity market returns, which are proxied by the error terms obtained from the regression equation

$$r_{c,t} = \delta_{0\,c,t} + \delta_{1\,c,t}r_{c,t-1} + \varepsilon_{c,t}$$

where $r_{c,t}$ is the weekly equity returns of each individual economy.

Figure 4.19: Share of Variance in Equity Returns Explained by Global and Regional Shocks (%)

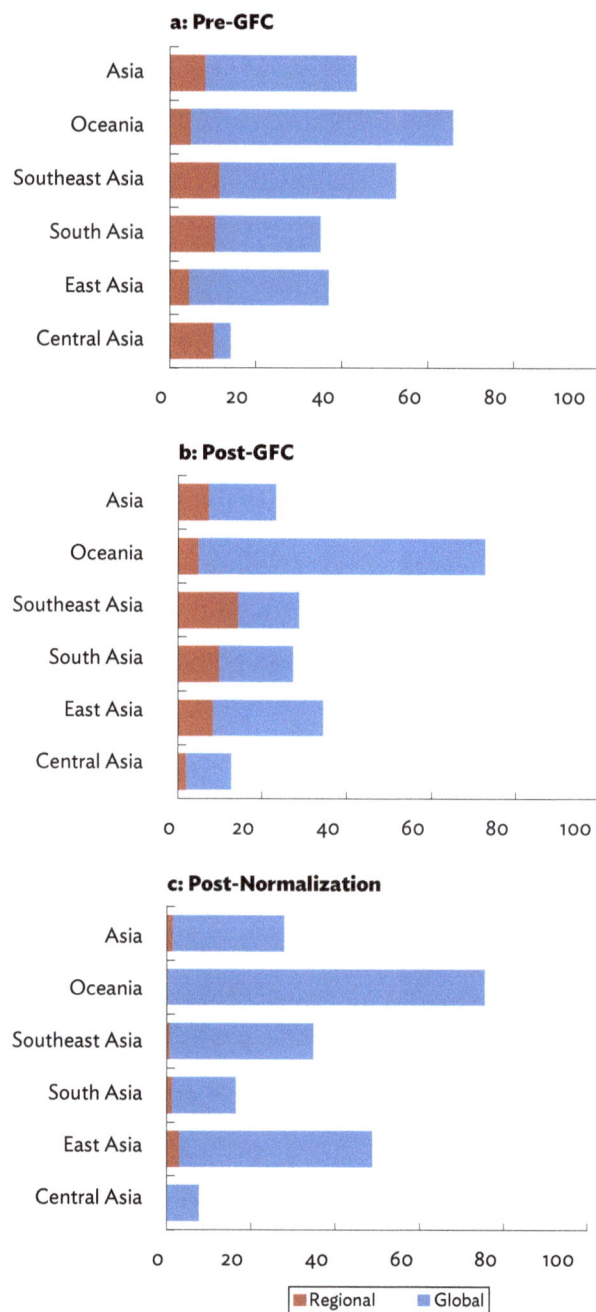

GFC = global financial crisis; Pre-GFC = January 1999–September 2007; Post–GFC = July 2009–December 2015; Post–Normalization = January 2016–June 2017.
Notes: Central Asia includes Georgia, Kazakhstan, and the Kyrgyz Republic. East Asia includes the People's Republic of China; Hong Kong, China; Japan; the Republic of Korea; Mongolia; and Taipei,China. South Asia includes Bangladesh, India, Nepal, Pakistan, and Sri Lanka. Southeast Asia includes Indonesia, the Lao People's Democratic Republic; Malaysia; the Philippines; Singapore; Thailand; and Viet Nam. Oceania includes Australia and New Zealand. Asia includes Central Asia, East Asia, South Asia, Southeast Asia, and Oceania.
Sources: ADB calculations using data from Bloomberg; CEIC; and World Bank. World Development Indicators. http://data.worldbank.org/data-catalog/world-development-indicators (all accessed July 2017); and methodology by Lee and Park (2011).

to the increase in the share of Asia's equity variance explained by global shocks between post-GFC and post-normalization periods.

Debt

The influence of external shocks on local bond return variance grew larger in the post-GFC period, as the global share to total variance has become more significant particularly in the recent post-normalization period.

The global share to Asia's total variance in local bond returns increased during the post-normalization period, while the external (both global and regional) shock exert more significant influence broadly across local currency bond markets in the post-GFC periods, reflecting a gradual global and regional integration of these markets (Figure 4.20). During post-normalization, in particular, the global share to Singapore, the Philippines, the Republic of Korea, the PRC, and Australia increased more significantly than other economies.

Bond Returns Convergence

The cross-border dispersion of Asia's 10-year local currency government bond yields continued to show yield convergence in 2016, both with regional markets and the US.

Estimating the cross-border dispersion of 10-year local currency government bond yields—using σ-convergence of regional local currency government bond yields with a 10-year maturity—shows that convergence of Asia's bond return fluctuations both within the region and with the US continued in 2016, suggesting increased co-movement after Brexit in June 2016 (Figure 4.21).[22] While's East Asia's local bond returns seemed to diverge slightly during the 2013 taper tantrum, its σ-convergence declined afterward—although it has been up slightly more recently.

Since 2006, Asia's local currency bond yields have been linked more to the US bond yields than intraregional bond markets. Asia and the US bond yields converged

Figure 4.20: Share of Variance in Local Bond Returns Explained by Global and Regional Shocks (%)

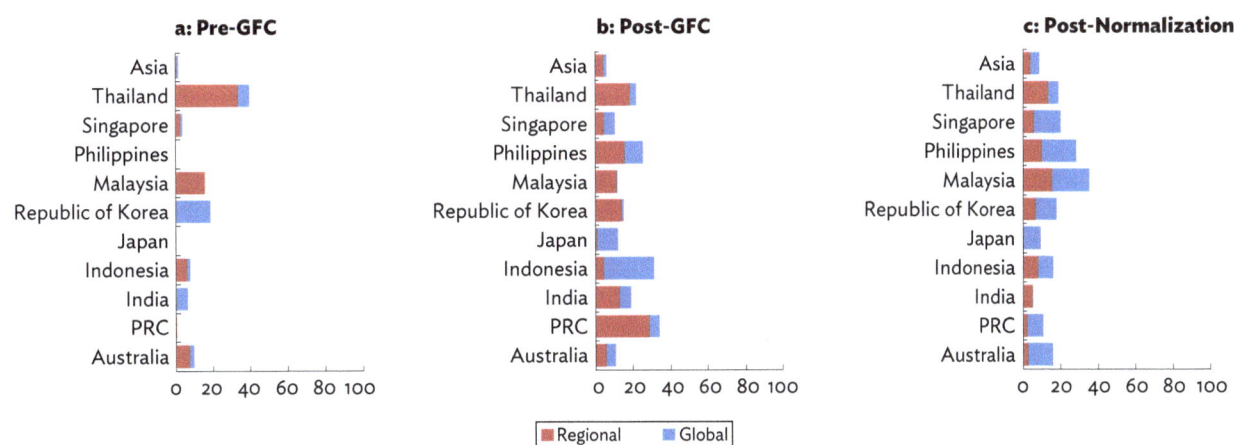

GFC = global financial crisis, PRC = People's Republic of China, Pre–GFC = January 2005–September 2007, Post–GFC = July 2009–December 2015, Post–Normalization = January 2016 – June 2017.
Sources: ADB calculations using data from Bloomberg; World Bank, World Development Indicators. http://data.worldbank.org/data-catalog/world-development-indicators (both accessed July 2017); and methodology by Lee and Park (2011).

---

22   To compute for the dispersion or σ-Convergence, each pairwise dispersion of bond yields r between economies i and j was obtained by

$$\sigma_{ijy} = \left[\frac{1}{n-1} \sum_{\forall t}^{n} \left(r_{it} - r_{jt} \right)^2 \right]^{1/2}$$

The formula was applied on a rolling basis, with 52 weekly data points. Each economy's σ-convergence is the simple mean of all its pairwise dispersions. The subregional and Asia σ-convergence are the unweighted mean of each included economy's σ-convergence.

Figure 4.21: σ-Convergence of 10-year Government Bond Yields—Asia

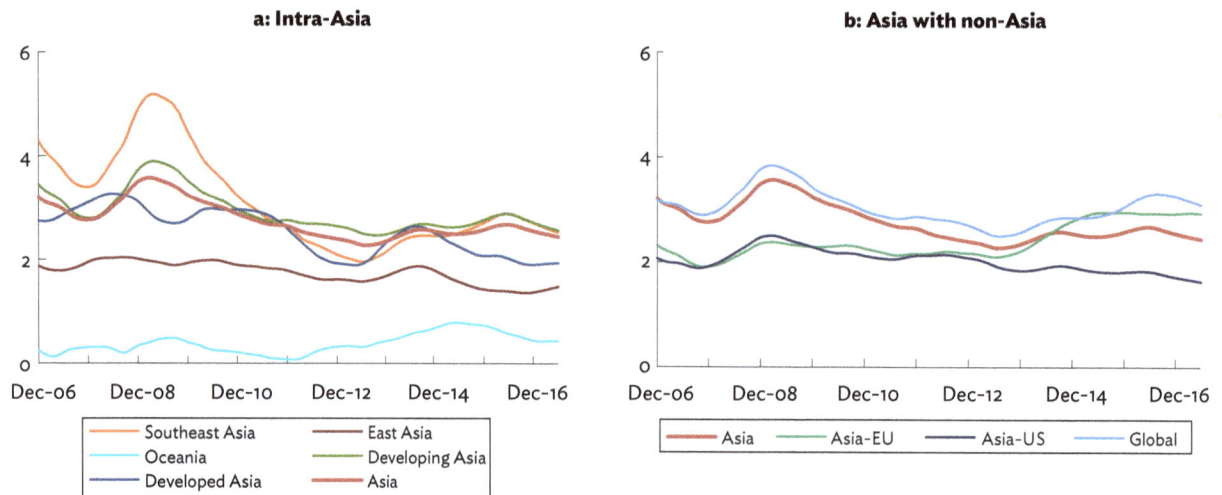

a: Intra-Asia

b: Asia with non-Asia

EU = European Union, US = United States.

Notes:

(i) Values refer to the unweighted mean of individual economy's σ-convergence, included in the subregion. Each economy's σ-convergence is the simple mean of all its pairwise standard deviation. Data are filtered using Hodrick-Prescott method.

(ii) East Asia includes the People's Republic of China; Hong Kong, China; Japan; the Republic of Korea; and Taipei,China. Southeast Asia includes Indonesia, Malaysia, the Philippines, Singapore, and Thailand. Oceania includes Australia and New Zealand. Developed Asia includes Japan and Oceania. Developing Asia includes Southeast Asia and East Asia. Asia includes Developed Asia and Developing Asia. Global includes Asia, Colombia, the EU, Mexico, and the US.

Sources: ADB calculations using data from Bloomberg; CEIC; and methodology by Espinoza et al (2010), and Park (2013).

further following the taper tantrum. While Asia's local currency bond yields were more linked to the EU bond yields between 2006 and 2013—the onset of the taper tantrum—it changed as Asia-EU bond yields diverged. Convergence has remained benign since.

Capital Flow Volatility

With increasing financial integration and a growing appetite for financial assets outside the region, Asia's capital flow volatilities of debt, FDI, and financial derivatives and other investments have increased, although equity volatility declined between post-GFC and post normalization periods.

Capital flow volatility of portfolio debt, FDI, and financial derivatives and other investments increased between post-GFC and post-normalization periods, while portfolio equity decreased (Table 4.9).

FDI remained the least volatile type of financial flow in the region during post-normalization (0.64). Against the post-GFC period, the increased volatility of FDI in the post-normalization period is attributed to Central Asia,

East Asia, and South Asia. The increase in portfolio debt volatility (from 0.96 during the post-GFC period to 1.27 afterward) was mainly due to the increase in Oceania's portfolio debt volatility (from 2.86 to 3.20), as well as the increase in Southeast Asia's portfolio debt volatility (from 0.83 to 1.06). The increase in volatility for financial derivatives and other instruments (from 1.37 post-GFC to 1.45 afterward) is also mainly attributed to South Asia and Oceania.

Table 4.9: Capital Flow Volatility—Asia (standard deviation of net capital inflow levels as % of GDP)

Subregion	Portfolio (Debt)			**	Portfolio (Equity)			**
	Pre-GFC Q1 1999–Q3 2007	Post-GFC Q3 2009–Q4 2015	Post-Normalization Q1 2016–Q4 2016		Pre-GFC Q1 1999–Q3 2007	Post-GFC Q3 2009–Q4 2015	Post-Normalization Q1 2016–Q4 2016	
Central Asia	4.21	4.38	3.18	▼	1.88	1.03	0.39	▼
East Asia	1.94	1.39	1.39	▲	1.99	1.21	1.02	▼
South Asia	0.00	0.85	0.73	▼	0.90	1.04	0.65	▼
Southeast Asia	1.11	0.83	1.06	▲	1.05	0.70	1.01	▲
Oceania	3.33	2.86	3.20	▲	3.54	1.96	1.00	▼
Asia	**1.44**	**0.96**	**1.27**	▲	**1.61**	**0.93**	**0.72**	▼

Subregion	FDI			**	Financial Derivatives and Other Investments[a]			**
	Pre-GFC Q1 1999–Q3 2007	Post-GFC Q3 2009–Q4 2015	Post-Normalization Q1 2016–Q4 2016		Pre-GFC Q1 1999–Q3 2007	Post-GFC Q3 2009–Q4 2015	Post-Normalization Q1 2016–Q4 2016	
Central Asia	4.20	2.68	3.69	▲	4.27	6.59	5.69	▼
East Asia	0.69	0.63	0.74	▲	3.42	1.85	1.67	▼
South Asia	0.29	0.55	0.91	▲	1.65	1.33	2.71	▲
Southeast Asia	1.77	1.20	0.59	▼	3.04	2.89	2.31	▼
Oceania	3.55	1.47	0.84	▼	2.89	1.91	4.96	▲
Asia	**0.67**	**0.48**	**0.64**	▲	**2.52**	**1.37**	**1.45**	▲

** = direction of capital flow volatility between post-GFC and post-normalization, ▼ = decrease, ▲ = increase.
– = no data available, FDI = foreign direct investment, GDP = gross domestic product, GFC = global financial crisis.
[a] "Other Investments" includes: (i) other equity; (ii) currency and deposits; (iii) loans (including use of International Monetary Fund (IMF) credit and IMF loans); (iv) nonlife insurance technical reserves, life insurance and annuities entitlements, pension entitlements, and provisions for calls under standardized guarantees; (v) trade credit and advances; (vi) other accounts receivable/payable; and (vii) special drawing rights (SDR) allocations (SDR holdings are included in reserve assets).
Notes: Central Asia includes Armenia, Azerbaijan, Georgia, Kazakhstan, the Kyrgyz Republic, and Tajikistan. East Asia includes the People's Republic of China; Hong Kong, China; Japan; the Republic of Korea; and Mongolia. South Asia includes India and Sri Lanka. Southeast Asia includes Brunei Darussalam, Indonesia, Malaysia, the Philippines, Singapore, Thailand, and Viet Nam. Oceania includes Australia and New Zealand. Asia includes Central Asia, East Asia, South Asia, Southeast Asia, and Oceania.
Sources: ADB calculations using data from CEIC; and International Monetary Fund. Balance of Payments and International Investment Position Statistics. http://www.imf.org/external/np/sta/bop/bop.htm (both accessed May 2017).

References

Asian Development Bank. 2014. *Basic Principles on Establishing a Regional Settlement Intermediary and Next Steps Forward: Cross-Border Settlement Infrastructure Forum.* Manila.

_____. 2016. *Asian Economic Integration Report: What Drives Foreign Investment in Asia and the Pacific?* Manila.

L. Baele, A. Fernando, P. Hördahl, E. Krylova, and C. Monnet. 2004. Measuring Financial Integration in the Euro Area. *ECB Occasional Paper Series.* No. 14. Frankfurt: European Central Bank.

Bank for International Settlements. Locational Banking Statistics. https://www.bis.org/statistics/bankstats.htm (accessed May 2017).

_____. 2006. *Cross-border Collateral Arrangements.* Basel.

R. Espinoza, A. Prasad, and O. Williams. 2010. Regional Financial Integration in the GCC. *IMF Working Paper.* No. 10/90. Washington, DC: International Monetary Fund.

J. Fichtner. 2016. The Anatomy of the Cayman Islands Offshore Financial Center: Anglo-America, Japan, and the Role of Hedge Funds. *Review of International Political Economy.* 23 (6). pp. 1034-1063.

M. Hinojales and C.Y. Park. 2010. Stock Market Integration: Emerging East Asia's Experience. in M. Devereaux, P. Lane, C.Y. Park, and S.J. Wei, eds. *The Dynamics of Asian Financial Integration: Facts and Analytics.* London and New York: Routledge.

International Monetary Fund. 2015. *Global Financial Stability Report: Navigating Monetary Policy Challenges and Managing Risks.* Washington, DC.

_____. Coordinated Direct Investment Survey. http://cdis.imf.org (accessed February 2017).

_____. Coordinated Portfolio Investment Survey. http://cpis.imf.org (accessed September 2017).

W.R. Lam. 2013. Cross-border Activity of Japanese Banks. *IMF Working Paper.* No. 13/235. Washington, DC: International Monetary Fund.

J.W. Lee and C.Y. Park. 2011. Financial Integration in Emerging Asia: Challenges and Prospects. *Asian Economic Policy Review.* 6 (2). pp. 176-198.

C.Y. Park. 2013. Asian Capital Market Integration: Theory and Evidence. *ADB Economics Working Paper Series.* No. 351. Manila: Asian Development Bank.

Reuters. 2016. The Irony of Negative Rates: Japanese Investors Flock to Europe & Vice-Versa. 24 March.

Stooq. Stooq Online. https://stooq.com/q/?s=^sti (accessed July 2017).

World Bank. World Development Indicators Online. http://data.worldbank.org/data-catalog/world-development-indicators (accessed July 2017).

05

Remittances and Tourism Receipts

Remittances and Tourism Receipts

Remittance Flows to Asia

Remittances are an important and stable source of external finance.

Along with foreign direct investment (FDI), tourism receipts, and portfolio investments, remittances are an important source of capital inflows for many economies in Asia (Figure 5.1). Close to half (45%) of global remittances flowed to Asia—the world's largest source of international migrants (United Nations 2015).

By value, India, the People's Republic of China (PRC), and the Philippines receive the most remittances in the region (Figure 5.2a). Remittances to the Kyrgyz Republic, Nepal, and Tonga are proportional to about 30% of gross domestic product (GDP) (Figure 5.2b). In per capita terms, Tonga, Samoa, and the Marshall Islands receive the most (Figure 5.2c). Large proportions

Figure 5.1: Financial Inflows to Asia by Type ($ billion)

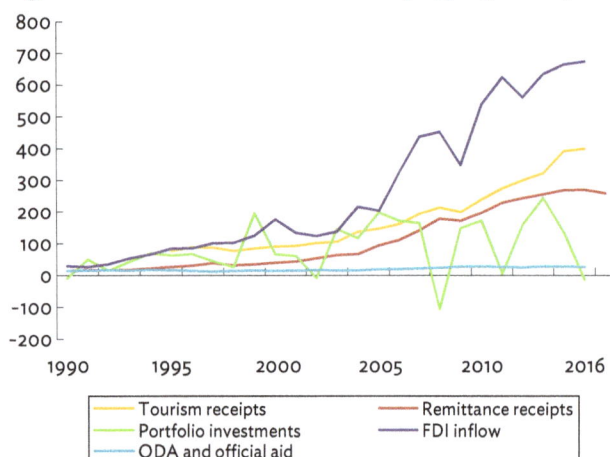

FDI = foreign direct investment, ODA = official development assistance.
Note: Portfolio investments include net equity inflows only.
Source: ADB calculations using data from World Bank. World Development Indicators. http://databank.worldbank.org (accessed June 2017).

Figure 5.2: Top 10 Remittance-Recipient Economies—Asia (2016)

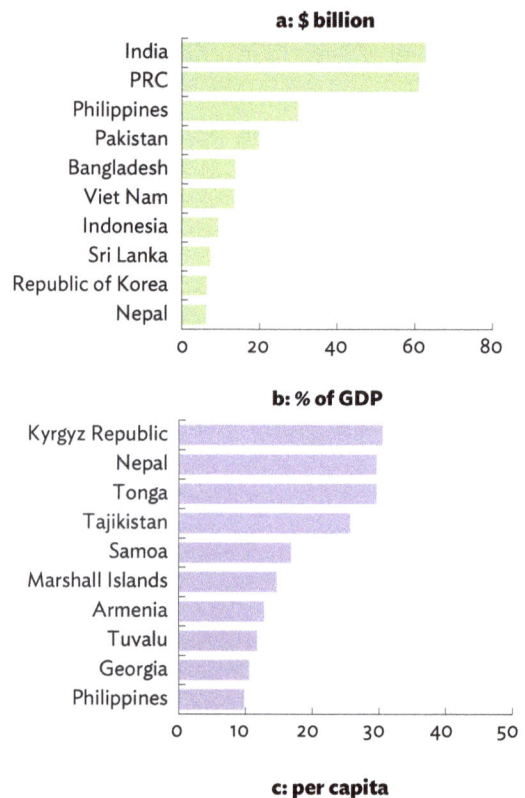

GDP = gross domestic product, PRC = People's Republic of China.
Sources: ADB calculations using data from International Monetary Fund. World Economic Outlook April 2017 Database. https://www.imf.org/external/pubs/ft/weo/2017/01/weodata/index.aspx (accessed June 2017); United Nations. Department of Economic and Social Affairs, Population Division. World Population Prospects 2015. https://esa.un.org/unpd/wpp/Download/Standard/Population/ (accessed April 2017); and World Bank. World Development Indicators. http://databank.worldbank.org (accessed June 2017).

of people from the Pacific migrate to Oceania and North America. For example, 50% of Tonga's population resides in Organisation for Economic Co-operation and Development countries.

Sources of Remittances to Asia

In 2016, some 28% of remittances to Asia were intraregional—down from 33% in 2011.

Subregional data show East Asia and Oceania sourced a substantial portion of remittances from economies within the same subregion (Figure 5.3). The Hong Kong, China–PRC corridor was the largest. The bulk of remittances to the Pacific came from other subregions, primarily Oceania. South Asia, Central Asia, and Southeast Asia subregions received most remittances from outside Asia. The Middle East was the largest source of remittances to Asia (Figure 5.4).

Figure 5.3: Subregional Remittance Share by Source— Asia (%)

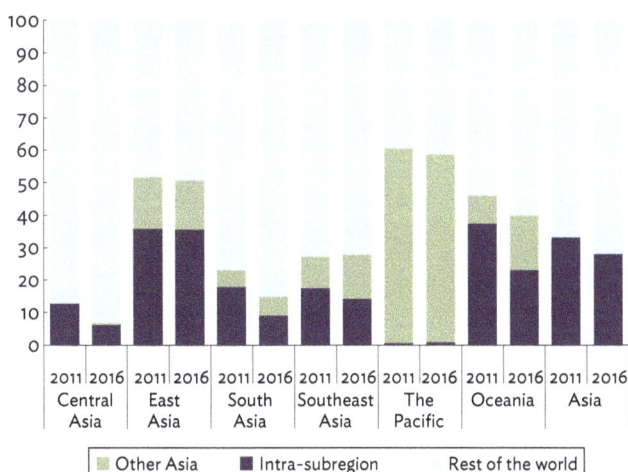

Notes:
(i) Intra-subregional share refers to the remittances within subregion *i* as a percentage of remittances from the world to subregion *i*.
(ii) Other Asia share refers to the remittances from other Asian subregions to subregion *i* as a percentage of remittances from the world to subregion *i*.
(iii) Rest of the world share is remittances from non-Asian economies to subregion *i* as a percentage of remittances from the world to subregion *i*.
(iv) 2016 numbers are estimated using 2015 remittance data and methodology used by Ratha and Shaw (2007).
Source: ADB calculations using data from World Bank. World Bank Migration and Remittances Data. http://www.worldbank.org/en/topic/migrationremittancesdiasporaissues/brief/migration-remittances-data (accessed June 2017).

Figure 5.4: Remittance Inflows to Asia by Source, 2016 ($ billion, % share)

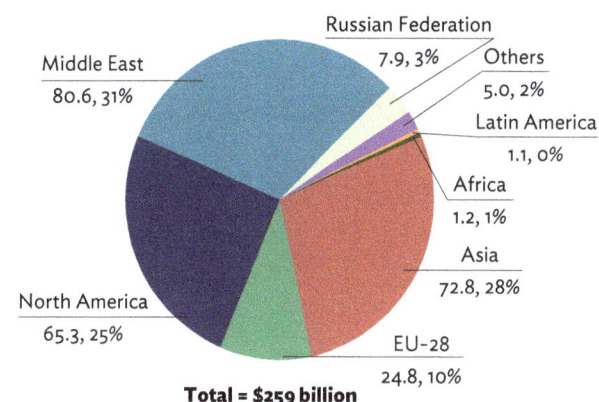

Total = $259 billion

EU = European Union.
Sources: ADB estimates using data from World Bank. World Bank Migration and Remittances Data.http://www.worldbank.org/en/topic/migrationremittancesdiasporaissues/brief/migration-remittances-data (accessed June 2017); and the methodology used by Ratha and Shaw (2007).

Remittances to Asia in 2016

Remittances to Asia declined in 2016 for the first time since the global financial crisis; down 4.0% to $259 billion, lowering its global share from 46.3% to 45.0%.

Remittances to the region fell 4.0% from $269 billion in 2015 to $259 billion in 2016. The $10-billion drop was actually larger than the $6-billion decline in 2009. Total global remittances contracted for the second consecutive year—falling first by 2.4% to $582 billion in 2015 and again by 1.2% to $575 billion in 2016 (Figure 5.5).

The recent fall in remittances is generally attributed to the slow recovery of major economies and low commodity prices—including crude oil—reducing employment demand for international migrants. But the effect has been uneven across subregions.

Central Asia continued to see a sharp decline in remittances for the third year running (Figure 5.6). In 2016, remittances to Azerbaijan were down 49%; those to Uzbekistan and Tajikistan fell 25.9% and 21.3%, respectively. Overall, remittances to Central Asia dropped 14% less than the 35% fall in 2015.

Figure 5.5: Remittance Inflows—Asia and World
($ billion, % share)

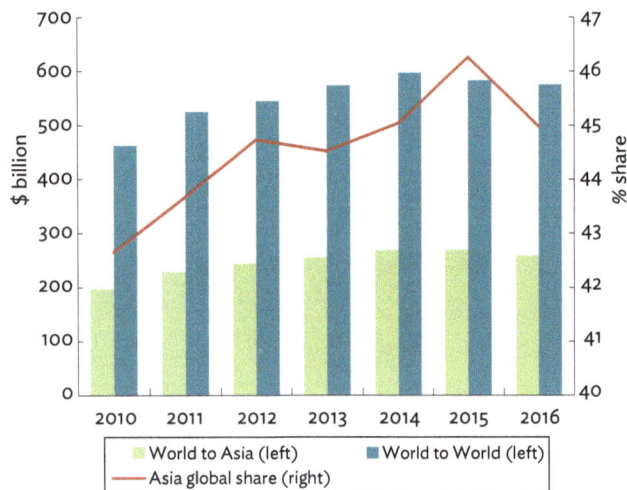

Note: Asia global share refers to the remittance inflows from world to Asia as a percentage of total global remittance inflows.
Source: ADB calculations using data from World Bank. World Bank Migration and Remittances Data. http://www.worldbank.org/en/topic/migrationremittancesdiasporaissues/brief/migration-remittances-data (accessed June 2017).

Figure 5.7: Remittance Inflows to Asia by Source
(% change, year-on-year)

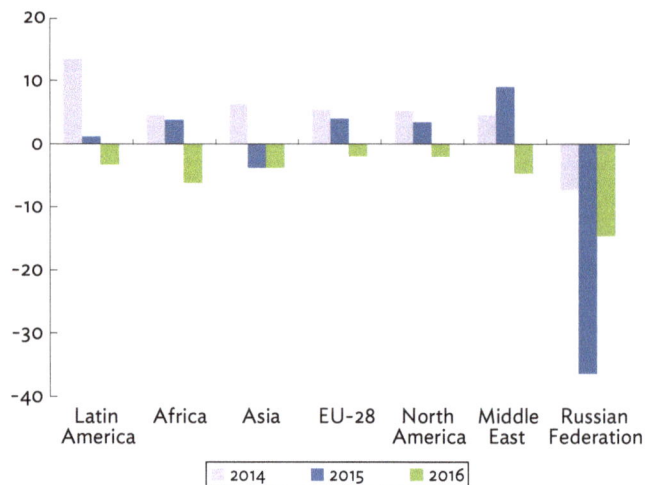

EU = European Union.
Notes: 2016 numbers are estimated using 2015 remittance data and methodology used by Ratha and Shaw (2007).
Sources: ADB calculations using data from World Bank. World Bank Migration and Remittances Data. http://www.worldbank.org/en/topic/migrationremittancesdiasporaissues/brief/migration-remittances-data (accessed June 2017); and the methodology proposed by Ratha and Shaw (2007).

Figure 5.6: Remittance Inflows to Asia Subregions
(% change, year-on-year)

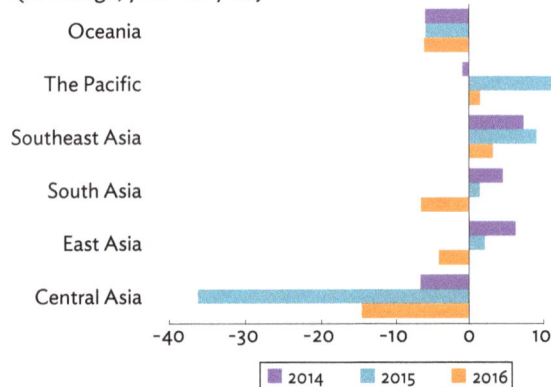

Note: 2016 numbers are estimated using 2015 remittance data and methodology used by Ratha and Shaw (2007).
Source: ADB calculations using data from World Bank. World Bank Migration and Remittances Data. http://www.worldbank.org/en/topic/migrationremittancesdiasporaissues/brief/migration-remittances-data (accessed June 2017).

The decline in remittances to Central Asia derives from the weak economy in the Russian Federation—the top migrant destination for all eight Central Asian economies (Figure 5.7). For example, the number of workers leaving Tajikistan—mostly for seasonal and temporary work in the Russian Federation—declined 11.5% between 2014 and 2015 (Statistical Agency of Tajikistan 2016).

Remittances to South Asia dropped for the first time since the global financial crisis (GFC). India's remittances contracted 8.9% ($6.2 billion), along with Bangladesh (11%) and Nepal (6.7%). Low global oil prices resulted in reduced remittances from the Middle East to these countries. Large proportions of workers from South Asia in the Middle East are employed in sectors susceptible to economic cycles—such as construction and transport. As a result, departures of unskilled workers from India fell from 781,000 in 2015 to 506,000 in 2016 (Ministry of External Affairs, India 2016). Remittances to Pakistan grew 2.8%, but departures of overseas workers from Pakistan to major Gulf destinations such as Saudi Arabia and United Arab Emirates declined in 2016, and remittances from these countries began to decline in early 2017.

A sharp decline in remittances can place a recipient economy and its households at risk, particularly for those highly dependent on remittances (see Figure 5.2). Remittances increase and smooth consumption, stimulate spending on physical and human capital, and allow construction of more disaster-resistant homes (Matsumoto et al. 2006, Mohapatra et al. 2012, and Yang 2008). Reduced remittances can have symmetric, damaging effects. If a large proportion of migrants come from the poor, a reduction can increase the poverty ratio

(ADB 2012). If the decline is only temporary, better-off migrants and their families may be able to minimize the shock by using savings and assets.

In contrast, remittances to Southeast Asia continued to grow.

Remittance inflows continued to grow in 2016 across much of Southeast Asia. Remittances to Viet Nam rose

2.9%, along with Lao People's Democratic Republic (2.7%), and Myanmar (2.3%). The Philippines remained the largest recipient in the subregion, receiving a record $29.9 billion, a 4.9% increase. Still, departures from the Philippines to the Middle East—largely housemaids; service workers; and skilled workers in medicine, engineering, and management—remained unaffected. Labor demand in these sectors is less susceptible to business cycles (Box 5.1).[23]

Box 5.1: Understanding the Sources of Fluctuations in Remittance Inflows

Remittance inflow trends have diverged across economies in Asia, with sharp declines in some economies and continued growth in others. The sources of remittance volatility are examined from the perspective of variations in migration patterns across economies, while controlling for key economic and social indicators that may also cause remittance fluctuations (following Jackman 2013). Variables include: (i) changes in migrant stock, (ii) the proportion of female workers (often employed in sectors less affected by business cycles and who remit regularly), (iii) the degree of concentration of migrants in a single destination (diversifying sources of shocks), and (iv) the proportion of migrants working in Organisation for Economic Co-operation and

Development destinations (where wages are generally higher and longer-term contracts are more frequent).

Results suggest that the high proportion of female migrants among migrant populations contribute to lowering fluctuations. Having a moderate concentration of migrants in one destination country can stabilize remittance inflows, but excessive concentration (above 49%) will result in losing the benefit. The change in size of migrant population also generates volatility as expected. The analysis also shows that providing assurance of property rights can mitigate fluctuations.

Sources of Volatility in Remittance Inflow (Dependent Variable = 3 year rolling SD of remittance annual growth)

	Coefficients		Coefficients
Migrant population (% growth)	0.046* (0.027)	Proportion of migrants in OECD countries (%)	0.022 (0.064)
Ratio (%) of migrants in top destination (TOP)	-0.970** (0.427)	Proportion of college graduates among migrants (%)	-1.335 (3.259)
TOP_squared	0.010** (0.005)	GDP, exchange rate, and interest rate volatilities of origin and destination countries	Yes
Female migration dummy (= 1 if % female migration>55)	-10.214** (4.387)	Year dummy	Yes
Natural disaster occurrences	0.253 (0.819)	Subregion dummy	Yes
		Constant	63.720*** (-17.801)
Property rights assurance at origin country (= rule of law index)	-4.052* (2.285)		
Proportion of migrants against total population (%)	-18.459 (15.817)	Number of observations	378
		R-squared	0.257

*** = significant at 1%, ** = significant at 5%, * = significant at 10%, GDP = gross domestic product, OECD = Organisation for Economic Co-operation and Development, SD = standard deviation.
Notes: Robust standard errors are shown in parentheses. The ordinary least square analysis uses data of 38 economies in Asia between the period of 2000–2016.
Sources: ADB calculations using data from Artuc et al. (2015); Centre for Research on the Epidemiology of Disasters. EM-DAT The International Disaster Database. http://www.emdat.be/ (accessed June 2017); International Monetary Fund. World Economic Outlook April 2017 Database. https://www.imf.org/external/pubs/ft/weo/2017/01/weodata/index.aspx (accessed June 2017); World Bank. World Development Indicators. http://databank.worldbank.org (accessed June 2017); World Bank. Migration and Remittances Data. http://www.worldbank.org/en/topic/migrationremittancesdiasporaissues/brief/migration-remittances-data (accessed June 2017); and United Nations. Department of Economic and Social Affairs, Population Division. World Population Prospects 2015. https://esa.un.org/unpd/wpp/Download/Standard/Population/ (accessed April 2017).

---

23   Heterogeneous impacts of economic shocks on remittances inflows observed in 2016 are highly consistent with what occurred during the GFC in 2009. The impact may vary depending on the nature of migration such as destinations and sectors that employ foreign migrants, and workers' skill level (ADB 2012).

Remittances to most Pacific developing member countries (Pacific DMCs) grew moderately, with the exception of Tuvalu, where remittances fell 2%. In East Asia, remittances to the PRC fell 4.6% ($2.9 billion).

Remittances are expected to recover as global economic recovery gains momentum.

With the global economic outlook improving and crude oil prices appearing to bottom out, global remittances as well as inflows to Asia are expected to rebound in 2017. Departure statistics of migrant workers from key origin economies—including Central Asia and South Asia—indicate that labor migration to key destinations began gaining momentum in early 2017. However, stricter immigration policies, if enforced, can reduce remittances as the size of the migrant population could be limited.

Tourism Receipts

Trends in 2015

Tourism receipts reached $398.6 billion in 2015 after growing at an average 10.1% between 2012 and 2015. Growth is expected to continue.

Tourism is rapidly growing in Asia, with increasing numbers of outbound tourists from the region generating higher revenues. Tourism receipts—the sum of expenditures by international visitors to pay for goods and services—contribute significant financial flows to the region (see Figure 5.1).

Worldwide, Asia is the second-largest beneficiary of tourism receipts ($398.6 billion) after Europe ($431 billion) (Figure 5.8). Overall, receipts grew 10.1% between 2012 and 2015. But, in 2015, Europe and the Middle East suffered substantial declines of 11% and 25%, respectively. These declining trends elsewhere resulted in Asia's increased share of world tourism receipts—from 24% in 2014 to 28% in 2015 (Figure 5.9).

Brunei Darussalam (77%), Timor-Leste (46%), Myanmar (34%), Japan (31%), Sri Lanka (21%), Palau (19%), Thailand (15%), and Samoa (13%) are some of the countries that had robust annual growth in tourism receipts in 2015.

Figure 5.8: Tourism Receipts by Region ($ billion)

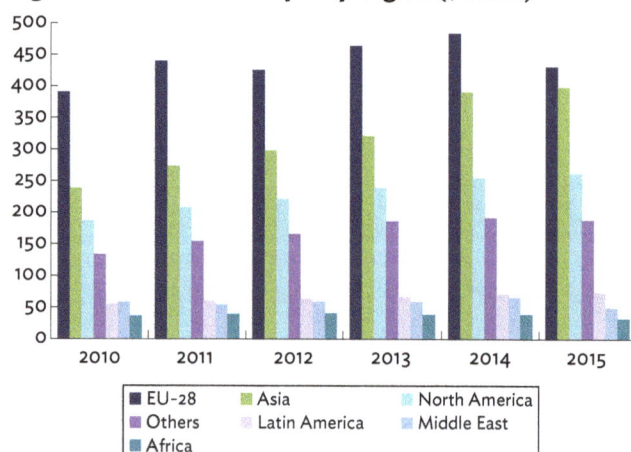

EU = European Union.
Source: ADB calculations using data from World Bank. World Development Indicators. http://databank.worldbank.org (accessed June 2017).

Figure 5.9: Tourism Receipts (% of world total)

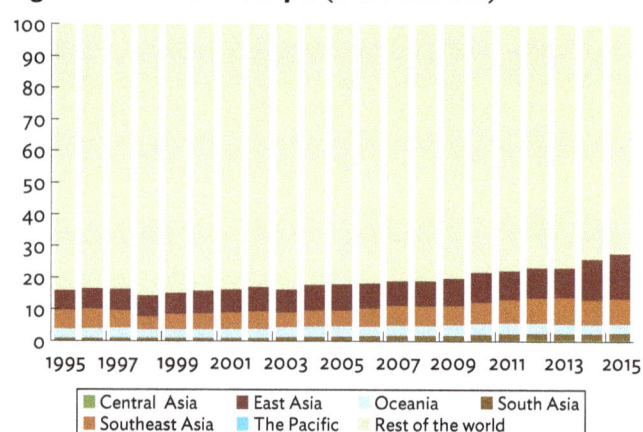

Source: ADB calculations using data from World Bank. World Development Indicators. http://databank.worldbank.org (accessed June 2017).

In 2015, outbound tourists from the PRC—which has had double-digit growth since 2004 except during the GFC—increased 12% to 90.0 million. Some 61% of PRC tourists visited Asian destinations.

By value, the PRC; Thailand; and Hong Kong, China are the top three tourist economies (Figure 5.10a). Economies that depend on tourism for GDP are the Pacific DMCs and Maldives—which derives 83.5% of its GDP from tourism (Figure 5.10b). Palau (54.9%), Vanuatu (34.4%), and Fiji (23.6%) also receive proportionately large amounts from tourism.

Figure 5.10: Economies by Tourism Receipts—Asia (2015)

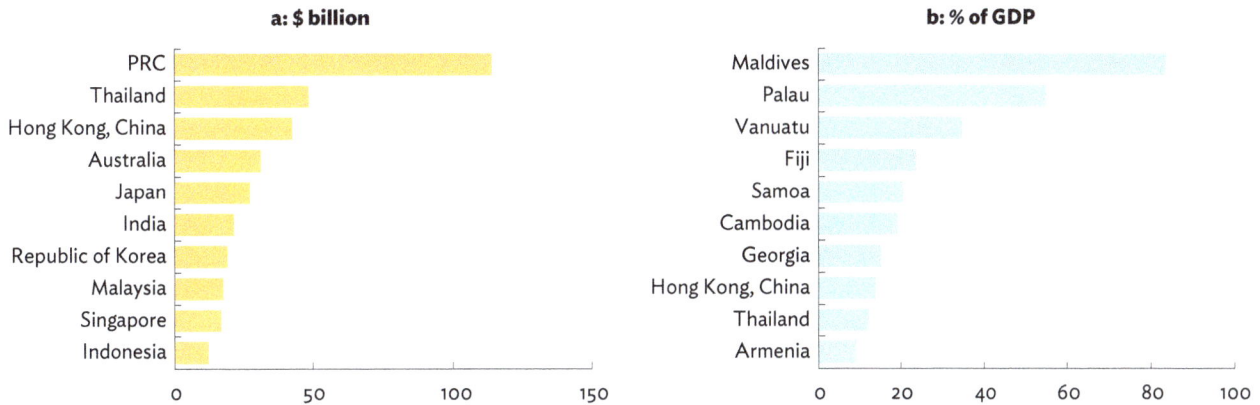

a: $ billion

b: % of GDP

GDP = gross domestic product, PRC = People's Republic of China.
Sources: ADB calculations using data from World Bank. World Development Indicators. http://databank.worldbank.org (accessed June 2017); and International Monetary Fund. World Economic Outlook April 2017 Database. https://www.imf.org/external/pubs/ft/ weo/2017/01/weodata/index.aspx (accessed June 2017).

Regional Share of Tourism Receipts

International tourism in Asia is largely intraregional.

In 2015, the share of Asian tourists among total visitors from the world to Asia was 78%, up from 75% in 2010. About 72% of Asian outbound tourists visited destinations in Asia.

Flows of international tourists in the region have considerably diversified over the past decade (Figures 5.11a, 5.11b). In East Asia, outbound tourism from the PRC has grown substantially, while Southeast Asia has come to accommodate a greater number of inbound and outbound tourists within Asia.

Figure 5.11: Tourism Flows—Asia (million)

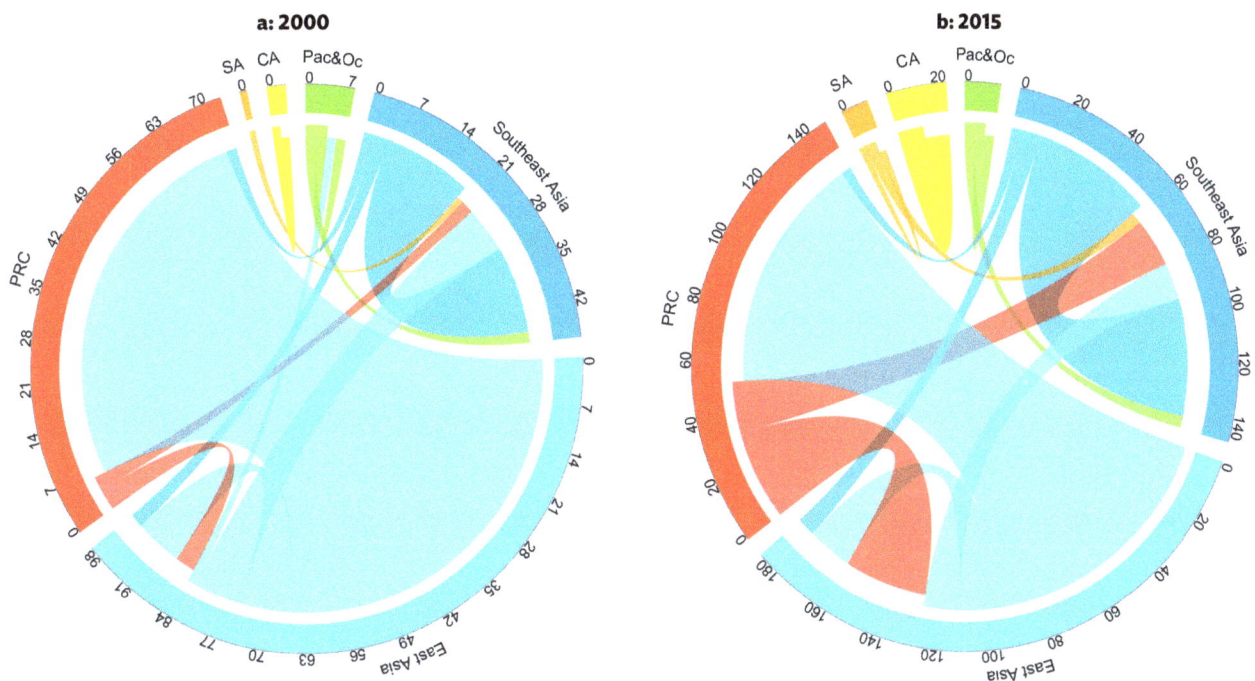

a: 2000

b: 2015

CA = Central Asia, Pac&Oc = the Pacific and Oceania, PRC = People's Republic of China, SA = South Asia.
Note: Figures are produced following Abel et al. (2014).
Source: ADB calculations using data from World Tourism Organization. 2017. Tourism Statistics Database.

Figure 5.12: Subregional Tourism Share—Asia
(% of total tourist arrivals to each subregion)

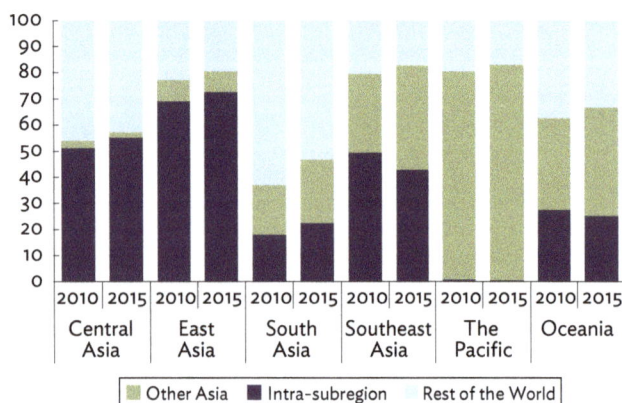

Notes:
(i)   Intra-subregional share refers to the tourist arrivals within subregion *i* as a
      percentage of tourist arrivals from the world to subregion *i*.
(ii) Other Asia share refers to the tourist arrivals from other subregions to
      subregion *i* as a percentage of tourist arrivals from the world to subregion *i*.
(iii) Rest of the world share is tourist arrivals from non-Asian economies to
      subregion *i* as a percentage of tourist arrivals from the world to subregion *i*.
Source: ADB calculations using data from World Tourism Organization. 2017.
Tourism Statistics Database.

At the subregional level, East Asia is the largest market
in number of receiving visitors, mostly intra-subregional
tourists (Figure 5.12). In contrast, South Asia has a
relatively small subregional tourism market with more
than half of its visitors arriving from outside its subregion.
The Pacific DMCs receive large majority of tourists from
other subregions, particularly Oceania (42%).

References

N. Abel, R. Bauer, and J. Schmidt. 2014. Visualizing Migration
    Flow Data with Circular Plots. *Vienna Institute of
    Demography Working Papers*. No. 2/2014. Vienna:
    Austrian Academy of Sciences.

E. Artuc, F. Docquier, C. Ozden, and Ch. Parsons. 2015. A
    Global Assessment of Human Capital Mobility: The Role
    Non-OECD Destinations. World Development. 65. pp.
    6-26.

ADB. 2012. *Global Crisis, Remittances, and Poverty in Asia.*
    Manila.

Centre for Research on the Epidemiology of Disasters. EM-
    DAT The International Disaster Database. http://www.
    emdat.be/ (accessed June 2017)

Government of India, Ministry of External Affairs. 2016. *Annual
    Report 2015-16*. Delhi.

International Monetary Fund. World Economic Outlook April
    2017 Database. https://www.imf.org/external/pubs/ft/
    weo/2017/01/weodata/index.aspx (accessed June 2017)

M. Jackman. 2013. Macroeconomic Determinants of
    Remittance Volatility: An Empirical Test. International
    Migration. 51 (s1). pp. e36-e52.

T. Matsumoto, Y. Kijima, and T. Yamano. 2006. The Role of
    Local Nonfarm Activities and Migration in Reducing
    Poverty: Evidence from Ethiopia, Kenya and Uganda.
    Agricultural Economics. 35(s3). pp. 449–458.

S. Mohapatra, G. Joseph, and D. Ratha. 2012. Remittances and
    Natural Disasters: Ex-post Response and Contribution
    to Ex-ante Preparedness. *Environment, Development and
    Sustainability*. 14(3). pp. 365–387.

D. Ratha and W. Shaw. 2007. South-South Migration and
    Remittances. *World Bank Working Paper*. No. 102.
    Washington DC: World Bank.

Statistical Agency under President of the Republic of Tajikistan.
    Migration of population, 1998–2015. http://www.stat.
    tj/en/database/socio-demographic-sector/ (accessed
    July 2017)

World Bank. Migration and Remittances Data.
    http://www.worldbank.org/en/topic/
    migrationremittancesdiasporaissues/brief/migration-
    remittances-data (accessed June 2017)

————. World Development Indicators. http://databank.
    worldbank.org (accessed June 2017)

World Tourism Organization. 2017. Tourism Statistics
    Database. statistics.unwto.org (accessed June 2017).

United Nations, Department of Economic and Social Affairs,
    Population Division. 2015. *Trends in International Migrant
    Stock: The 2015 Revision*. New York.

————. World Population Prospects 2015. https://esa.un.org/
    unpd/wpp/Download/Standard/Population/ (accessed
    April 2017).

D. Yang. 2008. International Migration, Remittances and
    Household Investment: Evidence from Philippine
    Migrants' Exchange Rate Shocks. *The Economic Journal*.
    118 (528). pp. 591–630.

06

Subregional Cooperation Initiatives

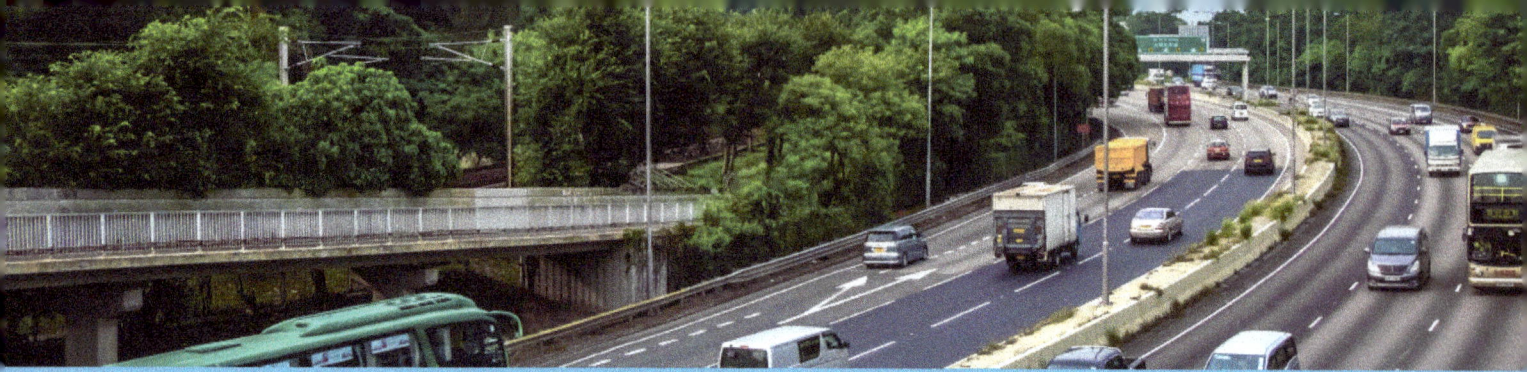

Subregional Cooperation Initiatives

Central and West Asia: Central Asia Regional Economic Cooperation Program[23]

The Central Asia Regional Economic Cooperation program has made important strides to connect countries within the region, and with East Asia and South Asia, the Russian Federation, and Europe.

The Central Asia Regional Economic Cooperation (CAREC) Program has established six corridors that crisscross the region, shortening structural distances for people and freight. It continues to chip away at barriers to trade by improving hardware and software elements that require cooperation between neighbors and the region in general.

Overview

Established in 2001, CAREC promotes regional economic cooperation through common infrastructure development and policy dialogue. The trading environment and investment climate have been improving through a network of multimodal transport corridors. These are opening economic opportunities by lowering trade costs, enhancing the flow of trade and people, and providing energy security and efficiency. They link CAREC members to each other and the rest of the world (Table 6.1). CAREC has grown from

Table 6.1: Selected Economic Indicators, 2016—CAREC

	Population (million)	Nominal GDP ($ billion)	GDP Growth (%, 2012–2016, average)	GDP Per Capita (current prices, $)	Trade Openness (total trade, % of GDP)
Afghanistan	33.4	18.9	3.9	566	49.4
Azerbaijan	9.8	37.8	1.6	3,876	38.4
PRC	1,378.2	11,185.1	7.3	8,116	33.3
Kazakhstan	17.8	135.0	3.4	7,584	45.9
Kyrgyz Republic	6.1	6.6	4.5	1,078	81.2
Mongolia	3.0	11.3	7.0	3,755	74.1
Pakistan	192.8	283.6	4.1	1,470	24.0
Tajikistan	8.7	7.4	6.9	854	51.3
Turkmenistan	5.4	36.6	8.9	6,722	32.7
Uzbekistan	31.8	67.1	8.0	2,108	26.5
CAREC	**1,687.1**	**11,789.4**	**7.2**	**6,988**	**33.3**

CAREC = Central Asia Regional Economic Cooperation, GDP = gross domestic product, PRC = People's Republic of China.
Note: CAREC average GDP growth rate is weighted using nominal GDP. Georgia joined CAREC in October 2016.
Source: ADB calculations using data from World Bank. World Development Indicators. http://databank.worldbank.org (accessed May 2017).

[23] Contributed by Shaista Hussain, Regional Cooperation Specialist, Central and West Asia Department (CWRD), Guoliang Wu, Senior Regional Cooperation Specialist, CWRD, and Ronaldo J. Oblepias, ADB Consultant, CWRD.

Figure 6.1: CAREC Loans and Grants by Sector, as of end-2016 ($ billion)

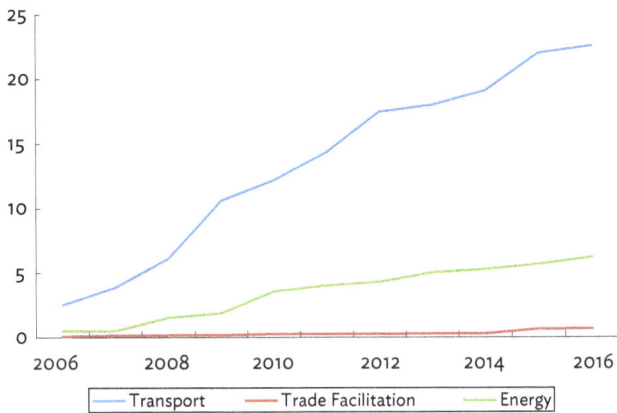

CAREC = Central Asia Regional Economic Cooperation.
Source: ADB. CAREC Program Portfolio.

six members in 2001 to 11 members in 2016. From six transport projects in 2001 worth $241 million, there were 176 projects in transport, energy, and trade facilitation worth $29.4 billion in 2016 (Figure 6.1). Of this, $10.4 billion (35%) was financed by ADB, $11.8 billion (40%) by other donor organizations, and $7.2 billion (24%) by CAREC governments (Figure 6.2).

In recent years, there has been a surge of interest among donors and governments to support economic cooperation initiatives in Central Asia. For example, there is the Belt and Road Initiative (BRI) and Silk Road Fund from the People's Republic of China (PRC), the New Silk Road pioneered by the United States (US), the Republic of Korea's Eurasia Initiative, and Quality Infrastructure sponsored by Japan. These offer new opportunities for cooperation, but also risk overlaps and competition if not coordinated and harmonized well. CAREC is now preparing a new long-term strategy to better position the group within a rapidly changing regional and global landscape.

Performance and Progress over the Past Year

CAREC continues to prioritize transport and energy, along with trade facilitation and trade policy; most investment projects involve infrastructure connectivity.

Transport. By 2016, road and railway projects had already surpassed CAREC's 2020 targets as outlined in its Transport and Trade Facilitation Strategy (TTFS) 2020 and Work Plan (CAREC 2017a) (Figure 6.3). With 1,363 kilometers (km) of expressways or national highways built, upgraded or improved in 2016, cumulative road infrastructure reached 8,592 km, well beyond the 7,800 km corridor length targeted for construction or improvement by 2020. In 2016, Turkmenistan completed 85 km of new railways, while 509 km of railways were improved in Azerbaijan and Uzbekistan. Thirteen projects in other transport subsectors (two ports, two logistics centers, three border crossing points [BCP], and six civil aviation projects) are being implemented. A new Railway Strategy and Road Safety Strategy were endorsed by CAREC ministers for 2017–2030.

Energy. In December 2016, ADB approved a $240-million loan for the fifth phase of the Turkmenistan–Uzbekistan–Tajikistan–Afghanistan–Pakistan (TUTAP) Power Interconnection Framework.

Figure 6.2: CAREC Projects by Funding Source, as of end-2016 ($ billion)

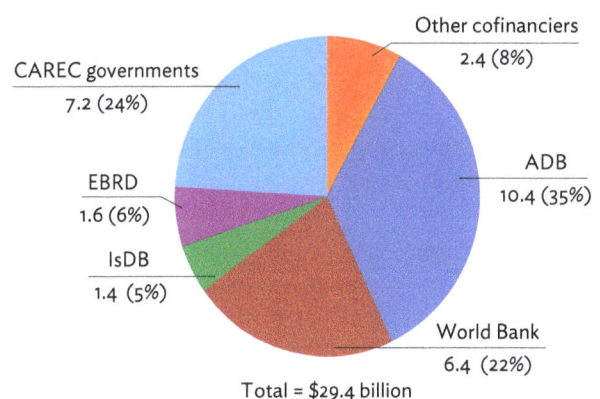

CAREC = Central Asia Regional Economic Cooperation, EBRD = European Bank for Reconstruction and Development, IsDB = Islamic Development Bank.
Source: ADB. CAREC Program Portfolio.

Figure 6.3: Progress of Multimodal Corridor Network Development (kilometers)

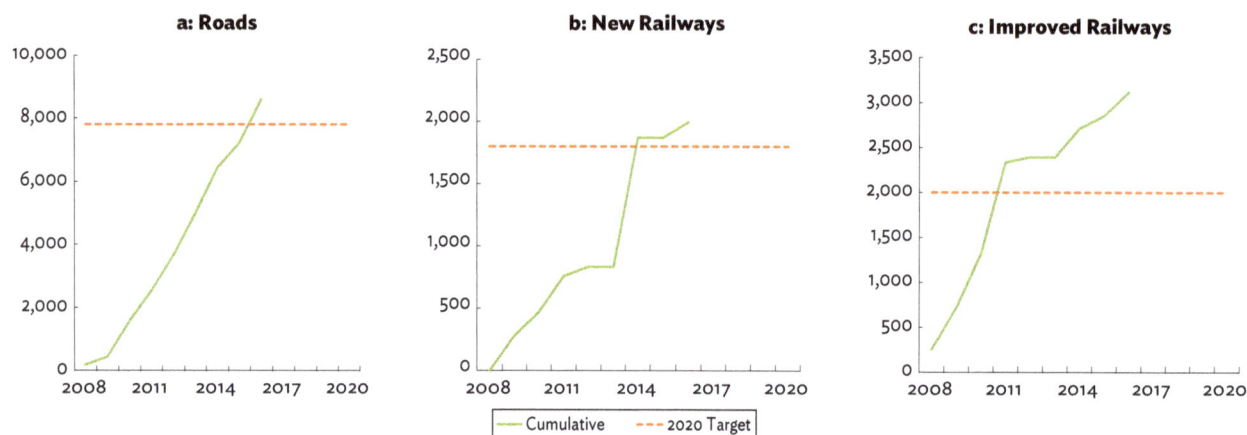

a: Roads

b: New Railways

c: Improved Railways

— Cumulative --- 2020 Target

Source: ADB. 2017a. CAREC Transport Sector Progress Report. June.

Through its unified grid, TUTAP will allow Afghanistan to supply power to its eastern and southern provinces, including Kabul. Another flagship project, the 2000-megawatt (MW) Turkmenistan–Afghanistan–Pakistan (TAP) Power Interconnection Project moved forward with the signing by the three countries of a joint ministerial statement and project framework that paves the way for project preparatory work. TAP would complement TUTAP power interconnections under the Central Asia South Asia Regional Energy Markets framework. In December 2016, under the Turkmenistan–Afghanistan–Pakistan–India Natural Gas Pipeline Project (TAPI), TAPI Pipeline Company Limited was awarded the project's front-end engineering design and project management and supervision contract (CAREC 2017c).

Trade Facilitation and Trade Policy. Seven CAREC countries have ratified the World Trade Organization's (WTO) Trade Facilitation Agreement (TFA)—Afghanistan, the PRC, Georgia, Kazakhstan, the Kyrgyz Republic, Mongolia, and Pakistan. CAREC continues to support Turkmenistan's and the Kyrgyz Republic's accession to the Revised Kyoto Convention through capacity building activities. CAREC's trade facilitation strategy also includes the Regional Improvement of Border Services program, which coordinates infrastructure improvement and simplification of border crossing clearance procedures in select BCPs in the Kyrgyz Republic, Mongolia, Pakistan, and Tajikistan. The CAREC Common Agenda for Modernization of Sanitary and Phytosanitary (SPS) Measures for Trade Facilitation promotes SPS reforms in policies,

investments in laboratory capacities, and improvement of border SPS management. In 2017, CAREC is piloting two new initiatives: the CAREC Advanced Transit System (CATS) and CAREC Customs Information Common Exchange (ICE) along CAREC sub-corridor 2a (Azerbaijan, Georgia and Kazakhstan) (CAREC 2017b). CATS will streamline and harmonize transit documentation, replace manual processes with a single electronic messaging system, and provide a modern, risk-based and affordable guarantee mechanism. Under ICE, the Customs Data Exchange Protocol will enable the electronic exchange of data and promote real-time collaboration between customs administrations.

Other CAREC Operational Priorities. The Almaty–Bishkek Economic Corridor (ABEC) seeks to transform the corridor into a single space, where the exchange of ideas, movement of goods, and people-to-people contact are faster, easier, and barrier-free. In November 2016, the Intergovernmental Council chaired by the prime ministers of Kazakhstan and the Kyrgyz Republic signed a protocol establishing the ABEC Subcommittee. An investment pipeline is being considered by governments and early-action projects are being developed. CAREC's capacity development agenda involves the CAREC Institute (CI)—physically established in March 2015 in Urumqi, PRC and legally set up as an inter-governmental organization in September 2017—which provides knowledge and relevant training to CAREC partners and promotes use of international best practices.

Prospects

At the 15th Ministerial Conference in October 2016, CAREC members agreed to begin working on a new development strategy following an extensive Mid-Term Review. To ensure relevance, ownership, and effective implementation, the process for formulating the new long-term strategy, CAREC 2030, involves consultations and participation from officials of all 11 CAREC members, multilateral and bilateral partners, the private sector, think tanks, and civil society. CAREC 2030 will bring a coordinated response to the multi-dimensional development challenges the subregion faces and consider new multilateral frameworks and initiatives—including the possibility of a broader mission and sectoral coverage to complement national efforts in achieving sustainable development goals and the 21st Conference of the Parties targets as an open and inclusive regional platform.

With much of Central Asia interconnected by road and rail—and with links to the rest of Asia and Europe—the logical next step is to build seamless air connectivity. Due to its strategic location, CAREC could become an aviation hub of both passenger and freight transport. Thus, CAREC 2030 calls for concerted actions of CAREC member countries to enhance aviation cooperation toward a regional open skies agreement.

Policy Challenges

The CAREC region has historically been susceptible to external economic shocks. Designing and implementing appropriate countercyclical policy responses in periods of the economic downturns remain challenging for the CAREC countries. CAREC countries find challenges with the pursuit of economic diversification, particularly with the expansion of trade in services. Against the backdrop of global trade growth slowing down, it becomes even more imperative for CAREC countries to further reduce technical barriers to trade and rationalize SPS measures to facilitate trade. Among the 11 member countries, eight countries are WTO members. Newly acceded countries are obliged to fulfill their WTO commitments by conducting necessary policy reforms for which the government require capacity building and knowledge solutions. CAREC, as an influential regional cooperation platform, thus plays an important role in helping connect

people, policies, and projects for shared and sustainable development for the CAREC region.

Southeast Asia: Greater Mekong Subregion Program[24]

Cambodia, the PRC (Yunnan Province and Guangxi Zhuang Autonomous Region), the Lao People's Democratic Republic (Lao PDR), Myanmar, Thailand, and Viet Nam make up the Greater Mekong Subregion (GMS) Program. In over 25 years of cooperation, the GMS has created an interconnected subregion that continues to see improved economic growth amid enhanced connectivity and competitiveness.

Overview

The GMS—with a regional GDP growth of 5.9% in 2016—continues its robust economic growth supported by increased regional transport connectivity (Table 6.2). Road density, defined as kilometers of road per square kilometer (km/km^2), increased 30% from 0.24 km/km^2 in 2006 to 0.31 km/km^2 in 2014, primarily due to new road transport networks being developed in Yunnan, Guangxi, Viet Nam, and Cambodia. These are contributing to the development of new urban centers and economic zones. Foreign direct investment (FDI) to the subregion increased from $10.8 billion in 2005 to $33.1 billion in 2015, while aggregate intraregional FDI increased from $8.3 billion in 2001–2006 to $29.2 billion in 2010–2015.

The program continues to be guided by the GMS Strategic Framework 2012–2022 (ADB 2011), which is anchored on economic corridor development. Strategic sectors of cooperation include: (i) strengthening transport linkages; (ii) delivering sustainable and secure energy; (iii) developing and promoting tourism along the Mekong as a single destination; (iv) promoting competitive, climate-friendly, and sustainable agriculture; (v) enhancing environmental performance; and (vi) supporting human resource development (HRD) to facilitate GMS integration.

---

[24] Contributed by the GMS Secretariat.

Table 6.2: Selected Economic Indicators, 2016—Greater Mekong Subregion

	Population (million)	Nominal GDP ($ billion)	GDP Growth (2012–2016 average, %)	GDP per Capita (current prices, $)	Trade Openness (total trade, % of GDP)	FDI Openness (total FDI inflows, % of GDP)
Cambodia	16	20.0	7.2	1,268.80	107.3	9.4
Guangxi, PRC	48	274.2	9.1	5,668.50	17.5	0.6
Yunnan, PRC	47	223.5	10.1	4,713.70	9.5	1.4
Lao PDR	7	13.8	7.3	1,921.10	79.7	9.9
Myanmar	52	58.9	7.6	1,127.90	23.1	4.5
Thailand	69	407.0	3.4	5,900.60	96.4	2.7
Viet Nam	93	201.3	5.9	2,173.20	174.5	6.1
GMS	**333**	**1,198.80**	**6.7**	**3,604.30**	**73.5**	**2.8**

FDI = foreign direct investment, GDP = gross domestic product, GMS = Greater Mekong Subregion, Lao PDR = Lao People's Democratic Republic, PRC = People's Republic of China.
Notes: GMS average GDP growth rate is weighted using nominal GDP. Total trade is the sum of exports and imports. FDI openness is based on 2015 data.
Sources: ADB calculations using data from CEIC; and Greater Mekong Subregion Statistical Database. www.greatermekong.org/statistics/ (accessed May 2017).

Projects across these key sectors are consolidated under the GMS Regional Investment Framework (2013–2022) (GMS Secretariat 2013) to develop projects and mobilize financing for regional connectivity. Progress is tracked, monitored, and refined through the GMS Program Secretariat and various working groups involving national line ministries. A 2016 *Study on Strengthening the Greater Mekong Subregion Program's Institutional Framework* (GMS Secretariat 2016a) found that through nearly 25 years of GMS Program cooperation, the GMS Program demand is for an activities- and projects-based initiative using a results-oriented approach.

Performance and Progress over the Past Year

The GMS Program expanded GMS Economic Corridors to continue to advance its transport network, focusing on strengthened regional connectivity. Projects support regional health security, transport and trade facilitation, new urban center development along GMS corridors and border areas, and regional industry and trade through tourism and agricultural value chains.

Progress in the GMS is underpinned by improvements in cross-border connectivity and enhanced transport networks. Other sectors of cooperation include energy, urban development, tourism, agriculture, the environment, and HRD. Substantial financial resources have contributed to this progress. As of 2016, for example, a total of $19.1 billion have been invested in GMS projects by GMS governments and multilateral and bilateral development partners. Of this, ADB has contributed $7.3 billion in 84 investment projects in the GMS (Figure 6.4).

Cross-border Physical Connectivity. In 2016, physical connectivity across the GMS benefited from the completion of three new bridges along GMS economic corridors—the Lao PDR–Myanmar Friendship Bridge over the Mekong River at Xiengkok–Kyainglap; the Tsubasa Bridge in Neak Loeung, Cambodia along the GMS Southern Economic Corridor; and a railway bridge between Cambodia and Thailand at Poipet–Klong Loeuk. Sections of the East–West Economic Corridor in Myanmar—Eindu–Kawkareik and the Mae Sot–Myawaddy border with Thailand—are also under construction.

To keep pace with the shifting patterns of trade, investment, tourism, and other economic flows—and the opening of Myanmar's economy in recent years—a review of the current configuration of the major GMS economic corridors was conducted in 2016. Following the study, the 21st GMS Ministerial Conference in December 2016 approved the extension and expansion of the GMS economic corridors to link all GMS capitals, major economic centers, and important GMS maritime gateways—including missing sections in Myanmar, as well as important new sections in the Lao PDR.

Figure 6.4: Sectoral Distribution of GMS Investment Projects Financed by ADB, 1994–2016

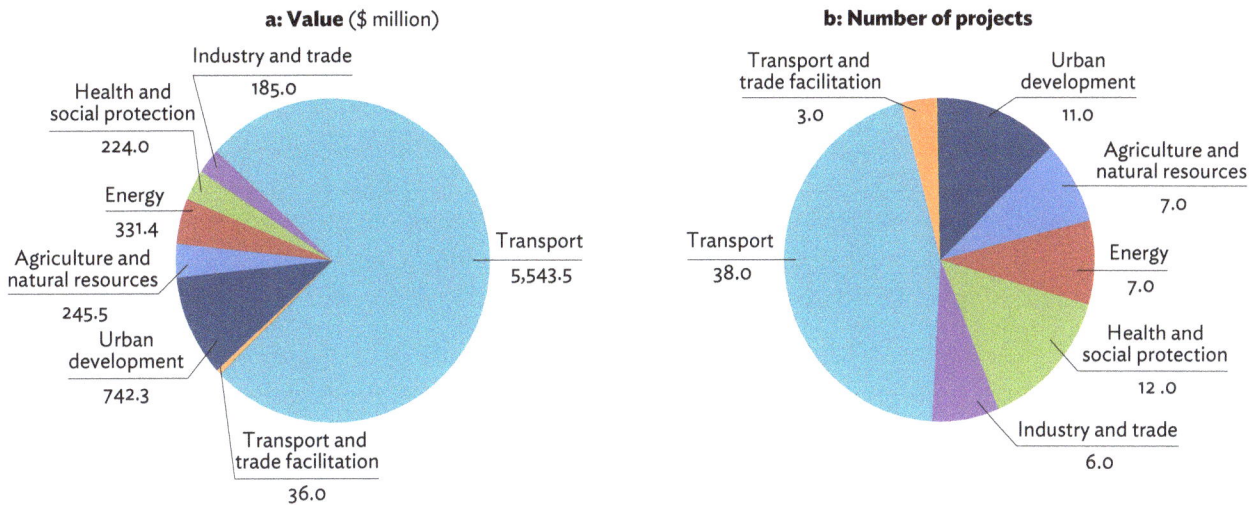

a: Value ($ million)

Industry and trade
185.0

Health and social protection
224.0

Energy
331.4

Agriculture and natural resources
245.5

Urban development
742.3

Transport and trade facilitation
36.0

Transport
5,543.5

b: Number of projects

Transport and trade facilitation
3.0

Urban development
11.0

Agriculture and natural resources
7.0

Energy
7.0

Health and social protection
12.0

Industry and trade
6.0

Transport
38.0

Source: ADB, Greater Mekong Subregion Secretariat.

Transport and Trade Facilitation. Progress in implementing the GMS Cross Border Transport Facilitation Agreement (CBTA) through transport and trade facilitation (TTF) activities included: (i) developing a revised CBTA to align its existing transit arrangements with those under the Association of Southeast Asian Nations (ASEAN) Customs Transit System; (ii) expanding traffic rights and routes through bilateral and trilateral arrangements; (iii) implementing standard customs reforms and improving national information technology systems in Cambodia, the Lao PDR, Myanmar, and Viet Nam; (iv) launching single stop/single window inspection for goods traffic at Mukdahan (Thailand) and Savannakhet (Lao PDR)—to be followed by border crossings at Lao Bao (Viet Nam)–Dansavanh (Lao PDR) and Moc Bai (Viet Nam)–Bavet (Cambodia); and (v) enhancing SPS arrangements for GMS trade through three ADB loan-assisted projects.

Energy. The GMS Regional Power Trade Coordination Committee continues to foster power trade and interconnections for seamless regional energy trade. Two working groups on: (i) performance standards and grid code (WGPG) and (ii) regulatory issues (WGRI) are helping harmonize regional power trade policy. In 2016, the WGRI concentrated on two important aspects of regulatory harmonization: (i) third party access and (ii) a methodology for calculating wheeling charges. The WGPG continues to work toward establishing common GMS technical performance standards.

Urban Development. The Corridor Towns Development Project Phase 1 is developing urban services in corridor towns in Viet Nam (Dong Ha, Lao Bao, Moc Bai), the Lao PDR (Kaysone Phomvihane, Phine, Dansavanh), and Cambodia (Battambang, Bavet, Neak Loeung, Poipet). The project also includes spatial planning in special economic zones (SEZs) and adjacent areas to provide guidance on investments that create more quality jobs in border areas. A 2016 *Study on the Role of Special Economic Zones in Improving Effectiveness of GMS Economic Corridors* (GMS Secretariat 2016b) identified and assessed key success factors in harnessing SEZs. In border area development, the ADB-supported Guangxi Regional Cooperation and Integration Promotion and Investment Program ($450 million) was approved in December 2016 and covers small and medium-sized enterprises (SMEs) development, development of border economic zones (BEZs), facilitation of cross-border investment and financial transactions, and further improvements in cross-border connectivity along the PRC–Viet Nam border.

Agriculture. The GMS Core Agriculture Support Program Phase II (CASP2) for 2011–2020 focuses on increasing the subregion's agricultural competitiveness through enhanced regional and global market integration and improved connectivity. In 2016, CASP2 completed setting up a participatory guarantee system for farmer groups in each GMS member and the first study on low-input rice value chains focusing on three rice-producing countries—Cambodia, Thailand, and Viet Nam. It conducted vital national and regional capacity building, piloted climate-friendly and gender-responsive agriculture practices at the farm production level, and applied research and extension work on climate-and environment-friendly agricultural practices.

Tourism. With 57.9 million tourist arrivals in 2015 generating $65 billion in the GMS—contributing as much as 15% of GDP in Cambodia and allowing 89% of tourists visiting the Lao PDR to arrive by land—regional transport connectivity is having a deep impact on several GMS economies. A new GMS Tourism Sector Strategy for 2016–2025 was recently completed, setting out a framework to guide cooperation between GMS national tourism organizations and other tourism industry stakeholders. The strategy outlines five strategic directions: HRD, improving tourism infrastructure, enhancing visitor experiences and services, encouraging creative marketing and promotion, and facilitating regional travel. Corresponding programs and projects were selected for each strategic area based on their potential to enable more competitive, balanced, and sustainable destination development.

Human Resource Development. HRD covers education, technical and vocational skills, cooperation on health, and labor and migration. The GMS, ASEAN, and national development programs are working to increase and support regional labor mobility. Mutual recognition of skills and qualifications was expanded to cover additional areas of logistics, machinery, and food processing. The Quality Assurance System—using established ASEAN University Network standards—and the Academic Credit Transfer System Framework for Asia among GMS universities have both shown progress. A GMS University Consortium of 24 GMS universities has been established to further foster networking in tertiary education among GMS members. Communicable disease control and management has been further strengthened—including implementing malaria and tuberculosis prevention and treatment initiatives for migrant and mobile populations in Cambodia, the Lao PDR, Myanmar, and Viet Nam. A new GMS Health Security Project was approved for ADB financing for these four countries to contribute to the enhancement of GMS public health security and strengthen national and regional capacity for disease surveillance and response, risk assessment, case management, and subregional collaboration.

Environment. The GMS continues to strengthen management of transboundary environmental issues. This includes: (i) developing national environmental policies and strategies in Cambodia, the Lao PDR, and Viet Nam; (ii) supporting the application of sound environment management policies and tools—including the launch of Myanmar's environmental impact assessment procedure and environmental quality guidelines, applying land use planning simulation modeling in Cambodia and the Lao PDR, and industrial pollution projection modeling in Cambodia and Myanmar; (iii) jointly developing transboundary biodiversity landscape monitoring and evaluation framework; (iv) creating transboundary conservation plans for rare species; and (v) promoting fuel efficient technologies, eco-driver training, and improved logistics measures—successfully tested in the Lao PDR and Viet Nam, and under way in Thailand.

Prospects and Future Strategies

As the GMS Program celebrates 25 years of cooperation, a Midterm Review of the GMS Strategic Framework 2012–2022 and several sector strategies are under way covering the next 5 years. Through 2017, a Strategy and Action Plan for Promoting Safe and Environment-Friendly Value Chains in the GMS is being developed, focusing on strengthening GMS competitive advantage through value-chain integration—particularly for smallholder farmers, rural women, and agricultural SMEs. The Action Plan will outline key GMS investments through the GMS Regional Investment Framework as well as policy and institutional measures. The Strategy and Action Plan will strengthen member commitment to food safety, market access for small producers, and inclusive food safety. HRD conducted a review of the latest Strategy and Action Plan to formulate and shape new strategic directions covering health, education, labor and migration, and social development. The new strategies on agriculture value chains and regional HRD cooperation—along with the new economic corridor alignment and GMS Tourism Sector Strategy 2016–2025—will drive investments in regional connectivity for the foreseeable future.

Policy Challenges

Implementing the GMS Cross-Border Transport Facilitation Agreement is a major challenge for the subregion.

As regional transport networks expand, tourism grows, and agricultural and industrial trade integrates across the region, the greatest challenge will be implementing the GMS CBTA fully. The GMS ministers of the National Transportation Facilitation Committee are committed, on a pilot basis, to test the GMS Road Transport Permit—allowing approved vehicles to travel freely across GMS country borders—as first step in implementing the CBTA. They are committed to full CBTA implementation by 2019. On transport facilitation, trade facilitation measures will also need to accelerate—in areas like SPS systems—to support intra-GMS trade in agriculture, food, and forest products.

The financing gap for GMS infrastructure investment is $6.4 billion, estimated in the 2016 Midterm Review of the Regional Investment Framework Implementation Plan. Greater participation and investments from the private sector—in the form of public private partnerships (PPP)—can help close the gap. This will require the GMS governments to strengthen PPP policy frameworks, bidding, and risk allocation to attract private sector investment.

East Asia: Support to CAREC and GMS Programs[25]

ADB supports regional cooperation and integration (RCI) in East Asia through the CAREC and GMS programs. It works to maximize synergies with new cooperation initiatives led by government stakeholders (including the BRI, for example). ADB has strengthened lending support to the PRC and Mongolia for RCI operations; covering connectivity, border economic zone development, SME development, border-crossing improvement, and single-window customs clearance, among others.

Performance and Progress over the Past Year

ADB continues to support projects in Mongolia and the PRC that relate to CAREC and GMS economic cooperation.[26]

Mongolia. Under the Western Regional Road Corridor Development Program, ADB supports development of about 300 km of the 743 km corridor in CAREC Corridor 4a. The corridor—part of Asian Highway 4—runs north–south from Mongolia's border with the Russian Federation at Ulaanbayshint to its border with the PRC at Yarant. As of 2016, paved roads covered just over 5% of Mongolia's total road network with the majority of roads unimproved road tracks.

Under CAREC, ADB is helping Mongolia implement two loan projects—Regional Improvement of Border Services (RIBS) and the Mongolia Upgrades of Sanitary and Phytosanitary Measures for Trade (MUST). RIBS addresses inefficient trade processes by rehabilitating BCP facilities; upgrading the Customs Automated Information System; constructing access roads in border areas; and developing the national single-window customs platform for international trade. The project will improve connectivity and cross-border cooperation to reduce BCP costs and processing time.

Mongolia is taking the lead in implementing the CAREC Common Agenda for Modernization of SPS Measures through its MUST project. The project will improve laboratories, inspection and quarantine facilities at the key BCPs in three *aimags* (provinces), establish an integrated SPS inspection management system, and align SPS control and inspection with international standards. A regional technical assistance project on Transforming SPS Measures for Trade Facilitation was proposed in 2017 to further help implement the project.

Joint customs control is a priority under the CAREC Customs Cooperation Committee work program to share a common set of information and reduce repetitive customs inspections. A pilot joint customs project

25 Contributed by Ying Qian, Director and Yuebin Zhang, Principal Regional Cooperation Specialist, East Asia Department.

26 ADB's East Asia Department (EARD) provides technical and administrative support for the CAREC Trade Facilitation program. EARD also provides direct support to Mongolia for participating in CAREC, and to selected provinces and autonomous regions of the PRC involved with CAREC and the GMS.

between Mongolia and the PRC reported increased international cooperation and better management and coordination between the two customs administrations. It improved consistency in implementing customs control measures and saw a significant decrease in fraud (for example, less undervaluation and underweighting goods). A case study documenting the success factors of the pilot project and recommendations on how to replicate the experience at other BCPs is being finalized.

The People's Republic of China. RCI is an integral part of ADB operations in the PRC, and one of the five strategic priorities of its Country Partnership Strategy 2016–2020 with the PRC. In 2016, ADB processed a multitranche financing facility and the first tranche of the Guangxi Regional Cooperation and Integration Promotion Investment Program to support Guangxi's involvement in regional cooperation—particularly the GMS program. The investment program uses a holistic approach to address the wide range of RCI issues Guangxi faces. The project is also intended to be a model for future investment projects in other border provinces participating in RCI programs.

ADB continues to support PRC participation in GMS economic cooperation. It supports the memorandum of understanding (MOU) between the PRC and Viet Nam on jointly developing BEZs. A new regional technical assistance project further supports BEZ development by (i) formulating policy recommendations for coordinated BEZ development, (ii) strengthening coordination mechanisms for the development and management of the BEZs and public–private coordination, and (iii) conducting capacity building for government stakeholders. The MOU should boost trade and investment, contributing to the development of the GMS North–South Economic Corridor.

ADB and the PRC government jointly organized a regional knowledge sharing workshop on Development of Special Economic Zones as Catalysts for Economic Corridors in September 2016 in Shanghai. The workshop brought together more than 50 participants from ADB's developing member countries (DMCs) to share lessons and experience on SEZ development and economic corridors.

In 2017, the $50-million second replenishment of the Poverty Reduction and Regional Cooperation Fund—established in 2005—came into effect. The PRC led the establishment of the CI with CAREC to conduct a Time Release Study and Corridor Performance Measurement and Monitoring subregional workshop in April 2017—to improve border management efficiency. There are plans to partner with the CI on a Regional Knowledge Sharing Initiative with the CAREC Federation of Carrier and Forwarder Association to discuss harmonizing standards for logistics operators in the subregion (in compliance with international best practices).

CAREC Trade Facilitation Program. A new CAREC Trade Facilitation Strategic Framework will be formulated to further broaden and deepen (i) implementation of the WTO TFA in close cooperation with trade policy agencies and related stakeholders, including the private sector; (ii) the current customs and integrated trade facilitation agenda; (iii) potential work on people mobility; and (iv) resolution of cross-sectoral trade facilitation issues anchored on economic corridor development like SEZs and cross-border economic zones (CBEZs), participation in regional and global value chains, e-commerce, cross-border finance, and access to trade by SMEs, among others.

Consultations with the PRC on the new CAREC Strategy 2030 led to three government recommendations on connectivity: (i) to focus on expanding connectivity, enhancing transport efficiency, and promoting green transportation—in particular the PRC–Kyrgyz Republic–Uzbekistan railway project—and liberalizing aviation markets by coordinating security and aviation infrastructure development, if possible with the BRI; (ii) to provide capacity building support on customs cooperation and standardizing customs procedures, developing CBEZs, and implementing WTO TFA provisions; and (iii) to facilitate negotiations on regional trade agreements, promote e-commerce to link SMEs to regional value chains, and enhance the region's digital economy.

Prospects

The PRC's BRI—Silk Road Economic Belt and 21st Century Maritime Silk Road—aims to promote connectivity and strengthen economic partnerships across Asia, Europe, and Africa. It highlights five priorities for cooperation: (i) fostering economic and development policy coordination; (ii) strengthening connectivity through energy, transport, and telecommunications infrastructure; (iii) promoting trade and investment; (iv) deepening financial cooperation and integration; and (v) promoting people-to-people exchanges. The potential to enhance synergies between ADB-supported RCI programs and BRI is significant.

Policy Challenges

Implementing the TFA within CAREC is a challenge that will require technical assistance.

With TFA effectivity, CAREC countries who are WTO members will need to: (i) have a National Committee on Trade Facilitation in place, (ii) notify WTO of Category A designations, (iii) implement Category A designations, and (iv) notify WTO of Category B and C designations

along with indicative dates for implementation. An assessment of the readiness of CAREC countries (both WTO members and nonmembers) to implement the TFA has been done to determine appropriate technical assistance required. Coordinated support from donors will be critical to help make TFA implementation a priority.

South Asia: South Asia Subregional Economic Cooperation[27]

In 2001, Bangladesh, Bhutan, India, and Nepal launched the South Asia Subregional Economic Cooperation (SASEC) initiative, with ADB assistance, to help address constraints of size, geography, and institutional capacity hindering development in South Asia (Table 6.3). Maldives and Sri Lanka joined in 2014, followed by Myanmar in 2017, expanding the potential for RCI from a subregional to inter-regional level. ADB acts as lead financier, secretariat, and development partner. Its support covers: (i) capacity building and institutional strengthening, (ii) regional initiatives, and (iii) financing for projects and technical assistance.

Table 6.3: Selected Economic Indicators, 2016—SASEC

	Population (million)	Nominal GDP ($ billion)	GDP Growth (%, 2012–2016, average)	GDP Per Capita (current prices, $)	Trade Openness (total trade, % of GDP)
Bangladesh	162.9	221.4	6.5	1,359	33.1
Bhutan	0.8	2.1	5.3	2,695	102.7
India	1,326.9	2,259.6	6.9	1,703	27.4
Maldives	0.4	3.8	3.9	9,021	65.5
Nepal	28.9	21.2	3.4	735	40.3
Sri Lanka	21.2	81.3	5.3	3,843	34.3
SASEC	**1,541.0**	**2,589.4**	**6.7**	**1,680**	**28.3**

GDP = gross domestic product, SASEC = South Asia Subregional Economic Cooperation.
Note: SASEC average GDP growth rate is weighted using nominal GDP.
Sources: ADB calculations using data from ADB. 2017. *Asian Development Outlook 2017*. Manila; CEIC; International Monetary Fund. Direction of Trade Statistics. https://www.imf.org/en/Data; and World Bank. World Development Indicators. http://databank.worldbank.org (all accessed May 2017).

[27] Contributed by Rose McKenzie, Senior Regional Cooperation Specialist, South Asia Department (SARD) and Jesusito Tranquilino, ADB Consultant, SARD.

Overview

SASEC connectivity has focused on developing intraregional trade corridors.

Since 2001, ADB has assisted SASEC members invest more than $9.17 billion in 46 projects in three strategic areas of cooperation—transport, trade facilitation, and energy (Figure 6.5). Developing intraregional trade corridors has improved access to key markets and gateway ports, and boosted prospects for participating in regional and global value chains. Trade facilitation projects and other activities have made trade processes more efficient and robust, while reducing the time and cost of intraregional trade. Transport facilitation efforts have helped SASEC members negotiate groundbreaking motor vehicle agreements that will ultimately create a seamless flow of passenger, personal and cargo vehicular traffic between and among participating countries in South Asia. Investments in energy have focused on enhancing energy security nationally, while building bilateral and regional arrangements to promote cross-border interconnection and electricity trade.

SASEC is institution light and project heavy, with senior officials meeting annually—at strategic and working group levels—to review progress and operational priorities. Technical subgroups support implementation of multi-track, multi-speed national investments that lead to regional development outcomes. SASEC closely aligns its strategic direction and planning with South Asian Association for Regional Cooperation initiatives and the Bay of Bengal Initiative for Multi-Sectoral Technical and Economic Cooperation.

Performance and Progress over the Past Year

The SASEC Program was significantly ramped up in 2016, as ADB approved nine projects at $2.43 billion, of which ADB provided $1.43 billion. This was markedly higher than the $500 million annual average value approved during the previous 15 years of the program. This can be partially credited to the adoption in June 2016 of the *SASEC Operational Plan 2016-2025* (SASEC OP) (ADB 2016), the program's first long-term operational plan—which identified projects aligned with the SASEC OP priorities in transport, trade facilitation, energy and economic corridor development. In 2016, ADB also supported the preparation of *SASEC Powering Asia in the 21st Century* (SASEC Vision) (ADB 2017)—a comprehensive blueprint for accelerating SASEC growth by leveraging the subregion's resource strengths, making SASEC an engine to help power Asia's growth in the 21st Century.

Transport. Transport cooperation continued to focus on improving the national and regional connectivity critical to seamless movement of goods and people across the subregion. Various SASEC road connectivity projects in Bangladesh, Bhutan, Nepal, and India's northeastern regions have helped improve parts of the Asian Highway Network, constructing alternate routes and developing access roads while improving land customs stations and customs systems.

The $257 million Nepal SASEC Roads Improvement Project approved in 2016 is integral to the international and regional road network system connecting Nepal to India and will contribute to raising Nepal's export competitiveness. India's $715 million New Bihar Ganga Bridge project and its approach road network will improve connectivity both within Bihar and with Nepal. It is essential to the regional road network system connecting Nepal to India, facilitating closer trade integration and contributing to Nepal's export competitiveness.

Figure 6.5: SASEC Projects by Sector ($ million)

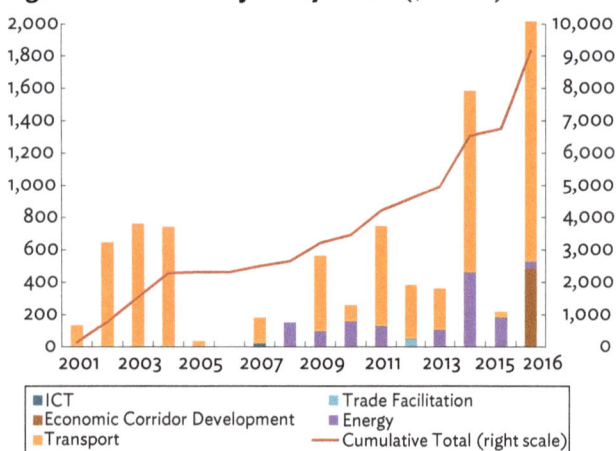

ICT = information and communication technology, SASEC = South Asia Subregional Economic Cooperation.
Source: ADB. SASEC Project Portfolio 2017.

Two ADB-supported railway enhancement projects in Bangladesh, approved in 2016 with a combined value of $890 million will improve the international connectivity of the rail system. These include sections of the Dohazari–Cox's Bazar route along the overall Chittagong–Cox's Bazar trade corridor, moving the SASEC–Myanmar Corridor toward completion—promoting inter-regional connectivity with Southeast Asia.

An additional $4 million in financing for Bhutan's airports supports development of a safe, reliable, and efficient air transport system connecting urban and rural centers in Bhutan, improving accessibility, promoting tourism and high-value agriculture.

Trade Facilitation. SASEC's Trade Facilitation Strategic Framework 2014–2018 (ADB 2014) focuses support to SASEC countries in five priority areas: (i) customs modernization and harmonization; (ii) standards and conformity assessments, primarily SPS and technical barriers to trade (TBT) measures; (iii) improvement of cross-border facilities; (iv) transport facilitation; and (v) institutional capacity building.

The SASEC Customs Subgroup coordinates subregional and national projects designed to promote trade facilitation, strengthen inter-agency cooperation and provide a regional knowledge-sharing platform. Projects focus on improving cross-border procedures and providing support to users of the Automated System for Customs Data World system. National and regional diagnostic studies in SPS and TBT will help identify and address nontariff barriers in the subregion. An electronic cargo tracking system initiative was launched in SASEC to speed up transit movement, simplify border-crossing procedures, and reduce congestion—by using satellite positioning systems, cellular communications, radio frequency identification, electronic seals, and monitoring software. Electronic tracking system technology also improves security of goods in transit and opens the way for off-border customs processes for exports, leading to substantial savings in time and cost for traders. Implementing the WTO TFA is a key area for coordinated capacity building in coordination with other development partners.

Energy. Energy cooperation continues to focus on enhancing electricity trade to expand and diversify the subregion's energy supply—to meet energy needs and secure power reliability. SASEC countries are forging arrangements for energy trade. Bhutan and Nepal are developing hydropower for export to neighbors. Meanwhile, transmission projects are strengthening Nepal's national power grid in preparation for energy trade. Nepal's power system expansion was approved in 2016—to support installation of utility-scale solar power to augment energy supply and expand domestic power transmission capacity for better power trade with India.

The SASEC Electricity Transmission Utility Forum completed its review of a transmission master plan study in December 2016, affirming the net economic benefits from interconnecting power systems in the subregion for power trading. Larger benefits will accrue from multi-country arrangements and from mitigating greenhouse gases as hydropower replaces fossil fuels. The SASEC countries agreed on the need to examine alternative scenarios that account for recent and future changes in each country's energy situation. They also agreed on the need for an enhanced forum for capacity building, knowledge sharing and consensus-building on transmission plans along with technical and other issues involving regional power trade.

Economic Corridor Development. A new area of SASEC focus, economic corridor development (ECD) builds on the backbone of transport corridors, by leveraging—in the case of SASEC—infrastructure connectivity and cities as growth centers to unlock full market potential. This means SASEC transport connectivity and trade facilitation efforts will be augmented and strengthened by a multi-sector approach that includes developing special economic/industrial zones and logistics centers—backed by better coordinated planning and policies that raise the competitiveness of domestic enterprises.

India's $484-million Visakhapatnam–Chennai Industrial Corridor (VCIC) Development Program was approved by ADB as the first SASEC ECD investment. It will complement ongoing efforts in Andhra Pradesh to enhance industrial growth and create high-quality jobs, focusing on priority infrastructure in VCIC with concomitant support for policy reform and institutional development. The VCIC is the first phase of India's East Coast Economic Corridor (ECEC), which runs from Kolkata to Kanyakumari—a multimodal, regional maritime corridor that should help integrate India's economy with the dynamic global value chains in Southeast Asia and East Asia.

In Bangladesh, ADB is also supporting the development of the Khulna–Dhaka–Sylhet (KDS) Corridor to link the lagging southwest and northeast regions and integrate them with the vibrant growth centers of Dhaka and Chittagong. Phase 1 of the KDS Corridor involves preparing a comprehensive development plan for the Southwest Economic Corridor. In Sri Lanka, an ADB-funded conceptual study has identified potential economic corridors, gauging how best to strengthen domestic supply chains and join the global manufacturing supply chain. The Colombo–Trincomalee Economic Corridor (CTEC) will link the Colombo–Gampha west region with the central and eastern part of the island. CTEC can accommodate several industry clusters—including garments and new export-oriented manufacturing as well as agribusiness and tourism.

Prospects

SASEC Vision and Operational Plan. In April 2017, SASEC Finance Ministers launched their shared SASEC Vision, which articulates SASEC aspirations and how they can be achieved through regional collaboration. Framing the partnership in the larger context of the subregion's collective growth and development, it lays out a plan to transform the subregion by generating synergies and leveraging natural resource-based industries, promoting industry linkages to develop regional value chains, and expanding trade and commerce by developing subregional gateways and hubs.

The SASEC OP supports the SASEC vision by identifying strategic objectives and operational priorities for transport, trade facilitation, and energy, while introducing ECD as a new area of strategic cooperation. It expands the scope of SASEC investments to: (i) strengthen regional connectivity

in railways and through seaports and inland waterways, (ii) increase focus on maritime-based trade facilitation together with SPS and standards conformity, and (iii) develop more clean energy and accelerate development of South Asia's power trade. It examines the development impact of promoting synergies between economic corridors under development. The SASEC OP is supported by over 200 potential projects identified by SASEC partners worth more than $120 billion—to be implemented during 2016–2025.

Policy Challenges

Over the coming decade, SASEC will see the share of its working age population rise—a "demographic dividend" that presents both an opportunity and challenge for subregional development.

If harnessed properly, this demographic dividend could catapult the subregion into one of the fastest growing subregions in Asia. The SASEC Vision recognizes that upping the ante in RCI will improve the chances of realizing the economic potential of the demographic dividend.

Each SASEC member should take strong ownership of the Vision—a commitment to a challenging and dynamic process requiring multi-stakeholder involvement for cohesive planning and effective coordination of programs, projects, and policies. This process will entail several steps or layers, beginning with organizing cross-country advocacy forums, filtering both short- and long-term strategic initiatives for each country, sorting policies to guide both public and private investment, building consensus on needed interventions, agreeing on institutional mechanisms for moving the Vision forward, and putting in place risk management mechanisms covering project planning, financing, implementation, and monitoring and evaluation.

The Pacific: Regional Approach to Renewable Energy Investments[28]

A regional approach to renewable energy investments provides a unique opportunity for Pacific developing member countries to share experience and learn from innovation across the subregion.

The Framework for Pacific Regionalism—endorsed by Pacific Islands Forum Leaders in July 2014—is the current master strategy for strengthening RCI in the broader Pacific subregion, where climate change is a major priority. In December 2016, the Green Climate Fund (GCF) approved funding to support an ADB program to assist seven Pacific DMCs in transitioning to a renewable energy future. An initial $12-million grant for the Cook Islands to install energy storage systems and support private investment in renewable energy will spearhead a series of projects. A $5-million grant was also approved to improve the energy sector policies and institutions in the Pacific. The proposed program will help develop feasibility studies for renewable energy projects worth over $400 million in the remaining six Pacific DMCs. The program, however, may be extended to the other Pacific DMCs.

Overview

The Pacific Islands Renewable Energy Investment Program (PIREIP) was conceptualized as part of the GCF Pacific Roadmap developed during the GCF Pacific Regional meeting in August 2016, attended by leaders and Ministers from all Pacific island countries. PIREIP supports a shift from diesel power generation to renewable energy in the Cook Islands, the Republic of Marshall Islands, the Federated States of Micronesia (FSM), Nauru, Papua New Guinea, Samoa, and Tonga. A concerted move toward solar, hydropower, and wind energy will place these seven Pacific DMCs on a more sustainable and climate-resilient development pathway. The program is expected to support 22 solar

power plants, five wind farms, eight hydropower plants, seven energy storage facilities, and 25 renewable energy mini-grids. Combined, these investments will reduce greenhouse gas emissions by an estimated 120,000 tons of carbon dioxide equivalent per year.

A Paradigm Shift in Energy Production

The new energy pathway is low-carbon and climate resilient, while also expanding energy access to marginalized populations.

PIREIP is designed to help DMCs rapidly shift from their current traditional energy profile—which has been almost entirely dependent on fossil fuels—to a more progressive and sustainable pathway.

The program supports Pacific DMCs in overcoming the investment and technical barriers to integrate higher shares of renewables in their energy mix. Technical integration of intermittent renewable energy poses significant challenges, particularly on small grids managed by utilities with relatively limited system management capacity. To date, most Pacific DMCs have already gained valuable experience with small amounts of grid-connected solar and wind power, which existing diesel generator-dominated systems can integrate without much problem. However, as renewable energy shares increase, the relatively simple diesel grids will require significant upgrades—most notably in battery storage—and better system management. In general, the Pacific remains at the start of the investment cycle for renewable energy integration beyond small initial investments. This suggests that significant challenges are best addressed through a regional approach.

PIREIP also supports the promotion of greater private sector participation and investment to support the structural shift toward renewable energy. This is particularly important to those Pacific DMCs that lack sufficient sovereign financing and require technical support to manage the transition. Also, there exist significant financial disincentives for corporatized Pacific power utilities reliant on high-cost diesel-based generation centers to increase energy access for customers in remote areas. Most Pacific island countries lack the budgetary resources to support rural electrification programs. Renewable energy for rural

28 Contributed by Paul Curry, Principal Operations Coordination Specialist; and Rommel Rabanal, Senior Economics Officer, Pacific Department.

electrification offers low-cost power generation that allows utilities to extend grids and improve access at lower power generation costs. Lastly, the program will offer more opportunities for sharing lessons learned and best practices among Pacific utilities. A regional project management unit will facilitate the program, enhanced through regional workshops and knowledge products.

Regional Approach

A regional approach was selected to assist the Pacific's transition to a sustainable, resilient energy future, as it supports: (i) improved knowledge transfer and dissemination of lessons learned and best practices, (ii) better sector planning and reform on medium-term basis using program financing, (iii) more efficient procurement through contract bundling across small island states with centralized procurement support, and (iv) greater private sector investment.

Improved Knowledge Transfer. The regional approach allows comprehensive sharing of lessons learned and innovative approaches between the participating Pacific power utilities—that often experience similar technical and management issues. This becomes more important as grids increase shares of renewable energy and where management of integration issues can be more complex. The implementation of a single initiative over multiple countries over many years will mobilize a broad spectrum of stakeholders to participate in the initiative. This would include: (i) Pacific DMC governments and regulators expecting to benefit from the broad range of services and skills available; (ii) Pacific power utilities, also to benefit from the broad range of services and skills available; (iii) development partners; and (iv) implementing and executing agencies, seeing opportunities for capacity building and increased efficiency.

Facilitating Sector Planning and Reform. Financing certainty over the medium-term helps infrastructure planning and possibly encourages additional co-finance. Currently, medium-term infrastructure planning suffers from a lack of clarity over medium-term funding, with plans often being overly dependent on the availability of short-term development partner finance. Medium-term engagement supports sector reform. The type of reforms needed vary among Pacific DMCs, but will cover key issues such as sector planning (like roadmaps and grid integration studies), power utility management reform and capacity building, tariff review and reform, regulatory and policy frameworks, and promotion of private sector investment. Medium-term support for sector reform has consistently been more effective than uncoordinated short-term assistance.

More Efficient Procurement. The regional approach allows bundling of equipment and works packages across Pacific DMCs. This will increase package sizes and contribute to reducing costs. Larger contracts will also potentially attract additional bidders and encourage greater competition.

Promoting Private Sector Participation. Through longer-term perspective, a pipeline of suitable opportunities for complementary private investment can be identified that will likely attract broader private sector interest in renewable energy projects. Sovereign financing to help support investment, and provision of transaction advice, can also be used to promote greater private sector participation.

Expected Impacts

The cost of power generation in these seven Pacific DMCs is among the highest in the world. The reasons include: (i) reliance on imported diesel for generation, (ii) long supply chains of relatively small diesel quantities creating high transportation costs, and (iii) low economies of scale for relatively small grids. Many Pacific DMCs have small populations dispersed over vastly distant islands, and they are heavily dependent on diesel—five of the seven target countries rely on diesel for over 85% of electricity generation. The average supply cost for electricity across the Pacific is about $0.47 per kilowatt-hour, high by international standards. The cost of diesel power generation is even higher for smaller and more isolated grids in outer islands.

The proposed mitigation investments under the PIREIP will include the following:

- Solar power generation: 50 MW at approximately 22 sites in five Pacific DMCs
- Wind power generation: 10 MW at 5 sites in three Pacific DMCs
- Hydropower generation: 19 MW at 8 sites in two Pacific DMCs

- Energy storage facilities in seven Pacific DMCs
- Improved energy access through 25 renewable energy mini-grids (four Pacific DMCs) and solar home systems (two Pacific DMCs)

In total, these investments are expected to reduce greenhouse gas emissions across the seven target Pacific DMCs by about 120,000 tons of carbon dioxide equivalent a year (Table 6.4).

In addition to these mitigation projects, PIREIP also includes adaptation investments:

- Samoa: a flood diversion dam/hydropower reservoir to prevent flash flooding after cyclones
- Yap, FSM: floating solar panels on a water reservoir to minimize evaporation and contribute to securing adequate water supply
- Kosrae, FSM: relocation of distribution lines currently located along the main island coastline and threatened by coastal erosion and storm-surge flooding

All infrastructure built under the PIREIP program will incorporate climate proofing in technical designs to ensure sustainability and resilience to climatic shocks.

More reliable power supply—through increased renewable energy generation and reduced exposure to price volatility in the international fossil fuel market—will also help support the ongoing information and communication technology (ICT) expansion in the Pacific.

Toward Regional Connectivity

Connectivity brings important benefits. In the short run, they emanate from reductions in costs and time, and increases in trade volumes. In the long run, regional connectivity helps unlock the tremendous growth potential by removing constraints and bottlenecks to regional integration and economic growth. Investors see the changed structure of incentives and respond with new capital investments. Workers respond by moving to regions where they can make more money. Thus, regional connectivity allows changes in the factors of production that help accelerate growth and reduce poverty.

Cross-border Connectivity in CAREC and GMS

Trade facilitation and improved border-crossing procedures under CAREC and the development of border zones and towns under the GMS are expected to strengthen cross-border connectivity.

CAREC countries continue to make significant progress in implementing the CAREC TTFS 2020, which prioritizes: (i) multimodal corridor network development, (ii) trade and border crossing service improvements, and (iii) strengthened operations and institutions.

Table 6.4: Projected Emission Reductions with PIREIP Investments

	Renewable Energy (%)		National RE Target	Reduction in CO_2 Emissions (ton)
	Current	**After PIREIP**	**National RE Target**	**Emissions** (ton)
Cook Islands	15	50	100% by 2020	7,000
Marshall Islands	2	6	20% by 2020	10,000
FSM	5	TBD	30% by 2020	19,000
Nauru	3	38	50% by 2020	10,000
Papua New Guinea	50	TBD	No target	21,000
Samoa	48	TBD	100% by 2017	33,000
Tonga	13	57	50% by 2020	20,000
			Total	**120,000**

CO_2 = carbon dioxide, FSM = Federated States of Micronesia, PIREIP = Pacific Islands Renewable Energy Investment Program, RE = renewable energy, TBD = to be determined.
Source: ADB.

Implementing these is the joint responsibility of the Transport Sector Coordinating Committee (TSCC) leading in priorities: (i) and (iii), and the Customs Coordinating Committee leading in (ii). The TSCC maintains a 3-year rolling Transport Sector Work Plan, updated each year to ensure timely implementation. Under the current Work Plan (2016–2018), the physical investments (hard infrastructure) detailed in the TTFS 2020 is supported by a set of complementary soft-side initiatives covering four pillars: (i) road safety, (ii) railways, (iii) road asset management, and (iv) transport facilitation. As of 2016, road and railway projects already surpassed 2020 targets (Figure 6.3). With this connectivity in place, the focus is now on ensuring road and rail assets are properly managed and safe for users. And, as mentioned, CAREC's new aviation pillar holds much potential for additional regional benefits.

In addition to transport and trade facilitation policies to support cross-border connectivity, the GMS will also need to synchronize its hardware. This includes prioritizing inter-operability of regional transport—like railways—managed through the GMS Railway Association. In energy, harmonized power grids for cross-border power trade are developed through the working groups of the Regional Power Trade Coordination Committee.

An emerging area of cooperation within the GMS is the development of border zones and border towns. As the Guangxi–Viet Nam project demonstrates, border zones require multi-sector investments. And border towns, such as those under the GMS Corridor Towns Development Project, can provide the necessary urban infrastructure investments and border area access roads to accelerate cross-border cooperation and attract new economic activities. Additionally, border zones will require logistics centers and multi-modal transport exchanges, facilities to support skills development, communicable health control centers, and business facilitation centers.

During 2017–2019, ADB plans to process seven investment projects for the PRC under the broad framework of the GMS and CAREC—for which ADB will provide about $1.2 billion in loans—to further enhance PRC physical connectivity and trade links with its neighbors and support economic corridor development. For Mongolia, ADB plans to finance two RCI projects for about $80 million to build regional roads, and

improve infrastructure and urban services in South Gobi border towns.

Connecting South Asia and Southeast Asia

Developing multimodal connectivity between India's northeastern region, Bangladesh, and Myanmar holds the potential to unleash tremendous economic energy—creating opportunities for millions in the region.

In February 2017, Myanmar joined SASEC, opening the gateway to accelerate inter-subregional cooperation between South Asia and Southeast Asia. With Myanmar's strategic location at the crossroads of Asia, better inter-subregional connectivity in transport and logistics, as well as in energy, among others, are expected to bring significant benefits to all SASEC members and Asia in general.

Myanmar's membership reflects SASEC's determination to look beyond South Asia—to the significant mutual benefits of cooperating with new partners and opening new regional markets. It will boost supply-chain linkages for businesses between South Asia and Southeast Asia. Myanmar can be a bridge for mutually beneficial trade and transport linkages from South Asia into Southeast Asia. Road corridors in Myanmar are the key links between the two subregions, and Myanmar's ports can offer alternate routes and gateways to landlocked northeast India.

Digital Connectivity in the Pacific

Ongoing ICT expansion in the Pacific opens a range of economic opportunities.

In coordination with Pacific governments and development partners, ADB is supporting a suite of ICT infrastructure and services projects to strengthen the Pacific's digital connectivity. Better connectivity, in turn, is expected to promote inclusive economic growth and social development across the Pacific.

ADB's ICT investments in the Pacific include submarine cable projects—providing reliable and high-speed broadband internet connections in Tonga (2011), Samoa

(2015), and Palau (2015). Similar submarine cable projects are in the pipeline for the Cook Islands, Kiribati, and Nauru.

ICT-enabled education projects include the Samoa *Schoolnet* and Community Access Project and the Solomon Islands ICT for Better Education Services Project. For health, information management systems are planned for Papua New Guinea and Samoa, along with wider e-Government services in the Cook Islands and Tonga.

The Pacific Information and Communication Technology Investment Planning and Capacity Development Facility has been established through regional technical assistance to support ICT development in the subregion. The facility provides demand-driven technical advice and capacity building to help Pacific DMCs improve service delivery and expand economic opportunities through ICT.

References

ADB. CAREC Program Portfolio.

_____. 2011. *The Greater Mekong Subregion Economic Cooperation Program Strategic Framework 2012–2022.* Manila.

_____. 2014. *South Asia Subregional Economic Cooperation Trade Facilitation Strategic Framework 2014-2018.* Manila.

_____. 2016a. Mongolia: Supporting an Emergent Middle Income Economy. *Development Effectiveness Brief.* Manila.

_____. 2016b. *South Asia Subregional Economic Cooperation Operation Plan, 2016-2025.* Manila.

_____. 2016c. Pacific Islands Renewable Energy Investment Program: Funding proposal for the Green Climate Fund. November.

_____. 2017a. CAREC Transport Sector Progress Report. June.

_____. 2017b. ADB ICT Operations in the Pacific (infographic).

_____. 2017c. *SASEC Powering Asia in the 21st Century.* Manila.

_____. 2017d. ADB ICT Operations in the Pacific (infographic).

Central Asia Regional Economic Cooperation (CAREC). 2017a. Transport Sector Progress Report and Work Plan 2017–2019. Tbilisi. 17–19 May.

_____. 2017b. Trade Facilitation Sector Progress Report and Work Plan (October 2016–June 2017). Tbilisi. 20-21 June.

_____. 2017c. Energy Sector Progress Report and Work Plan (August 2016 - May 2017). Tbilisi, 20-21 June.

Government of the People's Republic of China (PRC). 2016a. Outline of the Thirteenth Five-Year Plan for National Economic and Social Development of the People's Republic of China. Beijing.

_____. 2016b. Outline of the Thirteenth Five-Year Plan for National Economic and Social Development of the People's Republic of China. Beijing.

Greater Mekong Subregion (GMS) Secretariat. 2013. *GMS Economic Cooperation Program: Regional Investment Framework Pipeline of Potential Projects (2013–2022).* Manila.

_____. 2016a. *Study on Strengthening the Greater Mekong Subregion Program's Institutional Framework.* Manila.

_____. 2016 b. *The Role of Special Economic Zones in Improving Effectiveness of GMS Economic Corridors.* Manila.

South Asia Subregional Economic Cooperation. http://www.sasec.asia/

State Council of the PRC. 2015. Vision and Actions on Jointly Building Silk Road Economic Belt and 21st Century Maritime Silk Road. Beijing.

07

Asia-Pacific Regional Cooperation and Integration Index

Asia–Pacific Regional Cooperation and Integration Index

This year's *Asian Economic Integration Report* introduces a new composite index to measure the progress of regional cooperation and integration in Asia and the Pacific.

Regional cooperation and integration (RCI) plays a pivotal role in accelerating economic growth and development, reducing poverty and economic disparity, raising productivity and employment, and strengthening institutions (ADB 2015). Deeper regional integration expands markets, helps maximize the efficiency of resource allocation, and boosts productivity and investment opportunities—all helping narrow development gaps between ADB's developing member economies. RCI can also generate considerable noneconomic benefits such as greater security and political stability. Recognizing its importance and its economic and noneconomic benefits, ADB adopted RCI as a key strategic priority for development assistance in Asia.

The Asia–Pacific Regional Cooperation and Integration Index allows Asian economies to track and monitor the progress of their regional integration efforts.

Understanding where the region stands on RCI is important to unlock its economic potential and maximize its benefits. Policy makers need mechanisms to monitor and evaluate progress against set goals. Against this backdrop, the *Asian Economic Integration Report* offers a new measure of RCI for Asia—using composite indexes constructed from 26 indicators categorized into six different socioeconomic dimensions. The weights of the composite indexes are obtained from a two-stage principal component analysis (PCA). In the first stage, the PCA is applied to the indicators in each dimension to create a dimensional composite index for the specific dimension. In the second stage, the PCA estimates weights for these six dimensional indexes to create an overall index of regional integration. The

detailed methodology for constructing these indexes is in Box 7.1.

The new index also builds on six dimensional indexes.

Regional integration is a multidimensional process. The index allows comparative analysis on multiple dimensions across different subregional groups and countries to capture the diversity in Asia's RCI process.[29] The six dimensional indexes are designed to reflect the core socioeconomic dimensions integral to the dynamic RCI process. These include: (i) trade and investment, (ii) money and finance, (iii) regional value chains, (iv) infrastructure and connectivity, (v) movement of people, and (vi) institutional and social integration. In turn, the Asia-Pacific Regional Cooperation and Integration Index (ARCII) will allow each subregional group and economy to identify its strengths and weaknesses across these six different socioeconomic dimensions.

---

[29] The Asia-Pacific Regional Cooperation and Integration Index covers 48 Asian economies following the ADB classification (number of economies in parentheses): Central Asia (8)—Armenia, Azerbaijan, Georgia, Kazakhstan, the Kyrgyz Republic, Tajikistan, Turkmenistan, and Uzbekistan. East Asia (6)—Hong Kong, China; Japan; the People's Republic of China; the Republic of Korea; Mongolia; and Taipei,China. Southeast Asia (10)—Brunei Darussalam, Cambodia, Indonesia, the Lao People's Democratic Republic, Malaysia, Myanmar, the Philippines, Singapore, Thailand, and Viet Nam. South Asia (8)—Afghanistan, Bangladesh, Bhutan, India, Maldives, Nepal, Pakistan, and Sri Lanka. The Pacific (14)—the Cook Islands, the Federated States of Micronesia, Fiji, Kiribati, the Marshall Islands, Nauru, Palau, Papua New Guinea, Samoa, Solomon Islands, Timor-Leste, Tonga, Tuvalu, and Vanuatu. Oceania (2)—Australia and New Zealand.

Box 7.1: Constructing the Asia-Pacific Regional Cooperation and Integration Index

The Asia-Pacific Regional Cooperation and Integration Index (ARCII) makes use of 26 socioeconomic indicators categorized into six different dimensions to measure the diversity of regional cooperation and integration efforts. The box table lists these indicators in each of the six dimensions. All indicators are based on bilateral data, as regional integration is expressed as a ratio of the intraregional sum (or average) to total sum (or average) of cross-border economic activity. There are three exceptions: R24 takes the difference between intraregional and total averages, whereas R43 and R44 only reflect national levels due to data availability. The indicators are drawn from the annual data for 2013, which have the most complete data for the composite indexes.

Design of the Asia-Pacific Regional Cooperation and Integration Index

R1. Trade and Investment	R11	Proportion of intraregional goods exports to total goods exports
	R12	Proportion of intraregional goods imports to total goods imports
	R13	Intraregional trade intensity index
	R14	Proportion of intraregional foreign domestic investment (FDI) inflows to total FDI inflows
	R15	Proportion of intraregional FDI inflows plus outflows to total FDI inflows plus outflows
R2. Money and Finance	R21	Proportion of intraregional cross-border equity liabilities to total cross-border equity liabilities
	R22	Proportion of intraregional cross-border bond liabilities to total cross-border bond liabilities
	R23	Pairwise dispersion of deposit rates average regionally relative to that averaged globally
	R24	Pairwise correlation of equity returns average regionally minus that averaged globally
R3. Regional Value Chain	R31	Ratio between the average trade complementarity index over regional trading partners and the averaged trade complementarity index over all trading partners
	R32	Ratio between the average trade concentration index over regional trading partners and the averaged trade concentration index over all trading partners
	R33	Proportion of intraregional intermediate goods exports to total intraregional goods exports
	R34	Proportion of intraregional intermediate goods imports to total intraregional goods imports
R4. Infrastructure and Connectivity	R41	Ratio between the average trade cost over regional trading partners and the average trade cost over all trading partners
	R42	Ratio between the average liner shipping connectivity index over regional trading partners and the average liner shipping connectivity index over all trading partners
	R43	Logistics performance index (overall)
	R44	Doing Business Index (overall)
R5. Movement of People	R51	Proportion of intraregional outbound migration to total outbound migration
	R52	Proportion of intraregional tourists to total tourists (inbound plus outbound)
	R53	Proportion of intraregional remittances to total remittances
	R54	Proportion of other Asian economies that do not require an entry visa
R6. Institutional and Social Integration	R61	Proportion of other Asian economies with which there is a signed free trade agreement
	R62	Proportion of other Asian economies that have an embassy
	R63	Proportion of other Asian economies with which there is a signed business investment treaty
	R64	Proportion of other Asian economies with which there is a signed double taxation treaty
	R65	Cultural proximity with other Asian economies relative to that with all other economies

Source: Huh and Park (2017).

Continued on next page.

Box 7.1 continued

The ARCII was constructed using the following steps and procedures. First, minimum-maximum scaling is used to normalize all indicators which convey quantitatively different information in different measurement units. The normalized indicators range between 0 and 1, with higher values denoting greater regional integration. Second, principal component analysis (PCA) is performed to calculate the weights for each component to aggregate them into a single composite index. A two-step procedure is used for the ARCII: (i) to perform PCA on the indicators in each dimension to construct a composite index for each of the six dimensions; and (ii) to use PCA again to combine the six composite indexes into an overall ARCII index. The box figure describes the two-step procedure.

Computing for ARCII

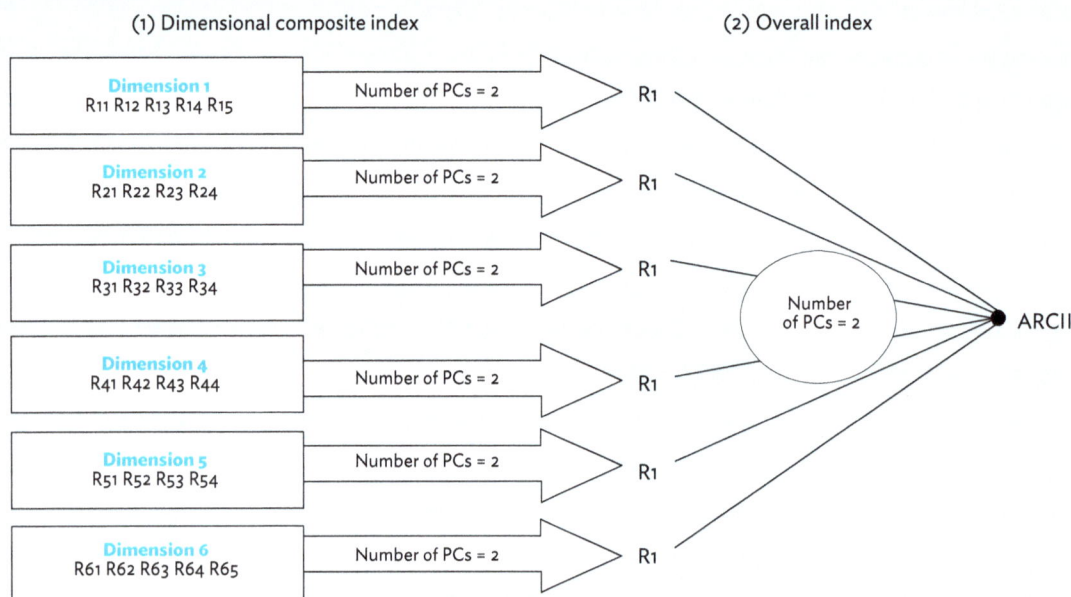

ARCII = Asia-Pacific Regional Cooperation and Integration Index, PCs = principal components.
Source: Huh and Park (2017).

Asia has made impressive progress in regional economic integration over the past few decades; however, significant variations remain across different subregions and economies.

The overall RCI index was estimated for 23 Asian economies in five subregions where data is available. Figure 7.1 presents the summary of the ARCII indexes for selected subregions in Asia. Southeast Asia ranks highest, with an average of 0.590, with its maximum and minimum values at 0.654 and 0.513, respectively. Five out of the top 10 countries in the overall ranking are from Southeast Asia.[30] The second and third go to East Asia and Oceania, with respective averages of 0.553 and 0.531. South Asia follows, with Central Asia

Figure 7.1: Overall Asia-Pacific Regional Cooperation and Integration Index by Subregion

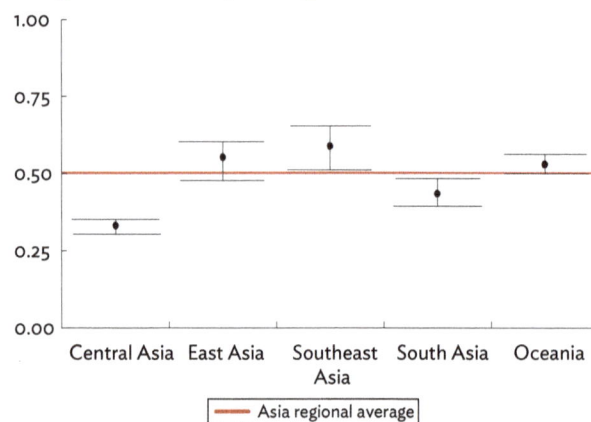

Notes: For each subregion, maximum (upper line), average (thick dot), and minimum (lower line) values of the overall index are reported. The horizontal line denotes Asia's regional average of 0.503. See Annex Table A7.1 for the list of economies covered.
Source: ADB calculations using updated data from Huh and Park (2017).

---

[30] Individual economy results for the ARCII are available upon request.

last—its maximum value of 0.351 is far below Asia's regional average of 0.503. The overall index could not be estimated for the Pacific due to lack of data.

Southeast Asia made major advances in regional integration, particularly in trade and investment and movement of people.

Figure 7.2 presents the six dimensional composite indexes for all six subregions, including the Pacific. Southeast Asia is the most regionally integrated, with the highest overall ARCII score among the six subregions. Its integration is driven largely by trade and investment and movement of people. East Asia comes second with its overall balanced and relatively high scores in all six dimensions. By contrast, inadequate infrastructure and connectivity keeps South Asia and Central Asia's regional integration low, while the Pacific subregion shows weak institutional and social integration.

Figure 7.2: Summary of Asia-Pacific Regional Cooperation and Integration Index by Subregion

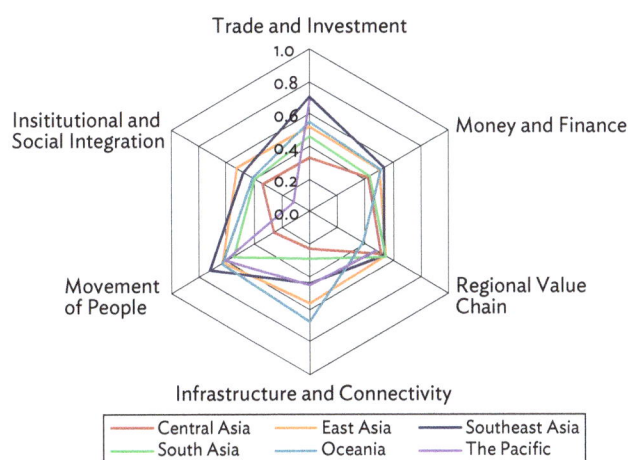

Note: See Annex Table A7.1 for the list of economies covered for each subregion and dimension.
Source: ADB calculations using updated data from Huh and Park (2017).

The ASEAN exhibits the highest degree of regional cooperation and integration among subregional initiatives; while weak infrastructure and connectivity keeps regional integration low in SASEC and CAREC.

The ARCII likewise shows the degrees of regional cooperation and integration in Asia's subregional initiatives across the six RCI dimensions. The

Figure 7.3: Asia-Pacific Regional Cooperation and Integration Index by Subregional Initiatives

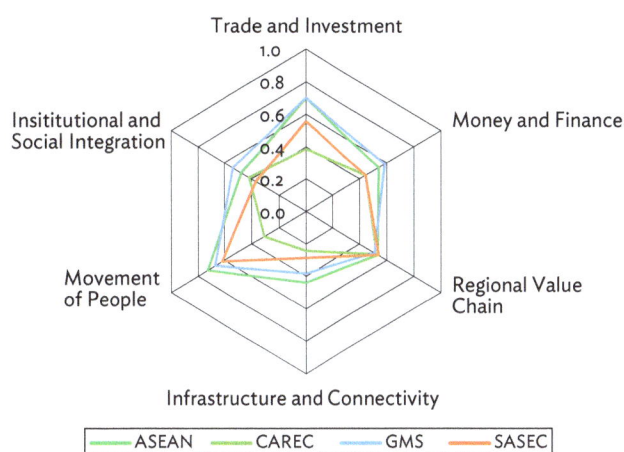

ASEAN = Association of Southeast Asian Nations, CAREC = Central Asia Regional Economic Cooperation, GMS = Greater Mekong Subregion, SASEC = South Asia Subregional Economic Cooperation.
Source: ADB calculations using updated data from Huh and Park (2017).

Association of Southeast Asian Nations (ASEAN) exhibits the highest degree of subregional cooperation and integration with an overall ARCII score of 0.569, particularly strong in the areas of trade and investment and movement of people (Figure 7.3). The Greater Mekong Subregion (GMS) is a very close second, with main contributors almost identical given the similarity of the member economies. The South Asia Subregional Economic Cooperation (SASEC), driven mainly by movement of people, trade and investment, and regional value chain, comes third. Finally, the Central Asia Regional Economic Cooperation (CAREC) appears to be the least regionally integrated. Meanwhile, weak infrastructure and connectivity keeps regional integration low in SASEC and CAREC.

The degree of RCI in Asia favorably compares to other regions of the world.

Regional integration indexes are also estimated for the European Union (EU), Latin America, and Africa. International comparisons can provide a more objective assessment of the degree of Asia's regional integration and help prioritize areas where progress may need to be accelerated. For compatibility, the same methodology was applied as ARCII in the makeup of the composite indexes and statistical procedures. Figure 7.4 shows the average overall regional integration index for the EU, Latin America and Africa, alongside Asia. The EU

Figure 7.4: Regional Integration Indexes Normalized Worldwide

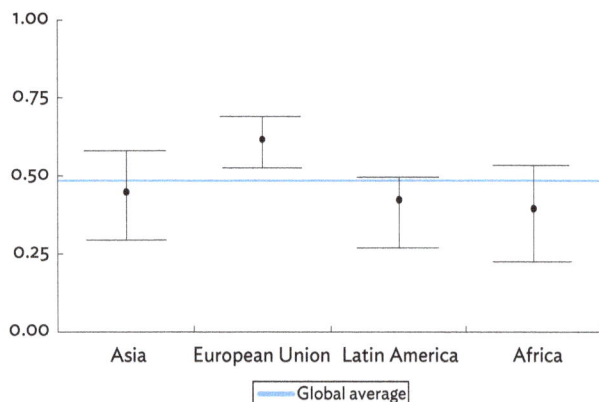

Notes: For each region, maximum (upper line), average (dot), and minimum (lower line) values of the overall index are reported. The horizontal line denotes global average of 0.484. See Annex Table A7.1 for the list of economies covered.
Source: ADB calculations using updated data from Huh and Park (2017).

Figure 7.5: Summary of Regional Integration Indexes Normalized Worldwide

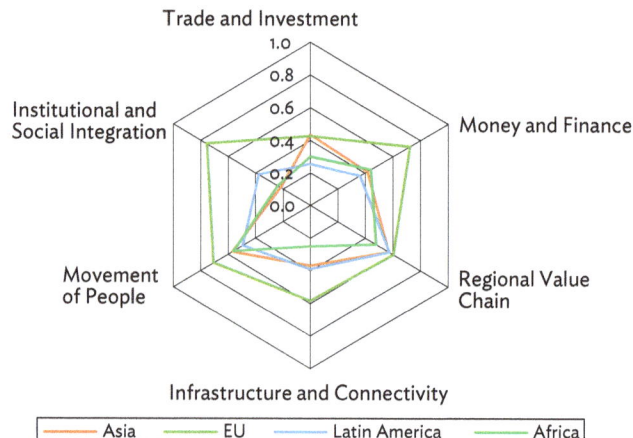

EU = European Union.
Note: See Annex Table A7.2 for the list of economies covered.
Source: ADB calculations using updated data from Huh and Park (2017).

outperforms all other regions, with an average of 0.617.[31] Asia comes second, where the overall index averages 0.448 but is 27% below the EU. Latin America performs slightly weaker than Asia, with an average of 0.423, and Africa closely follows, with an average of 0.395.

The EU has the highest scores on all but one dimensional indexes; but Asia outranks both Africa and Latin America.

Figure 7.5 summarizes the six dimensional composite indexes for four regions. The EU has the highest scores on all but one dimensional indexes. Its dominance is most pronounced in institutional and social as well as money and finance integration given its institutions of economic and monetary union. Only Asia's trade and investment integration is comparable in magnitude to the EU's. Asia also ranks second in movement of people. Regional value chain and movement of people are Asia's most regionally integrated components, while institutional and social integration is least. Latin America beats Asia as well as Africa for the remaining dimensions of regional value chain, infrastructure and connectivity, and institutional and social integration.

Overall, economic integration in East Asia and Southeast Asia is most advanced, driven by growing trade and FDI networks linked to global supply chains.

Trade and FDI liberalization accelerated in the 1980s and 1990s around Asia, with many economies entering free trade agreements (FTAs). As of July 2017, 147 FTAs were in effect with another 168 under negotiation or proposed in ADB's 48 regional member economies. However, regional integration in Asia has been largely market-led and bottom-up, lacking strong regional institutions and governance.

Southeast Asia is the most regionally integrated among the six subregions in Asia.

The region includes all members of the ASEAN, which was established in 1969 to promote intergovernmental cooperation and facilitates economic integration among its members. The region shows particularly strong integration in trade and investment and movement of people. East Asia ranks second overall for regional integration, closely followed by Oceania. Central Asia comes last, with all dimensional and overall indexes scoring below corresponding averages for other subregions.

---

[31]   Nearly all EU countries stand on top in world rankings. Malaysia, ranking 23rd, scores highest (0.585) among non-EU economies. Other top-ten performers in Asia attain high scores, with ranks between 26 and 43.

Trade and investment integration leads Asia's regional integration, while the institutional and social dimension is particularly weak.

Compared with the EU—which broadly outperforms Asia across all regional integration dimensions—Asia's trade and investment integration is the only one comparable in magnitude. Institutional and social integration is particularly weak in Asia. The empirical results suggest that other dimensions should be given as much, if not more, attention as trade and investment integration in advancing Asia's regional integration.

Collective actions can improve regional integration, particularly in the institutional and social dimension, including efforts to remove national barriers to regional integration, adopt regional standards, and institutionalize regional frameworks.

Regional integration is a dynamic, evolutionary process that offers everyone access to markets and resources, allows goods and services to move easily across borders, and lets citizens travel freely for leisure and work. It is also about unlocking the region's potential by encouraging capital and production to move and grow beyond national limits. The region's authorities need to: (i) progressively eliminate national obstacles to the movement of goods, services, capital, and labor; (ii) harmonize and coordinate national and regional policies; and (iii) institutionalize the regional framework, mechanisms and standards to promote regional integration. Greater collaboration among the region's economies—underpinned by a strong regional institutional framework—would further deepen regional integration across all dimensions.

References

ADB. 2015. *Thematic Evaluation Study: Asian Development Bank Support for Regional Cooperation and Integration.* Manila.

H. Huh and C.Y. Park. 2017. Asia-Pacific Regional Integration Index: Construction, Interpretation, and Comparison. *ADB Economics Working Papers.* No. 511. Manila: Asian Development Bank.

Annexes: List of Economies Covered

Table A7.1: Dimensional Indexes—Asia

	R1	R2	R3	R4	R5	R6
	Trade and Investment	Money and Finance	Regional Value Chain	Infrastructure and Connectivity	Movement of People	Institutional and Social Integration
Central Asia						
Armenia	✓		✓	✓	✓	✓
Azerbaijan	✓		✓	✓	✓	✓
Georgia	✓	✓	✓	✓	✓	✓
Kazakhstan	✓	✓	✓	✓	✓	✓
Kyrgyz Republic	✓	✓	✓	✓	✓	✓
Tajikistan	✓		✓	✓	✓	✓
Turkmenistan			✓	✓	✓	✓
Uzbekistan	✓		✓	✓	✓	✓
East Asia						
China, People's Republic of	✓	✓	✓	✓	✓	✓
Hong Kong, China	✓	✓	✓	✓	✓	✓
Japan	✓	✓	✓	✓	✓	✓
Korea, Republic of	✓	✓	✓	✓	✓	✓
Mongolia	✓	✓	✓	✓	✓	✓
Taipei,China	✓	✓		✓		✓
Southeast Asia						
Brunei Darussalam	✓		✓	✓	✓	✓
Cambodia	✓	✓	✓	✓	✓	✓
Indonesia	✓	✓	✓	✓	✓	✓
Lao People's Democratic Republic	✓	✓	✓	✓	✓	✓
Malaysia	✓	✓	✓	✓	✓	✓
Myanmar	✓		✓	✓	✓	✓
Philippines	✓	✓	✓	✓	✓	✓
Singapore	✓	✓	✓	✓	✓	✓
Thailand	✓	✓	✓	✓	✓	✓
Viet Nam	✓		✓	✓	✓	✓
South Asia						
Afghanistan	✓		✓	✓	✓	✓
Bangladesh	✓	✓	✓	✓	✓	✓
Bhutan	✓		✓	✓	✓	✓
India	✓	✓	✓	✓	✓	✓
Maldives	✓	✓	✓	✓	✓	✓
Nepal	✓	✓	✓	✓	✓	✓
Pakistan	✓	✓	✓	✓	✓	✓
Sri Lanka	✓	✓	✓	✓	✓	✓
Pacific						
Cook Islands			✓			✓
Fiji	✓		✓	✓	✓	✓
Kiribati			✓	✓	✓	✓
Marshall Islands	✓		✓	✓	✓	✓
Micronesia, Federated States of					✓	✓
Nauru						✓
Palau			✓	✓	✓	✓
Papua New Guinea	✓		✓	✓	✓	✓
Samoa	✓		✓	✓	✓	✓
Solomon Islands			✓	✓	✓	✓
Timor-Leste	✓		✓		✓	✓
Tonga			✓	✓	✓	✓
Tuvalu			✓		✓	✓
Vanuatu	✓		✓	✓	✓	✓
Oceania						
Australia	✓	✓	✓	✓	✓	✓
New Zealand	✓	✓	✓	✓	✓	✓

Source: ADB compilation.

Table A7.2: Overall Regional Cooperation and Integration Indexes

Asia (23)	**European Union** (26)	**Latin America** (16)	**Africa** (19)
Central Asia	Austria	Argentina	Algeria
Georgia	Belgium	The Bahamas	Benin
Kazakhstan	Bulgaria	Brazil	Botswana
Kyrgyz Republic	Cyprus	Chile	Ghana
East Asia	Czech Republic	Colombia	Kenya
China, People's Republic of	Denmark	Costa Rica	Malawi
Hong Kong, China	Estonia	Ecuador	Mauritius
Japan	Finland	Jamaica	Morocco
Korea, Republic of	France	Mexico	Mozambique
Mongolia	Germany	Nicaragua	Namibia
Southeast Asia	Greece	Panama	Nigeria
Cambodia	Hungary	Paraguay	Rwanda
Indonesia	Ireland	Peru	Seychelles
Lao People's Democratic Republic	Italy	Trinidad and Tobago	South Africa
Malaysia	Latvia	Uruguay	Sudan
Philippines	Lithuania	Venezuela	Swaziland
Singapore	Luxembourg		Tanzania
Thailand	Malta		Uganda
South Asia	Netherlands		Zambia
Bangladesh	Poland		
India	Portugal		
Maldives	Romania		
Nepal	Slovenia		
Pakistan	Spain		
Sri Lanka	Sweden		
Oceania	United Kingdom		
Australia			
New Zealand			

Source: ADB compilation.

The Era of Financial Interconnectedness: How Can Asia Strengthen Financial Resilience?

The Era of Financial Interconnectedness: How Can Asia Strengthen Financial Resilience?

Introduction

Twenty years after the Asian financial crisis (AFC), Asia stands strong, with more resilient financial systems and a solid economic outlook. The AFC triggered a wave of major economic and financial policy reforms, laying the foundations for a sustained period of high growth afterwards. The crisis exposed structural weaknesses and policy distortions in crisis-affected countries, combined with poorly planned financial liberalization and capital account opening. A surge in external capital inflows—driven in part by the region's economic success and fixed exchange rates—led to rapid credit growth and asset price bubbles across crisis-affected countries. These financial imbalances quickly unraveled, triggering the crisis and threatening long-term economic growth.

The global financial crisis (GFC) that followed 10 years later led to a major change in thinking about the links between macroeconomics and finance, triggering changes in policy making. In particular, the GFC showed how risks of unbridled financial flows in an era of globalized finance and tightly interconnected financial markets could lead to a buildup of systemic risk and widespread financial instability. In emerging market economies, increasing financial integration can bring about excessive risk-taking and leverage. If poorly regulated and supervised, it can amplify the effects of financial cycles, create financial instability and damage the real economy. Thus, Asia's increasingly integrated financial markets require a sound understanding of the associated risks and need to design appropriate policy responses.

The 2013–2014 "taper tantrum" exemplified the risks stemming from globalized finance. After the United States (US) Federal Reserve announced it was planning to end its ultra-loose monetary policy through gradual monetary policy normalization, many emerging market economies—including some in developing Asia[32]—were hit by sudden large capital outflows and short-term financial instability. Thus, it is also important to understand the channels through which changes in monetary policy and financial conditions in advanced economies can affect emerging market macroeconomic and financial conditions and prepare policies that can mitigate these effects on financial stability.

Although the region has taken great strides in improving its financial resilience in the two decades since the AFC, significant structural weaknesses remain and new challenges have emerged. Remaining challenges include: (i) diversifying out of bank-dominated Asian financial systems, (ii) controlling rising credit and private sector debt, and (iii) avoiding high foreign currency-denominated debt financing. The recent rise in nonperforming loans and heavy reliance on US dollar-denominated debts are reemerging challenges in some economies. New challenges include: (i) links between financial cycles and the real economy, (ii) more rapid risk transmission from greater financial interconnectedness, and (iii) rising volatility from macrofinancial interlinkages. Taken together, these existing, reemerging and new challenges can exacerbate the region's financial fragility. For example, a change in US dollar funding conditions transmits rapidly in a more interconnected and integrated global financial system, increasing the vulnerability of economies over-reliant on US dollar-denominated foreign debt.

This theme chapter analyzes these existing and new financial vulnerabilities and challenges. It identifies policy gaps, proposes policy considerations and offers suggestions on what can be done. In particular, it emphasizes policy options where increased regional cooperation can safeguard financial stability and promote financial resilience.

---

[32] See for example ADB (2014) and Estrada, Noland, Park, and Ramayandi (2015).

Experiences and Lessons from Past Crises

To better analyze current financial vulnerabilities in Asia and identify policy gaps, it is worth taking a thorough look at three relatively recent international economic and financial crises—the AFC, GFC, and the European sovereign debt crisis (EDC)—to examine the causes, policy responses, and lessons learned.

The Asian Financial Crisis

The AFC disrupted a period of high economic growth as a currency and banking crisis triggered a regional economic crisis.

After several years of high economic growth, the AFC began in Thailand in July 1997 and soon spread to Indonesia and Malaysia, before spilling over to other Asian economies with currencies tightly linked to the US dollar. The crisis originated in Thailand, triggered by the high volume of foreign capital that flooded into the country in the years leading to the crisis, fueling speculative markets in real estate and stocks alongside heavy domestic consumption. These contributed to a growing, unsustainable current account deficit. Authorities tried to defend the value of the Thai baht, but were ultimately forced to devalue the currency in early July 1997. In the following weeks, financial stress spread to neighboring economies as currency and then banking crises surfaced as the previously large capital inflows to the region slowed or reversed. It evolved into a more generalized regional economic crisis with deep impact on the real economy. In little more than a year, gross domestic product in Indonesia, Malaysia, the Philippines, the Republic of Korea, and Thailand fell a combined 30%. Banks succumbed to ever-expanding portfolios of nonperforming loans (NPLs). Investment rates plunged. And with several Asian economies amid deep recessions, spillovers affected trading partners across the region and around the globe.

Among other factors, the AFC was caused by: (i) the nature of foreign borrowing, (ii) financial sector weaknesses, (iii) fixed exchange rates, and (iv) a region-wide loss of confidence that precipitated substantial capital outflows.

The root of the AFC was the nature of foreign borrowing, which created a double maturity and currency mismatch. Much of the increasing foreign capital inflows were short-term (below 1-year) and unhedged. The lack of prudential supervision and proper regulations allowed these short-term inflows to be invested in long-term domestic projects—many in real estate and unproductive sectors (Sugisaki 1998, World Bank 1998). Thus, the maturity mismatch exposed the domestic financial systems to the risk that foreign loans might not be rolled over. The currency mismatch also arose from the *de facto* dollar peg in crisis-affected economies. The peg gave borrowers a false sense of security, encouraging them to take on increasing amounts of US dollar debt. It made domestic financial institutions less circumspect over exchange rate risks, in part due to the misplaced confidence that the US dollar loans could readily be repaid out of local currency earnings.

Weaknesses in the financial sector played a pivotal role as well. The region lacked the financial market infrastructure, supervision, and regulatory environment to efficiently allocate foreign capital inflows. Liberalizing local financial markets was premature and insufficiently regulated. Weak banking systems, poor corporate governance, and an overall lack of transparency exacerbated the loss of investor confidence in the region's financial systems.

The AFC prompted a wide array of reforms, including more flexible exchange rate regimes, stronger financial regulation and supervision, banking sector restructuring, and domestic and regional capital market development. Regional financial cooperation initiatives centered on: (i) establishing a regional mechanism for liquidity support and crisis management (the ASEAN+3 Chiang Mai Initiative [CMI] and the Chiang Mai Initiative Multilateralisation [CMIM]), (ii) strengthening regional macroeconomic and financial surveillance (the CMIM-associated ASEAN+3 Macroeconomic Research Office [AMRO]), and (iii) deepening regional capital markets—particularly through local currency bond market development (the ASEAN+3 Asian Bond Markets

Initiative [ABMI]). More recent regional initiatives to develop local capital markets include the ASEAN Capital Markets Forum and implementation plan,[33] and related initiatives under the Asia-Pacific Economic Cooperation forum (Goswami and Sharma 2011).

Among the lessons learned from the AFC were the need to: (i) develop long-term currency bond markets as an alternative to bank financing, (ii) enhance the infrastructure of local capital markets, and (iii) undertake prudential regulation and supervision.

One lesson from the crisis was the need to develop long-term local currency sovereign bond markets to avoid future currency and maturity mismatches and provide a more stable source of financing. More broadly, the crisis highlighted the need to develop the infrastructure of local capital markets and to establish mechanisms for adequate macroprudential regulation and supervision. Given the risks of foreign currency borrowing (and dollar funding in particular), local and international bank regulators need to maintain the safety and soundness of their domestic banking systems and be on the lookout for excessive capital inflows—specifically those that fund consumption or fuel local asset bubbles rather than contribute to expanding productive capacity. Apart from restrictions on short-term capital flows, protective measures designed to enhance financial resilience include ensuring adequate levels of foreign currency reserves and the development of cooperation mechanisms for cross-border crisis management (such as the CMIM). Finally, the AFC showed that the timing and sequence of external financial liberalization matters.

The Global Financial Crisis

The GFC began as a domestic mortgage crisis in the US, which rapidly spread worldwide after the failure of several "systemically important financial institutions".

The GFC unfolded largely because improperly designed regulatory systems facilitated overinvestment in real estate, financed by increasingly complex,

repackaged (and hard to trace) financial vehicles. It began as a domestic mortgage crisis in the US which rapidly spread across the world after the failure of Lehman Brothers Holdings, a major financial services company, and near-failure of American International Group (AIG), an insurance conglomerate. Financial institutions lost confidence in dealing with each other and international funding markets froze. The liquidity squeeze forced regulators worldwide to recapitalize financial institutions—including those not normally subject to bailouts—and become the lender of last resort for markets.

The GFC showed how greater financial integration could lead to greater financial vulnerabilities—stemming from weaknesses in SIFIs, the lack of macroprudential supervision and the lack of monitoring mechanisms for the early detection of systemic risk.

Aside from excessive borrowing and lending, poorly functioning credit markets, misaligned incentives, and a disconnect between regulatory structures and the rapidly integrated and sophisticated financial system, the GFC was also a product of the international transmission of systemic risk. The crisis underscored how increased financial integration and cross-border financial interlinkages can transmit risk globally—fueled by vulnerabilities and ultimate failure of "systemically important financial institutions" (SIFIs). The GFC also exposed the information gap between cross-border institutions and the inability of international and domestic regulatory structures to manage them effectively. It also exposed failures in financial market funding and the lack of prudential supervision (Arner 2009, Arner 2011). The excessive reliance on quantitative risk management mechanisms exacerbated the principal causes of the GFC (Arner 2009)—as they proved incapable of dealing with extreme market stress.

The GFC triggered a series of financial regulatory reforms aimed at enhancing the resilience of the global financial system.

The immediate government response was to inject massive amounts of capital to rescue SIFIs—an approach that differed from the International Monetary Fund (IMF) response to the AFC, which included very different measures, such as the closure of financial institutions and addressing of distressed assets

---

[33] The "Implementation Plan to Promote the Development of an Integrated Capital Market to Achieve the Objectives of the AEC Blueprint 2015" covers the adoption of international standards, progressive liberalization, and the sequencing of regional initiatives.

(Arner, Avgouleas, and Gibson 2017). Strengthening bank balance sheets and stabilizing financial systems ultimately restored banks' ability to resume lending.

The international Group of Twenty forum and newly created Financial Stability Board (FSB) established the foundations underlying the new regulatory framework.[34] They were charged with coordinating post-GFC responses and financial regulatory reforms, as well as setting financial standards and monitoring adherence to these standards. These reforms are still being implemented so their effectiveness cannot yet be fully gauged. Nonetheless, widening divergence in national regulatory practices has occurred recently along with a reluctance to abide by certain strictures—such as the capital adequacy frameworks set out in 2010 under Basel III.

The major lessons of the GFC included the need to: (i) provide adequate financial supervision and macroprudential regulation, (ii) devise early warning systems to detect and mitigate the buildup of systemic risk, and (iii) design a framework to resolve SIFIs.

Mechanisms for the early detection, mitigation, and effective resolution of crises and SIFIs are critical for financial stability and resilience. The inability to prevent and address systemic risk proved to be a crucial limitation of the regulatory architecture prevailing prior to the GFC (Arner 2009). Consequently, regulators need to identify and regulate SIFIs to mitigate the transmission of systemic risk. Moreover, they need to have the tools and mechanisms to ensure funding markets remain liquid under all market conditions.

More effective financial regulations and macroprudential supervision are critical to mitigating risks associated with complex financial instruments. Improving financial market infrastructure can likewise help contain possible sources of systemic risk (such as establishing central-counterparty clearinghouses). Regulatory bodies must possess the tools and mechanisms to assess and manage risks across the financial system as well as those that aggregate over time.

The absence of an effective SIFI resolution mechanism was a main factor behind the Lehman Brothers collapse and near collapse of AIG. A critical regulatory deficiency was the inability to adequately respond to the failure of large financial conglomerates and identify the risks inherent in cross-border interactions and interconnections. Regulatory bodies must have appropriate resolution powers and measures at their disposal to prevent serious financial instability in times of stress. The AFC and the GFC more broadly highlighted the need to establish appropriate responses and resolution systems—particularly for domestic or regional SIFIs. Regional dialogue has helped—especially in the context of executing the ASEAN Banking Integration Framework.

The European Sovereign Debt Crisis

The EDC unfolded as the euro area struggled to deal with weaknesses and failures of banks operating across borders.

The financial shocks during the GFC spilled over to most developed economies, including European Union (EU) members. Despite much discussion and work toward establishing a "Single Financial Market," no single EU regulator existed. Adequate crisis resolution mechanisms—particularly those dealing with cross-border issues—were unavailable for nearly all EU jurisdictions (Avgouleas 2012). The threat of widespread bank failures thus accompanied the near collapse of the region's financial systems. The banking crisis eventually gave way to a sovereign debt crisis, triggered by the excessive leverage in the banking systems of countries such as Cyprus, Ireland, and Spain. At the same time, markets became increasingly reluctant to roll over Greek debt, resulting in eventual IMF and EU rescue programs.

---

[34] These include: (i) building high-quality capital and liquidity standards and mitigating procyclicality, (ii) addressing SIFIs and resolution regimes, (iii) improving over-the-counter derivatives markets, (iv) strengthening accounting standards, (v) strengthening adherence to international supervisory and regulatory standards, (vi) reforming compensation practices to support financial stability, (vii) developing macroprudential frameworks and tools, and (viii) expanding and refining the regulatory perimeter (Arner 2011).

The crisis stemmed in part from the lack of transnational supervisory and regulatory structures to govern banks and other financial institutions.

In the immediate aftermath of the GFC, high public and private debt across euro area economies, a flawed macroeconomic framework, and the absence of institutions capable of handling cross-border banking crises contributed to the sovereign debt crisis. Also, regulatory and institutional features crucial to support financial stability were insufficiently robust or nonexistent. This was particularly relevant for those resolving cross-border financial institutions, deposit guarantee arrangements, and providing regulatory, supervisory, and fiscal arrangements. The severity grew given the tight links between financial institutions operating in a single market—as links amplified the transmission of shocks across market segments.

The EDC (and GFC) underscored a need to revisit existing models of financial market integration—to ensure they had institutions and structures that could underpin financial stability and economic growth.

The EDC triggered a wave of regional policy initiatives toward establishing a European banking union—including a new European emergency financial assistance facility, euro area banking supervision, and resolution mechanisms.

Four reforms are worth noting. First, the European Stability Mechanism was established, aimed at providing financial assistance to euro area economies and troubled banks during a crisis. Second, the Single Supervisory Mechanism (SSM) for euro area banks was organized under the European Central Bank (ECB). An October 2013 SSM Regulation gave the ECB investigatory and supervisory powers to: (i) license financial institutions in the European Monetary Union; (ii) monitor compliance with capital, leverage, and liquidity requirements; (iii) supervise financial conglomerates; and (iv) require banks to take remedial action when regulatory capital requirements are breached. Third, the EU plans for harmonizing members' resolution laws and introducing integrated resolution structures are being implemented. The single resolution mechanism (SRM) was established in 2014 to ensure continuity in essential banking operations; to protect depositors, assets and public funds; and to safeguard overall financial stability. The mechanism should ensure speedy and credible resolution of cross-border failures. Based on the EU's "Single Rulebook",[35] both the SSM and the SRM are pillars of the European banking union. And fourth, the development of common EU rulebooks for the single market by the European Supervisory Authorities is under way.

Financial stability risks rise as cross-border markets grow; international cooperation is needed to devise and implement measures that enhance financial stability.

With the failure of previous EU mechanisms to ensure financial market stability, the post-crisis reforms are milestones for greater integration and regionalism. The post-EDC response to further develop and run single market operations underscored the need to improve international and regional coordination.

The EDC highlighted the contagion risks inherent in a highly integrated system—a valuable lesson for Asia as financial integration and interconnectedness deepens. The EDC exposed weaknesses in national regulatory structures—particularly when addressing integrated financial markets. And it made clear the need for harmonized regulatory standards. Those most severely affected by the crisis had to adopt policies based on national circumstances, not necessarily harmonized or conforming to single market policies. This is increasingly relevant for Asia, given the region's heterogeneity in economic size, development, and sociopolitical context.

---

[35] The EU's "Single Rulebook" refers to a unified regulatory framework for the financial sector in the EU that seeks to ensure a consistent application of Basel III in the EU.

Financial Conditions, Vulnerabilities, and Cycles in Asia

The AFC and GFC led to a major revision in thinking about the relationship between macroeconomics and finance—in particular the impact macrofinancial linkages can have on the real economy.

The significance of macrofinancial linkages and the impact financial channels have on the real economy has surfaced only recently. The GFC showed how the various forms of finance can become channels of transmission, amplification, and propagation of shocks—and become the source of shocks themselves. Prior to the GFC, few studies explored how macroeconomics and finance intersected—they were usually treated as separate issues. A lesson from the GFC was how financial markets can be less than fully efficient and subject to a herding behavior—among other biases. Prominent academics (for example, Blanchard et al. 2016) acknowledged the importance of macrofinancial linkages and the real economic effects shocks have on financial supply and demand. Spurred by the GFC, more empirical evidence has been collected on macrofinancial linkages and financial cycles and is being analyzed.

This section outlines both existing and newly emerging financial vulnerabilities and challenges[36] in the region.

Current Status of Asia's Financial Conditions and Sources of Financial Vulnerability

While the region has taken great strides in enhancing financial resilience in the wake of the AFC, substantial challenges remain and new sources of vulnerabilities have emerged.

The AFC triggered a wave of major economic and financial policy reforms that laid a strong foundation for post-crisis recovery and sustained high growth. However, the GFC highlighted several remaining challenges, including: (i) the bank-dominated nature of Asian financial systems, (ii) the role of credit growth and rising private sector debt, and (iii) high exposure to foreign currency-denominated debt.

Banks remain the biggest source of corporate financing in emerging Asia. While stock market capitalization and bank credit were roughly equal sources of corporate funding in 1996 (59.1% and 59.4% of GDP, respectively), bank credit has ballooned in the two decades since. As of 2016, bank credit was 113.6% of corporate financing in emerging Asia (as a percentage of GDP), far outstripping stock market capitalization (68.1%) and corporate bonds (21.8%) (Figure 8.1).

Loans and leverage are rising in several economies, raising concerns of unsustainable credit booms.[37] And as credit increases and deviates from its long-run trend (Figure 8.2), credit gaps remain, if slightly narrowing. There was high credit growth during the pre-GFC period—particularly in Cambodia, India, Indonesia, the Lao People's Democratic Republic, Myanmar, the People's Republic of China (PRC), the Republic of Korea, and Viet Nam. However, others had low credit growth— Hong Kong, China; Japan; Malaysia; Taipei,China; and Thailand. Generally, credit growth has moderated since 2014, the result of a slowdown in net capital inflows—as global push factors grew bearish with the likely increase in the US Federal Fund rates, growth moderation in the PRC, and low global commodity prices.

---

[36] Online annex 2.A provides an overview of current financial and economic vulnerabilities compared with periods before the AFC and GFC. See also online annexes 2.B and 2.C for information on capital flows and exchange rate dynamics during past crises. https://aric.adb. org/aeir2017_onlineannex2.pdf

[37] See online annex 2.D for an overview on domestic credit growth and loan-to-deposit ratios since the pre-AFC period. https://aric.adb.org/ aeir2017_onlineannex2.pdf

Figure 8.1: Corporate Financing as % of GDP—Emerging Asia (excluding HKG and SIN)

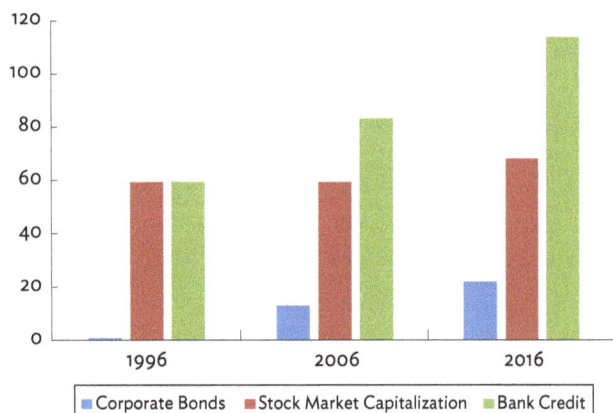

GDP = gross domestic product, HKG = Hong Kong, China, SIN = Singapore.
Note: Emerging Asia (excluding Hong Kong, China and Singapore) includes the People's Republic of China; India; Indonesia; the Republic of Korea; Malaysia; the Philippines; Thailand; and Viet Nam.
Sources: ADB calculations using data from AsianBondsOnline. https://asianbondsonline.adb.org; International Monetary Fund (IMF). International Financial Statistics. www.imf.org/en/Data; CEIC; and IMF. World Economic Outlook October 2016 Database. https://www.imf.org/external/pubs/ft/weo/2017/01/weodata/index.aspx (all accessed March 2017).

Figure 8.2: Deviation of Credit-to-GDP from Long-Run Trend (%)

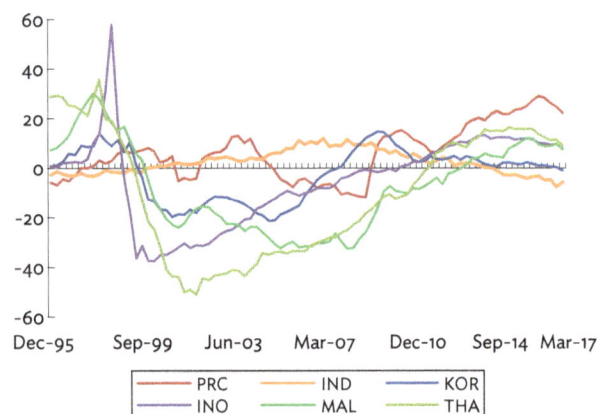

GDP = gross domestic product, IND = India, INO = Indonesia, KOR = Republic of Korea, MAL = Malaysia, PRC = People's Republic of China, THA = Thailand.
Notes: The credit-to-GDP ratio, published in the Bank for International Settlements database of total credit to the private nonfinancial sector, captures total borrowing from all domestic and foreign sources. In terms of financial instruments, credit covers the core debt, which is here equal to loans and debt securities. A credit-to-GDP gap is defined as the difference between the credit-to-GDP ratio and its long-term trend, in percentage points. The long-term trend is calculated using a one-sided Hodrick-Prescott filter with a smoothing parameter of 400,000.
Source: Bank for International Settlements. https://www.bis.org/ (accessed September 2017).

Figure 8.3: Credit to Private Nonfinancial Sector—Selected Asian Economies (% of GDP)

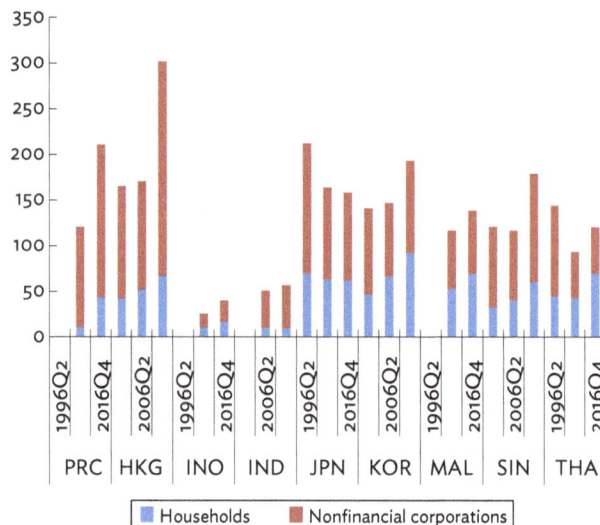

GDP= gross domestic product; HKG = Hong Kong, China; IND = India; INO = Indonesia; JPN = Japan; KOR = Republic of Korea; MAL = Malaysia; PRC = People's Republic of China; SIN = Singapore; THA = Thailand.
Notes: Credit covers core debt, equal to loans plus debt securities, and is provided by domestic banks, all other sectors of the economy and non-residents. Nonfinancial corporations include both private-owned and public-owned corporations; households include households and non-profit institutions serving households. For India, data starts second quarter of 2007.
Source: Bank for International Settlements. https://www.bis.org/ (accessed July 2017).

The combination of high leverage and slowing economic growth lowered the debt service capacity of many countries, raising the question of debt-at-risk. Corporate and household debt (and leverage) continues to be a concern for several economies in the region (Figure 8.3). The PRC's leverage ratio, for instance, rose from 73% in March 2010 to 90% in March 2017, mostly due to growing corporate debt. The household debt-to-GDP ratio in the PRC more than doubled from 19% in March 2009 to 43% by September 2016. The Republic of Korea shows the same pattern—household debt increased from 74% of GDP in late 2008 to nearly 92% by September 2016. Thailand and Malaysia show similar trends. Mian, Sufi and Verner (2017) show that, in particular, an increase in the household debt-to-GDP ratio predicts lower GDP growth and higher unemployment in the medium run. Hence, these ratios could prove unsustainable should interest rates rise sharply—from rapid US monetary policy normalization, for example.

Compared with the AFC, external positions remain strong; although foreign borrowing has increased over the past decade.

Overall, total external debt[38] in emerging Asia (excluding Singapore and Hong Kong, China) was $3.2 trillion in 2015—nearly 20% of the region's GDP (up from 15% in 2005) (Figure 8.4). External debt ratios in India, Malaysia, the Republic of Korea, and Thailand increased, while those in Indonesia and the Philippines decreased. The PRC has maintained its debt level at about 12% of GDP.

Short-term external debt ratios also increased slightly. For Asia, short-term debt grew from 5.8% of GDP in 2005 to 7.9% in 2015. Malaysia had the largest rise—from 24% to 31% of GDP. Large short-term external debt increases the risk of potential currency and maturity mismatches.

By and large, bank capitalization is strong in emerging Asia—banks in the region remain sufficiently capitalized

to withstand modest shocks (for example, a rise in loan-loss provisioning consistent with a deceleration in trend economic growth and rising NPLs). However, the combination of high corporate leverage, large asset price volatility, and slowing growth is affecting bank asset quality in some countries.

Furthermore, there has been an increase in nonbank financing across the region in recent years. While this form of financing can provide a useful alternative to bank-based funding in spurring economic activity, it could also present a potential source of risk, facilitated through pronounced linkages with the banking sector FSB 2017). As a share of total financial assets, nonbank financial intermediation[39] has remained steady in selected Asian economies[40] over the period 2010–2014 at around 22%. In absolute terms, there has been a slight increase from $17 trillion to $20 trillion in this measure. At the same time, assets of other financial intermediaries[41] across the region have increased

Figure 8.4: External Debt-to-GDP Ratio—Selected Asian Economies (%)

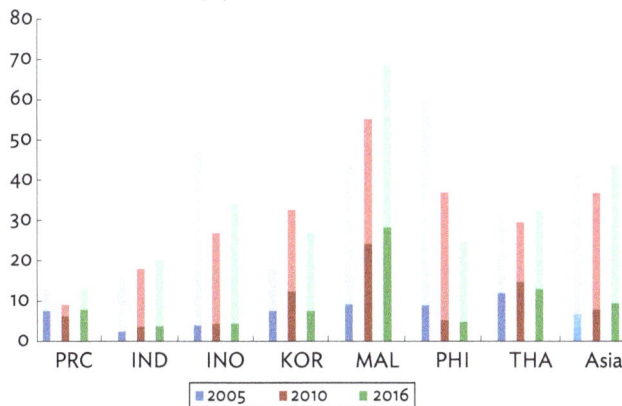

GDP = gross domestic product, IND = India, INO = Indonesia, KOR = Republic of Korea, MAL = Malaysia, PHI = Philippines, PRC = People's Republic of China, THA = Thailand.
Notes: Columns show the share of external debt as a percentage of GDP. The bold areas indicate the fraction of short-term external debt as a percentage of GDP.
Sources: ADB calculations using data from CEIC; and World Bank Quarterly External Debt Statistics SDDS. http://databank.worldbank.org/data/reports.aspx?source=quarterly-external-debt-statistics-sdds (accessed June 2017).

Figure 8.5: Narrow Measure of Shadow Banking for Selected Asian Economies

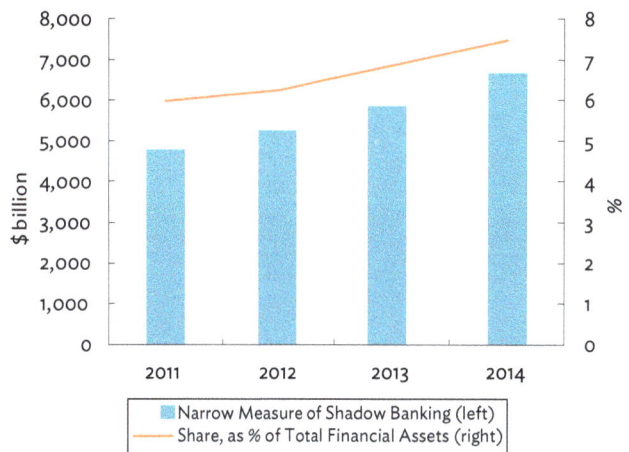

Notes: According to the Financial Stability Board's methodology, the narrow measure of shadow banking includes nonbank financial entity types that are considered by authorities to be involved in credit intermediation where financial stability risks from shadow banking may occur. The measure has been aggregated for the following economies: Australia; Hong Kong, China; India; Indonesia; Japan; the People's Republic of China; the Republic of Korea; and Singapore. The data spans from 2011 to 2014, due to availability.
Source: Financial Stability Board (2015).

---

[38]   The economies included are Cambodia; India; Indonesia; Kazakhstan; the Lao People's Democratic Republic; Myanmar; Malaysia; the People's Republic of China; the Philippines; the Republic of Korea; Sri Lanka; Taipei,China; Thailand; and Viet Nam. If Hong Kong, China and Singapore are included, the external debt level is $5.8 trillion, and the ratios for 2005 and 2010 are 30% and 33%, respectively.

[39]   The FSB (2017) defines this as a measure of all nonbank financial intermediation, comprised of other financial institutions (OFIs), insurance corporations, and pension funds.

[40]   This includes Australia; Hong Kong, China; India; Indonesia; Japan; the People's Republic of China; the Republic of Korea; and Singapore.

[41]   OFIs are comprised of all financial institutions that are not classified as banks, insurance corporations, pension funds, public financial institutions, central banks, or financial auxiliaries (FSB 2017).

from $7.3 trillion in 2010 to $9.7 trillion in 2014. Most strikingly, the narrow measure of shadow banking[42] across selected Asian economies has seen a rapid increase from $4.8 trillion in 2011 to $6.7 trillion in 2014, representing a relative increase of as much as 40% over that period (Figure 8.5) (FSB 2015).[43]

Reemerging Sources of Financial Vulnerability

Some pockets of financial vulnerability reemerge in Asia. In particular, the recent increase in NPLs and continued reliance on the US dollar-denominated debt in some Asian financial systems are potential problems.

Although moderate relative to the AFC, NPLs have increased alongside default risks and a buildup of financial vulnerabilities (Table 8.1).

The region's external debt positions have improved dramatically since the AFC; yet the US dollar remains the dominant currency for the region's international financial transactions.

A large portion of foreign currency-denominated external debt in emerging Asia is in US dollars. In the first quarter of 2017, 79% of outstanding international debt securities in Asia's major emerging economies was denominated in US dollars.[44] Generally, the ratio of outstanding US dollar-denominated international debt securities to total international debt securities for these economies has increased over time (Figure 8.6). While the share of dollar-denominated debt securities has fallen moderately since the GFC, there has been an upward trend since the pre-AFC period. A high concentration of foreign debt in US dollars deepens an economy's exposure to dollar liquidity risks and more general susceptibility to external shocks.

Figure 8.6: Evolution of the Share of Outstanding International Debt Securities Denominated in US Dollars (%)

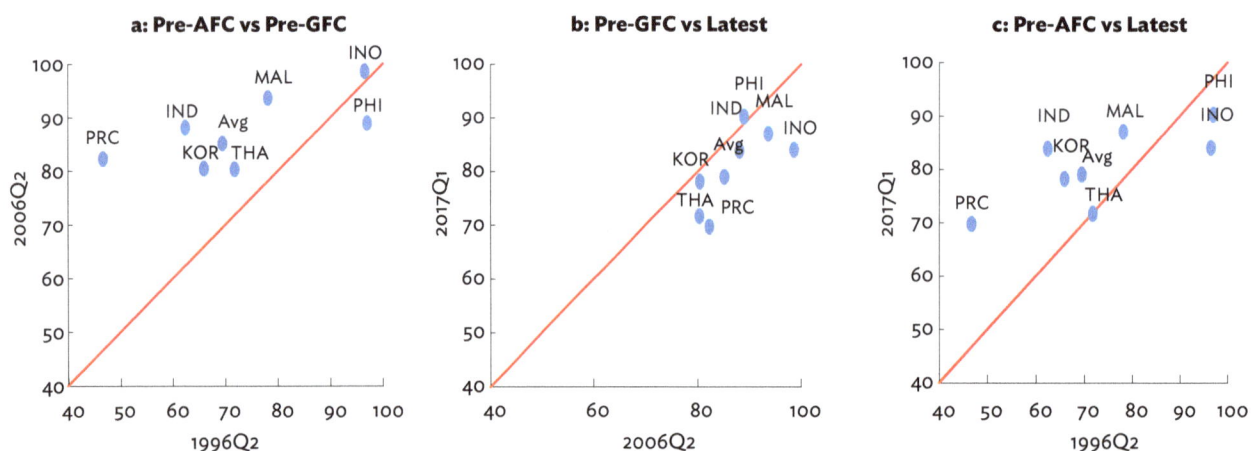

AFC = Asian financial crisis, Avg = Average, GFC = global financial crisis, IND = India, INO = Indonesia, KOR = Republic of Korea, MAL = Malaysia, PHI = Philippines, PRC = People's Republic of China, THA = Thailand.
Source: Bank for International Settlements. Debt Securities Statistics. http://www.bis.org/statistics/secstats.htm (accessed August 2017).

---

42   This includes nonbank financial entity types that are considered by authorities to be involved in credit intermediation where financial stability risks from shadow banking may occur (FSB 2017).

43   See FSB (2015) for the full dataset.

44   Emerging Asia includes India, Indonesia, the Republic of Korea, Malaysia, the PRC, the Philippines, and Thailand. Data are from the BIS International Debt Securities dataset.

Table 8.1: Bank Nonperforming Loans (% of gross loans)

Economy	1997	1998	1999	2000	2001	2002	2003	2004	2005	2006
Central Asia										
Afghanistan										
Armenia		6.0	8.0	17.5	24.4	9.9	5.4	2.1	1.9	2.4
Azerbaijan					28.0	21.5	15.1	9.5	7.2	
Kazakhstan						11.9	8.4	4.3	3.3	2.4
Kyrgyz Republic		10.1	30.9	30.9	13.4	13.3	11.2	8.0		6.2
Tajikistan										11.3
East Asia										
China, People's Rep. of			28.5	22.4	29.8	26.0	20.4	13.2	8.6	7.1
Korea, Rep. of	5.8	7.4	8.3	8.9	3.4	2.4	2.6	1.9	1.2	0.8
Mongolia										
South Asia										
Bangladesh		40.7	41.1	34.9	31.5	28.1	22.1	17.5	13.2	12.8
India	15.7	14.4	14.7	12.8	11.4	10.4	8.8	7.2	5.2	3.5
Maldives										
Pakistan	20.7	19.5	22.0	19.5	23.4	21.8	17.0	11.6	9.0	7.3
Southeast Asia										
Indonesia		48.6	32.9	34.4	31.9	24.0	6.8	4.5	7.3	5.9
Malaysia	4.1	18.6	16.6	15.4	17.8	15.9	13.9	11.7	9.4	8.5
Philippines	4.7	12.4	14.6	24.0	27.7	14.6	16.1	14.4	10.0	7.5
Thailand		42.9	38.6	17.7	11.5	16.5	13.5	11.9	9.1	8.1

Economy	2007	2008	2009	2010	2011	2012	2013	2014	2015	2016
Central Asia										
Afghanistan				49.9	4.7	5.0	4.9	7.8	12.1	15.2
Armenia	2.4	4.3	4.9	3.0	3.4	3.7	4.5	7.0	7.9	9.3
Azerbaijan			3.5	4.7	6.0	5.7	4.5	4.4	5.3	
Kazakhstan	2.7	7.1	18.9	20.9	20.7	19.4	19.5	12.4	8.0	7.9
Kyrgyz Republic	3.6	5.3	8.2	15.8	10.2	7.2	5.5	4.5	7.1	
Tajikistan	4.8	5.4	9.6	7.4	7.2	9.5	13.2	20.4	19.1	
East Asia										
China, People's Rep. of	6.2	2.4	1.6	1.1	1.0	1.0	1.0	1.1	1.7	1.7
Korea, Rep. of	0.7	0.6	0.6	0.6	0.5	0.6	0.6	0.6		
Mongolia		7.2	17.4	11.5	5.8	4.2	5.3	5.0	7.5	8.5
South Asia										
Bangladesh	14.5				5.8	9.7	8.6	9.4	8.4	
India	2.7	2.4	2.2	2.4	2.7	3.4	4.0	4.3	5.9	7.6
Maldives						20.9	17.6	17.5	14.1	11.1
Pakistan	7.4	9.1	12.2	14.7	16.2	14.5	13.0	12.3	11.4	11.1
Southeast Asia										
Indonesia	4.0	3.2	3.3	2.5	2.1	1.8	1.7	2.1	2.4	3.0
Malaysia	6.5	4.8	3.6	3.4	2.7	2.0	1.8	1.6	1.6	1.7
Philippines	5.8	4.6	3.5	3.4	2.6	2.2	2.4	2.0	1.9	2.0
Thailand	7.9	5.7	5.2	3.9	2.9	2.4	2.3	2.3	2.7	2.9

Notes: White cells denote a nonperforming loan ratio below 5%, yellow between 5% and 10%, and orange above 10%. Blank cells indicate data are unavailable.
Sources: ADB calculations using data from Bank of Mongolia; and World Bank. World Development Indicators. http://databank.worldbank.org/data/reports.aspx?source=world-development-indicators (accessed October 2017).

Box 8.1: The Influence of US Dollar Funding Conditions on Asia's Financial Markets

The US dollar has long been the major funding currency of international debt. With 79% of major emerging Asian economies' outstanding international debt securities denominated in US dollars as of the first quarter of 2017—the dollar liquidity and bilateral exchange rate movements have important implications for financial stability.[a]

Traditionally, based on the Mundell-Fleming model, analysts would argue a currency appreciation hampers trade by making exports more expensive to foreign buyers, and thus lowering output through the trade channel (Fleming 1962; Mundell 1963). However, recent evidence points to an alternative channel through which changes in the exchange rate could affect the economy. For instance, Borio and Lowe (2002), and Reinhart and Reinhart (2009) note currency appreciation is usually associated with

strong credit growth and loosening financial conditions, thus having expansionary effects on an economy. More recently, Hofmann, Shim and Shin (2017) investigate the financial channel, focusing on how the bilateral exchange rate against the US dollar affects financial conditions in emerging market economies. They suggest using a balance-sheet approach in understanding the underlying economic mechanism, implying that an appreciation in local currency against the US dollar would improve a country's balance sheet capacity as the value of (dollar-denominated) liabilities relative to assets decreases.

$$\Delta y_{i,t} = \alpha_i + \delta \Delta y_{i,t-1} + \alpha_1 \Delta BER_{t-1} + \alpha_2 \Delta NEER_{i,t-1}$$
$$+ \beta \Delta CPI_{t-1} + \gamma \Delta IP_{t-1} + \theta \Delta r_{i,t-1}$$
$$+ \eta_1 \Delta VIX_{t-1} + \eta_2 \Delta CPIUS_{t-1} + \eta_3 \Delta IPUS_{t-1} \quad (1)$$
$$+ \eta_4 \Delta MMUS_{t-1} + \mu_i + \varepsilon_{i,t}$$

Effect of Bilateral Exchange Rate Against US Dollar on Financial Conditions

	(1)	(2)	(3)	(4)	(5)
$\Delta BER_{i,t-1}$	-0.0561***	0.00848			0.00495
	(0.0171)	(0.0104)			(0.0103)
$\Delta NEER_{i,t-1}$	0.0873***		0.0390***	0.0340***	
	(0.0188)		(0.0115)	(0.0113)	
$\Delta BER\_orth_{i,t-1}$				-0.0833***	
				(0.0191)	
$\Delta NEER\_orth_{i,t-1}$					0.0784***
					(0.0195)
ΔVIX_{t-1}	0.00115*	0.00117*	0.00127**	0.00113*	0.00119*
	(0.000631)	(0.000635)	(0.000635)	(0.000627)	(0.000633)

*** = significant at 1%, ** = significant at 5%, * = significant at 10%. Standard errors in parentheses.
US = United States, ΔBER = month-on-month log change in bilateral exchange rate against US dollar (an increase indicates an appreciation of the local currency), $\Delta NEER$ = month-on-month change in nominal effective exchange rate (an increase indicates an appreciation of the local currency), ΔBER_orth = orthogonal residuals of ΔBER on $\Delta NEER$ regressions, separately for each economy in the sample, $\Delta NEER\_orth$ = orthogonal residuals of $\Delta NEER$ on ΔBER regressions, separately for each economy in the sample, ΔVIX = month-on-month log change in the Chicago Board Options Exchange volatility index.
Note: Other controls include the domestic and US change in year-on-year growth in consumer price index; the domestic and US change in year-on-year growth in the industrial production index; month-on-month change in lending rate, which is defined as the average short-term (1-year) lending rate of the commercial banks in the economies; the month-on-month change in 3-month money market rate in the US.
Sources: ADB calculations using data from Bank for International Settlements. Consumer Price Statistics. http://www.bis.org/statistics/cp.htm?m=6%7C348; Bank for International Settlements. Effective Exchange Rate Indices. http://www.bis.org/statistics/eer.htm?m=6%7C187; Bloomberg; Haver Analytics; and International Monetary Fund. International Financial Statistics. http://data.imf.org/?sk=388DFA60-1D26-4ADE-B505-A05A558D9A42 (all accessed August 2017).

---

[a]   Emerging Asian economies include India, Indonesia, Malaysia, the People's Republic of China, the Philippines, the Republic of Korea, and Thailand.

Empirically, Hofmann, Shim and Shin (2017) show that bilateral exchange rate fluctuations significantly impact financial conditions in emerging economies. In particular, they show that a local currency appreciation increases investors' bond inflows, suppresses local currency and foreign currency sovereign bond spreads, and consequently loosens financial conditions. Using a similar empirical approach but focusing on emerging Asian economies, a dynamic panel data model—using Anderson-

Hsiao's instrumental variable estimation (Anderson and Hsiao 1982)—offers some interesting results (box table).

The dependent variable is defined as the month-on-month change in local currency bond spread (LC spread)—an increase represents tightening domestic financial conditions.[b] It is regressed on the US dollar bilateral exchange rate (approximating the financial channel of exchange rates) and the nominal effective exchange rate (approximating the trade channel of the exchange rate). Monthly data from December 2006 to December 2016 for eight emerging Asian economies are used and five different model specifications are employed.[c]

First, a 1% appreciation of the domestic nominal effective exchange rate increases the LC spread by 8.7 basis points, indicating that exchange rates affect the economy through the trade channel. Second, a 1% appreciation of the domestic bilateral exchange rate against the US dollar decreases the LC spread by 5.6 basis points, thereby loosening domestic financial conditions. These results show exchange rates affect the economy through both trade and financial channels. Column (2) shows that without controlling for the trade channel, the bilateral exchange rate against the US dollar has a negligible net effect on financial conditions. On the other hand, column (3) indicates that without controlling for the change of bilateral exchange rate against the US dollar, the nominal effective exchange rate still has a significant impact on domestic financial conditions. Horse-race regressions between ΔNEER vs. BER_orth and ΔBER vs. NEER_orth reported in columns (4) and (5) further demonstrate pronounced pure effects of the financial and trade channels. In sum, the regression results are qualitatively matched with the findings of Hofmann, Shim, and Shin (2017)—that emerging Asian financial markets are particularly susceptible to changes in global dollar funding conditions.

Empirical evidence shows the significant impact of a change in bilateral US dollar exchange rates on sovereign bond spreads in selected emerging Asian economies with important implications for their financial conditions (Box 8.1). Generally, an appreciation of domestic currency against the US dollar improves the country's balance sheet capacity—decreasing the value of dollar-denominated liabilities relative to assets. Policy makers need to monitor this interplay between the bilateral exchange rate and local financial market conditions.

---

[b]   Defined as the difference between the 5-year sovereign local currency bond yield and the 5-year US Treasury yield.

[c]   Estimations are calculated for India, Indonesia, Malaysia, the People's Republic of China, the Philippines, the Republic of Korea, Thailand and Viet Nam.

New Global Financial Conditions and Vulnerabilities

This section briefly looks at the characteristics of financial cycles and how financial crises cause spillover effects. It also examines the emergence and impact of a global financial cycle.

Financial Cycles: Characteristics and Interplay with the Business Cycle

Financial cycles are longer lasting, more volatile, and more closely related to impending financial crises than business cycles.

In contrast to more frequently examined business cycles, financial cycles last longer, are associated with greater volatility and are more closely linked to impending financial crises. Financial cycles—typically related to credit, housing, or equity prices—can stretch over a decade or two, up to twice the typical 6 to 8 year length

Figure 8.7: Average Amplitude of Financial Booms and Busts

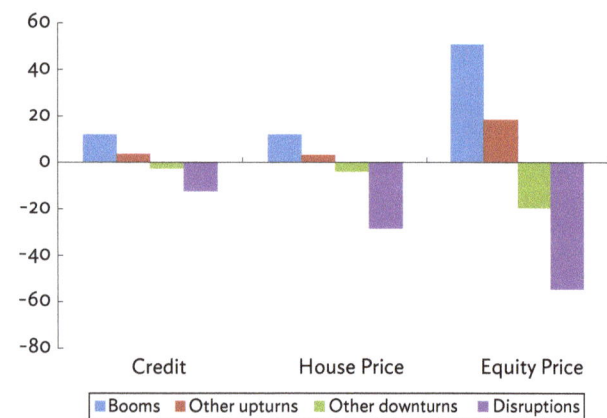

Notes: Figures reflect the average amplitude of upturns and downturns, measured in percentages. The amplitude for upturns (downturns) is calculated based on the 1-year change in each respective financial variable after its trough (peak). Booms are the top 25% of upturns calculated by amplitude. Disruptions (crunches, busts, and collapses) are the worst 25% of downturns calculated by amplitude. The dataset includes 21 Organisation for Economic Co-operation and Development (OECD) countries and covers quarterly data from 1960 to 2007 and draws from International Monetary Fund's International Financial Statistics and OECD (updated to account for data revisions).
Source: Claessens, Kose, and Terrones (2011) as in Claessens (2017).

of business cycles. Financial cycles also have particularly long boom periods and show higher volatility (Figure 8.7).[45] The heightened volatility arises from a myriad of factors—including deeper contraction phases relative to business cycles, lengthy downturns in housing prices and credit upturns, and the high coincidence of financial cycle peaks and subsequent financial turmoil. Cycles of credit, housing, and equity prices also tend to reinforce one another. In addition, these cycles coincide globally, underscoring the impact of growing cross-border interconnections.

While financial booms can enhance and lengthen expansions, ensuing financial disruptions will likely amplify and lengthen recessions.

The effects of financial cycles spillover to the business cycle, at times with strong interactions. This is evident as recessions coinciding with financial contractions are longer and deeper, and as credit fluctuations are strongly linked to changing output levels (Figure 8.8). Higher credit expansion prior to a financial crisis, for

Figure 8.8: Impact of Financial Disruptions on Recessions

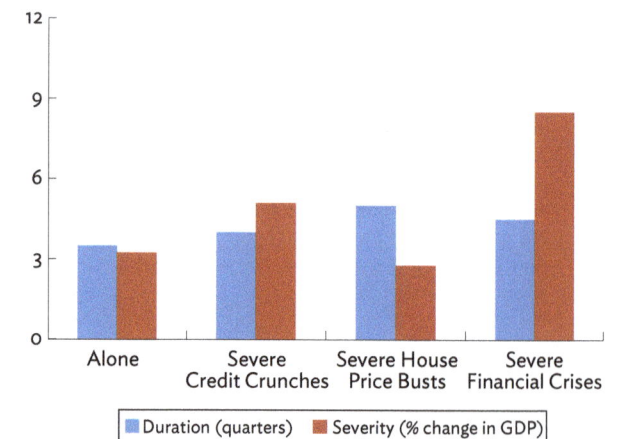

GDP = gross domestic product.
Notes: Severe credit crunches and equity or house price busts are in the top half of all crunch and bust episodes. Duration is the number of quarters from peak to trough in output. The dataset includes 21 Organisation for Economic Co-operation and Development (OECD) countries and covers quarterly data from 1960 to 2007. It draws from International Monetary Fund's International Financial Statistics and OECD (updated to account for data revisions).
Source: Claessens, Kose, and Terrones (2011 and 2014) as in Claessens (2017).

---

[45] Based on a dataset covering the following economies: Australia, Austria, Belgium, Canada, Denmark, Finland, France, Germany, Greece, Ireland, Italy, Japan, the Netherlands, New Zealand, Norway, Portugal, Spain, Sweden, Switzerland, the United Kingdom, and the United States. The same dataset is used for Figures 8.8–8.9.

Figure 8.9: Impact of Financial Booms on Expansions

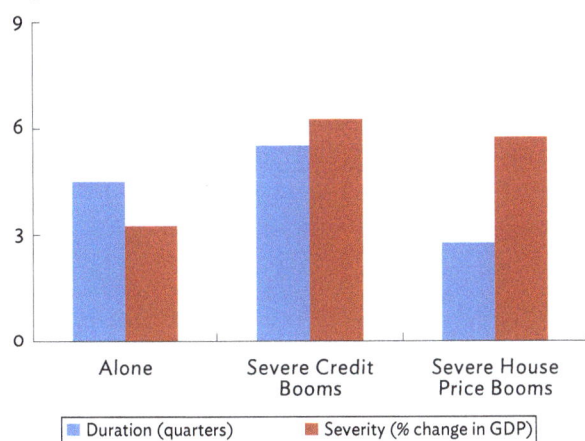

GDP = gross domestic product.
Notes: The dataset includes 21 Organisation for Economic Co-operation and Development (OECD) countries and covers quarterly data from 1960 to 2007. It draws from International Financial Statistics and OECD (updated to account for data revisions).
Source: Claessens, Kose, and Terrones (2011 and 2014) as in Claessens (2017).

instance, has been shown to stall post-crisis recovery (Taylor 2015). Co-movements between financial and business cycles can similarly occur during periods of economic and financial growth—with financial booms enhancing and lengthening output growth (Figure 8.9). Thus, the dynamics of the financial cycle needs to be better understood—to more effectively detect early signs of financial stress and the buildup of systemic risk. Financial regulation and macroprudential policies have an important role to play in moderating the negative impact of these cycles.

Financial crises are often preceded by rising asset prices—housing prices and credit. Their effects can include a substantial fall in credit volume and asset prices, impairments to financial intermediation, large-scale balance sheet problems, and a sudden stop in capital flows (particularly in emerging markets). These force public interventions or financial regulatory reforms.[46] Nonetheless, the government's response can benefit the economy in the long run, as crises can be the impetus to much needed and often difficult reforms—often politically difficult to implement during normal times.

The deeply interconnected nature of financial systems is underscored by the high degree of synchronization of financial cycles globally.

A global financial cycle—showing commonalities in credit, asset prices, and financial conditions across countries—appears in part driven by financial and economic conditions in major financial centers, such as the US, euro area, Japan, and the United Kingdom—the G4 (Rey 2013). US monetary policy, global liquidity conditions (especially US dollars), the strength of G4 banking systems, and global risk aversion all have important implications for the high synchronicity of global capital flows and its financial ramifications for Asia.

The global financial cycle matters for financial stability in emerging economies, with liquidity conditions in advanced economies affecting international capital flow dynamics.

Among the lessons from past crises have been the long-lasting destabilizing effects large and volatile capital flows can have on emerging market economies. In an increasingly integrated global financial system, this is even more crucial when designing effective policy responses given more rapid international risk transmission. This amplifies shock propagation and synchronization in the region, potentially undermining financial stability.

Empirical results suggest that monetary policy in advanced economies—in the form of low interest rates, quantitative easing, and market expectations about policy moves—heavily impacts capital inflows to Asia (see Bhattarai, Chatterjee, Park 2015; Kim 2014; Chen, Filardo, He, and Zhu 2012; Villafuerte 2017). Changes in monetary policy can also trigger increased capital flow volatility. These inflows create upward pressure on asset prices (currencies, equities, and bonds) and increase foreign ownership of local currency securities in target economies, thereby increasing local financial market sensitivity to swings in foreign investor sentiment.

---

[46] See Annex 8.1 for a chronological overview and description of past financial crises, theories, and policy advice.

Asia's Financial Interconnectedness, Transmission, and Spillovers of Shocks and Risks

Financial integration and interconnectedness allow for a more efficient allocation of financial resources and create greater opportunities for economic growth globally. But they could also lead to increased financial fragility. As the AFC and GFC demonstrated, deeper cross-border financial linkages and associated increased volumes of cross-border financial flows can be a source of financial volatility and contagion, in particular to emerging market economies.

In such a highly interconnected financial environment, shocks in one part of the system can be amplified and transmitted through exposures to common financial intermediaries or markets. Therefore, policy makers must better understand the mechanisms underlying the transmission of financial risk. They need to carefully monitor Asia's financial network development and understand how deepening financial interconnectedness relates to financial stability risks—such as vulnerability to external shocks, financial contagion, or liquidity risks stemming from foreign currency funding.

This section starts with an analysis of the evolution of Asia's financial network using equity market return data. Moreover, it features two empirical applications that analyze specific sources of risks stemming from financial interconnectedness. First, using bilateral cross-border data on bank liabilities between countries, it shows how large borrowing exposures to advanced economies can be a source of financial distress when a financial crisis strikes. The crisis can spread to borrowing economies, with a negative impact on regional financial stability. Second, the macrofinancial effects associated with NPLs in Asia are examined, with a discussion of the possible role inter-regional and intraregional spillover effects play.

Asia's Financial Sector Network

Since the late-1990s, international financial crises have highlighted the advantage of viewing the global financial system as a network of economies, where cross-border financial linkages play a fundamental role in the spread of systemic risk.

Daily equity market returns (in local currencies) from 42 markets around the world (15 from Asia) are used to analyze the changing nature of Asia's financial networks for six key periods over the past 20 years.

The empirical analysis is conducted to effectively model the changing network of financial markets within and between Asia and the rest of the world to capture its evolution through six time periods over the last two decades—before, during, and after the AFC and GFC, respectively. For each period, the direction of financial links between markets, the relative significance of those links and their strength is examined. It provides a comprehensive overview of Asia's financial network over time. The network structure allows an examination of the possible buildup of systemic risks within the network and identifies channels of contagion arising from financial market interconnectedness and cross-border financial linkages.

An advantage of network analysis is that it improves understanding of the way in which financial stress transmits between markets, helping facilitate policy making during times of financial distress.

The advantage of network analysis lies in its ability to better understand the mechanisms underlying the transmission of financial stress between markets, to help identify and monitor network nodes that act as critical links between regions and can therefore facilitate the transmission of shocks. More generally, it can help authorities design appropriate policy responses and targeted interventions to promote financial stability and resilience.

Data of 42 equity market indexes (in local currencies)—15 located in Asia—are used to provide a comprehensive analysis of Asia's financial network over 1996–2016.

The analysis draws on the approaches developed in Dungey et al. (2017b), Diebold and Yilmaz (2009, 2014), and Billio et al. (2012), primarily to document changes in the characteristics of Asia's financial network over time—changes in the number and strength of links between financial markets in the network. To derive a comprehensive representation, two main steps are

applied using vector autoregression (VAR) models (Box 8.2). First, a VAR considers the relationships between all of the asset markets. Within that framework, nested Granger Causality tests determine which links are statistically significant. Second, the relative strength of the identified links—a spillover measure—is assessed through a forecast error variance decomposition, whereby the sources of observed volatility in each return are attributed to shocks in source nodes. These network statistics allow for a detailed analysis of Asia's financial network and how it has evolved.

Box 8.2: Deriving Asia's Financial Sector Network: Data, Methodology, and Model

The data employed in the analysis is comprised of daily equity price indexes in local currencies of 42 markets over 1996–2016,[a] with 15 located in Asia. The observations are broken down into six phases covering the periods before, during and after the 1997/98 Asian financial crisis (AFC) and 2008/09 global financial crisis (GFC). Box tables 1 and 2 list the economies included, grouped by region and the time series observation in each subsample period.

Phase One and Phase Four correspond to the periods prior to the AFC and the GFC, respectively. Phases Two and Five indicate the crisis periods (see Dungey, Fry, and Martin 2006; and Dungey, Milunovich, Thorp, and Yang 2015 for more on the recognized crisis durations). Phases Three and Six cover the period following each crisis, and can be seen as recovery periods.

Using network analysis, the direction, relative significance, and strength of links between equity markets (or nodes) are determined. To study the changes in the networks across the six time periods, several aspects are assessed: (i) the changing completeness (or density) of the network; (ii) the changing number of links between nodes; (iii) the changing strength of links between nodes; (iv) the net and gross change in links between nodes; (v) "betweenness", closeness, and eigenvalue centrality (indicating the substitutability of a node, the sum of distances to all other nodes, and the proximity between nodes, respectively); and (vi) Jaccard statistics (or the similarity of networks

1: Markets Grouped by Region

Europe	Asia	North America
United Kingdom	Australia	Canada
	People's Republic of China	United States
Euro Area	Hong Kong, China	
Austria	India	**Latin America**
Belgium	Japan	Argentina
Finland	Republic of Korea	Brazil
France	Singapore	Chile
Germany		Mexico
Greece	*ASEAN4*	
Ireland	Indonesia	**Africa**
Italy	Malaysia	Egypt
Netherlands	Philippines	South Africa
Portugal	Thailand	
Spain		
	Other Asia	
Other Europe	New Zealand	
Czech Republic	Pakistan	
Denmark	Sri Lanka	
Hungary	Taipei,China	
Poland		
Sweden		
Switzerland		
Turkey		

Source: Dungey et al. (2017a).

[a] The analysis is conducted using demeaned returns and actual day dating.

Continued on next page

Box 8.2 continued

2: Time Series Observation in Each Subsample Period

Phase	Time period	Number of observations
All Phases	1 March 1995–30 December 2016	5738
Phase 1	1 March 1995–1 July 1997	650
Phase 2	2 July 1997–31 December 1998	391
Phase 3	1 January 1999–31 December 2002	1042
Phase 4	1 January 2003–14 September 2008	1287
Phase 5	15 September 2008–31 March 2010	602
Phase 6	1 April 2010–30 December 2016	1761

Source: Dungey et al. (2017a).

from one period to the next). However, the analysis finds that betweenness, closeness, and eigenvalue centrality of the nodes do not provide particularly useful information for tracking changes between different periods.

The analysis employs a vector autoregression (VAR) model to analyze the existence and strength of the links between markets. It draws on the methodological approaches developed in Dungey et al. (2017b) in identifying a network of financial linkages between nodes (represented by index equity market data for each economy), where the links between them (edges) are determined by an adjacency matrix that includes both the direction and strength of the links and a measure of their statistical significance. Existing links are identified through nested Granger causality tests of links between nodes. If one node Granger causes the other one, then the link is recognized as existing in the network. If the Granger causality is not significant, then the link is nonexistent. The relative strength of the links is determined by using a forecast error variance decomposition approach.

The combination of the two methodologies draws on the work of Diebold and Yilmaz (2009, 2014) and Billio et al. (2012). It is driven in part by the limitation that statistical significance is not a strong point of VAR models. The Granger causality approach is used to weed out the spuriously large or poorly estimated linkages from the adjacency matrix resulting from the VAR approach.

The use of data on equity rather than bank liabilities (utilized more frequently in other studies) was due in part to the availability and extensiveness of the data; to its ability to more accurately reflect market sentiment; and to the concern that concentrating analysis and reforms on one sector could create shocks that transmit through other markets.

Source: Dungey et al. (2017a)

Empirical results reveal a complex global financial network, highlighting the high degree of financial market interconnectedness.

Figure 8.10 maps the identified global financial network over the entire sample period. The thickness of the lines denotes the strength of the links, the size of the nodes increases with the number of outward links of each respective market, and the color indicates the outward spreading region in which the market is located.

The complexity of the relationships between nodes is evident as there are 1,722 possible connections between nodes. The markets involved are highly interconnected, though some nodes are relatively isolated. The diagram reflects the relatively strong significance of the relationships between European markets in the sample, particularly euro area members. Financial interconnectedness within Asian economies is also visible.

Tracking the development of the network over time shows that its density has changed substantially before and after crises.

Figure 8.11 illustrates the evolution of the financial network over time. During the transition from pre-crisis to crisis, a quick buildup of significant or strong links takes place. During periods of stress, markets become more interconnected (as demonstrated by the growing number of weaker connections coinciding with fewer strong connections). By contrast, after a crisis, many connections fail, with the decrease not offset by a rise in links elsewhere. In this way, crisis periods increase degrees of connectedness, while recovery phases reduce them.[47]

Table 8.2, Panel A indicates that the number of statistically significant edges in the network has grown less monotonically than what may initially be suggested by the panels. While only 12.2% of possible linkages were statistically significant before the AFC, it jumped by 45% (to 305 links) during the AFC before returning to close to pre-crisis numbers after the crisis. During the buildup

---

[47] It is worth noting the complications of using completeness statistics to understand the evolution of a network. The completeness of a network may fall due to an increased number of linkages outweighed by the fall in their average strength (similar to what occurred during the AFC) or it may rise due to an overwhelming increase in the number of links (as occurred during the GFC).

Figure 8.10: Network Plots for Entire Sample

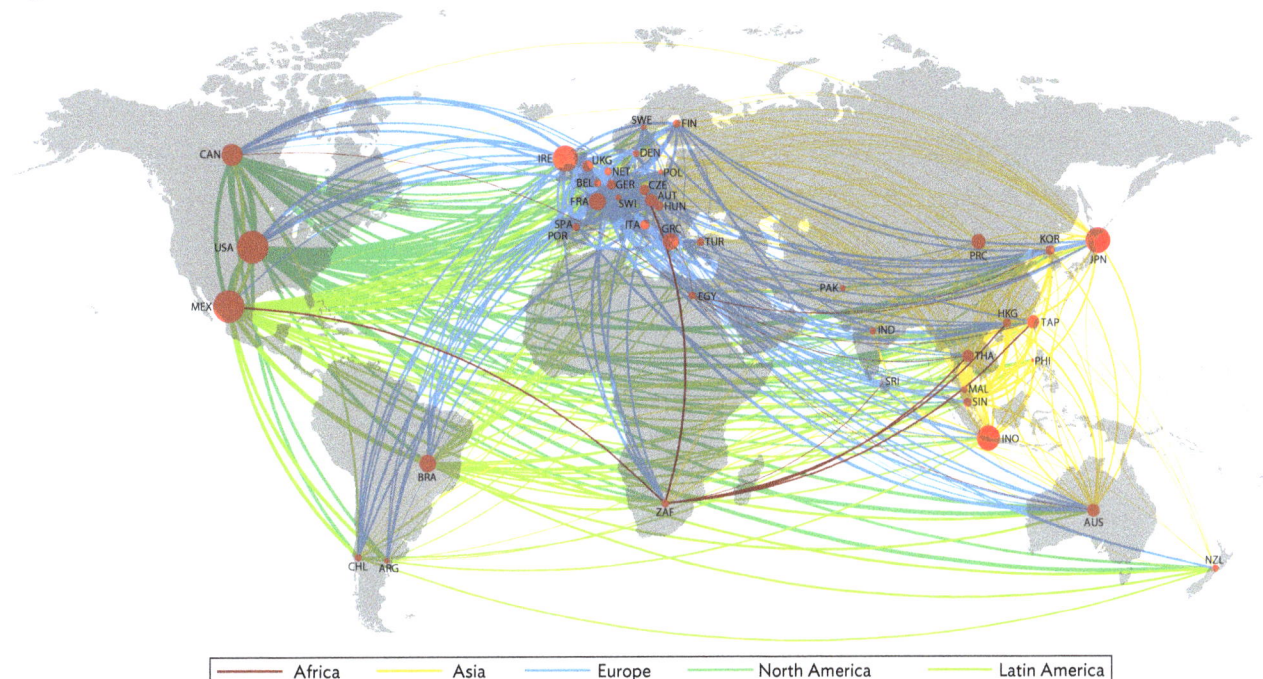

ARG = Argentina; AUS = Australia; AUT = Austria; BEL = Belgium; BRA = Brazil; CAN = Canada; CHL = Chile; CZE = Czech Republic; DEN = Denmark; EGY = Egypt; FIN = Finland; FRA = France; GER = Germany; GRC = Greece; HKG = Hong Kong, China; HUN = Hungary; IND = India; INO = Indonesia; IRE = Ireland; ITA = Italy; JPN = Japan; KOR = Republic of Korea; MAL = Malaysia; MEX = Mexico; NET = Netherlands; NZL = New Zealand; PAK = Pakistan; PHI = Philippines; POL = Poland; POR = Portugal; PRC = People's Republic of China; SIN = Singapore; SPA = Spain; SRI = Sri Lanka; SWE = Sweden; SWI = Switzerland; TAP = Taipei,China; THA = Thailand; TUR = Turkey; UKG = United Kingdom; USA = United States; ZAF = South Africa.
Notes: Sample period: 1 March 1995 to 30 December 2016. The figure displays the return-based network of markets. Edges were calculated with bivariate Granger causality tests between markets (nodes) at the 5% level of significance. The thickness of the lines indicates the relative strength of links between markets. The size of the nodes increases with the number of outward links of each respective market, and the colors indicate the outward spreading region in which the market is located. Connectivity lines (edges) and nodes were drawn using *ggplot* and *ggrepel* packages of R version 3.4.1 (Wickham 2009, Slowikowski 2016).
Sources: ADB calculations using data from Bloomberg (accessed February 2017). Methodology based on Dungey et al. (2017a). World map was taken from ADB. Climate Change Resilience in Asia's Cities (infographic). https://www.adb.org/news/infographics/climate-change-resilience-asias-cities.

to the GFC, the number of links again increased by 10% (to 237 links). During the GFC, the number of links jumped dramatically to 389 before declining again to a level similar to the AFC.

Overall, the empirical results show interconnectedness increases during periods of stress, followed by a decrease during recovery phases, with the average strength of linkages growing pre-crisis, before declining significantly. The changing magnitude of the linkages is also worth noting, as the strength of market connections change from being very tight to being loose, with the number of weak links growing and the number of strong links decreasing. The number of links common to two adjacent time periods—the Jaccard similarity statistic

(Table 8.3)—also increases over time before decreasing following the GFC.[48]

The analysis also suggests a general deepening of Asia's market connections with the rest of the world—as well as within the region—over the past two decades.

In charting the network changes over time, the role and changing links to and from specific economies can be

---

[48] It is worth noting that the Jaccard statistics depicted in the third row of Table 8.3 are low, reflecting few common links between two time periods. This reflects, in part, the significant growth in the number of links in the network over the sample period (with 45% more links post-GFC compared with pre-AFC) and that this growth leads to a reduction in the Jaccard statistic by construction. The first two rows of the table highlight stability in the network in terms of link retention across time periods. Apart from the post-GFC phase, the proportion of links removed during each phase is falling, from 80% to 65%. The links are therefore more likely to be retained over the sample period.

Figure 8.11: Evolution of Weighted Networks

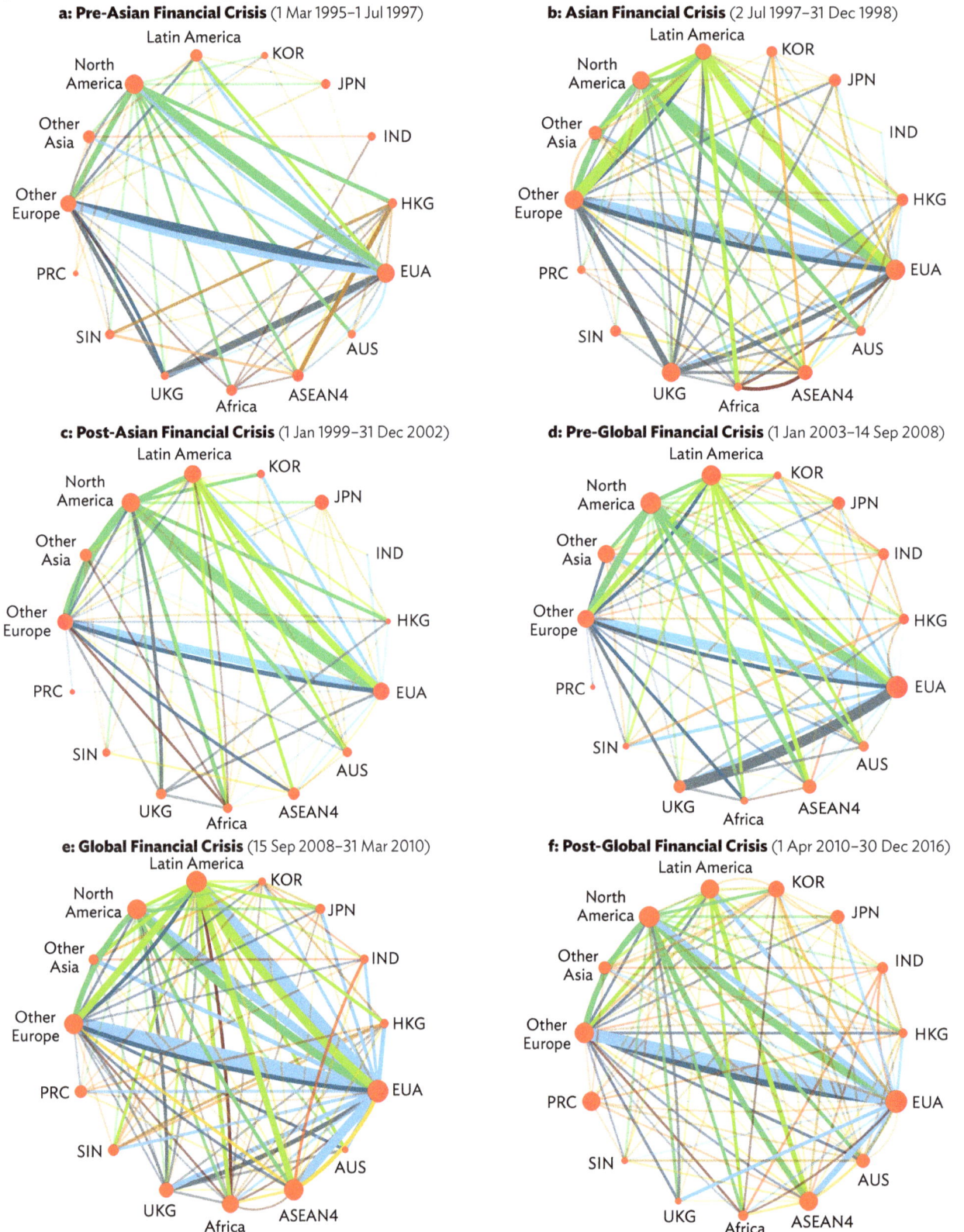

a: Pre-Asian Financial Crisis (1 Mar 1995–1 Jul 1997)

b: Asian Financial Crisis (2 Jul 1997–31 Dec 1998)

c: Post-Asian Financial Crisis (1 Jan 1999–31 Dec 2002)

d: Pre-Global Financial Crisis (1 Jan 2003–14 Sep 2008)

e: Global Financial Crisis (15 Sep 2008–31 Mar 2010)

f: Post-Global Financial Crisis (1 Apr 2010–30 Dec 2016)

ASEAN4 = Association of Southeast Asian Nation (Indonesia, Malaysia, Philippines, and Thailand); AUS = Australia; EUA = euro area; HKG = Hong Kong, China; IND = India; JPN = Japan; KOR = Republic of Korea; PRC = People's Republic of China; SIN = Singapore; UKG = United Kingdom.
Notes: The figure displays the returns-based network of 15 equity markets and regional groupings from 1 March 1995 to 30 December 2016. These are defined in Box 8.2. Edges were calculated using bivariate Granger causality tests between markets at the 5% level of significance. The thickness of the lines indicates the average relative strength of each market (or regional grouping). The size of the nodes increases with the number of outward links of each respective market (or regional grouping).
Sources: ADB calculations using data from Bloomberg (accessed February 2017): and methodology based on Dungey et al. (2017a).

Table 8.2: Network Statistics

	Phase 1	Phase 2	Phase 3	Phase 4	Phase 5	Phase 6
Panel A						
Average strength	0.0260	0.0235	0.0236	0.0276	0.0260	0.0225
Number of edges	210	305	214	237	389	306
Completeness	0.2570	0.2252	0.1820	0.2034	0.2734	0.1990

Panel B					
Phase 1 to Phase 2	**Phase 2 to Phase 3**	**Phase 3 to Phase 4**	**Phase 4 to Phase 5**	**Phase 5 to Phase 6**
Edges Formed					
0.0194	0.0169	0.0208	0.0225	0.0211
264	159	180	306	233
0.1608	0.0968	0.1163	0.1864	0.1424
Edges Removed					
0.0206	0.0196	0.0180	0.0207	0.0229
169	250	157	154	316
0.1640	0.1536	0.1020	0.0994	0.1957

Notes: The average link strength is estimated from the connectedness of each respective network. The number of edges was calculated using bivariate Granger causality tests between network nodes (entities). For the definition of phases 1-6, see Box 8.2.
Sources: ADB calculations using data from Bloomberg (accessed February 2017): and methodology based on Dungey et al. (2017a).

Table 8.3: Jaccard Statistic for All Economies in the Sample (%)

	Phases				
	1 to 2	**2 to 3**	**3 to 4**	**4 to 5**	**5 to 6**
Edges removed as proportion of Phase t-1	80.48	81.97	73.96	64.98	81.23
Edges formed as proportion of Phase t	86.56	74.30	75.95	78.66	76.14
Jaccard statistic for all edges	8.65	11.85	14.47	15.29	11.74

Notes: For the definition of phases 1-6, see Box 8.2.
Sources: ADB calculations using data from Bloomberg (accessed February 2017): and methodology based on Dungey et al. (2017a).

seen. Over the course of the period studied, the number of direct connections from the PRC grew; the PRC also grew more connected to ASEAN economies and North America. Following the AFC, Singapore and Hong Kong, China established increasing inward-linkages with Asian economies, highlighting their importance as critical avenues for connecting Asia's markets to the rest of the world.[49] Thus, shocks originating in Asia's markets could spread to the US and other developed markets via a conduit of regional hubs—Singapore and Hong Kong, China. This is in line with Remolona and Shim (2015), who highlight the special financial intermediary role played by Singapore and Hong Kong, China as regional

banking centers. In more recent years, however, many Asian markets have increased and strengthened direct links to external markets.

The analysis shows the complexity of expanding financial networks and highlights a growing internationalization and interconnectedness of Asian financial markets.

The analysis empirically illustrates the nature of the global and regional financial network, embedding the direction, statistical significance, and strength of interlinkages into a single framework. The evolution of the network over the sample period clearly indicates the growing internationalization and interconnectedness of Asia's markets. The analysis also highlights specific instances where this occurred through market

[49] See online annex 2.E for a tabulation of the in- and out-linkages of the markets included in the study. https://aric.adb.org/aeir2017_onlineannex2.pdf

interaction with local or regional hubs—particularly Hong Kong, China or Singapore. However, over time Asia's markets increasingly link directly with other regions.

Strikingly, the analysis shows just how interconnected Asia's financial markets are, and their associated shared risks and vulnerabilities. This underscores the need for coordinated action in designing and structuring policies aimed at making the region's financial systems more resilient. As past crises have taught us, economies cannot safeguard financial stability alone. Rather, national policies need to be supplemented regionally to make Asia more resilient.

Finally, one limitation inherent in the model follows from the use of the single dimension of asset markets in the analysis. Equity markets may not fully capture the complexities in overall financial linkages between economies. The challenge to researchers and policy makers is to include different asset markets and potentially different players to better reflect the complexity of multiple layers of financial interconnectedness between economies. Sovereign bond market networks will, for instance, differ from equity market networks (Dungey et al. 2017a), and real economy networks—such as trade networks or input-output production networks (Pesaran and Yang 2016)—are closely tied to financial networks, but the weights on the nodes can be different and multidimensional.[50]

Global Financial Interconnectedness of the Banking Sector

The GFC highlighted how financial weaknesses and vulnerabilities can intensify with greater financial interconnectedness.

Although the GFC originated in advanced economies—unlike the AFC—emerging economies were also hit due to the increasingly interconnected global financial system. Banks in emerging economies faced a liquidity crunch as some troubled banks in advanced economies unwound their international investment positions and

withdrew funds from emerging markets. These spillovers were exacerbated if the troubled banks were larger and more interconnected—SIFIs were responsible for transmitting financial distress to well-connected financial institutions.

Recent studies look at possible contagion through domestic banks' liability-side exposure to foreign banks during the GFC.

A few recent studies highlight the risk of financial spillovers emanating from bank exposures on the liabilities side. An examination of the Northern Rock bank run in the United Kingdom demonstrates how a potential financial disruption can unfold as creditors pull back leverage in an effort to limit risk exposure.

Given the importance of the liability side as a channel of financial contagion, an empirical investigation tests the contagion effect of an economy using bilateral data on bank claims between economies. The goal is to empirically measure the effect of direct and indirect exposures of emerging economies to crisis-affected economies and to test whether these exposures can account for the capital outflows from emerging economies. Using data from 27 different Bank for International Settlements (BIS) reporting economies, 62 counterparty emerging economies are chosen for the model. These also include 12 emerging Asian economies (Box 8.3).[51]

An emerging economy's direct and indirect exposures on the liability side to crisis-affected banks in advanced economies can explain the capital outflows experienced during the GFC.

The results reveal that both direct and indirect exposures to crisis-affected economies play an important role in explaining the capital outflows experienced by emerging market economies during the GFC. These findings highlight the importance of the banking channel for financial distress transmitted from advanced lending economies to borrowing emerging economies. Analyzing the impact of exposures to foreign liabilities on capital outflows during the GFC (Table 8.4) shows that the coefficients of direct exposure of the banking sector

---

[50] See online annex 2.F for a discussion on the use of high frequency data in assessing financial networks. https://aric.adb.org/aeir2017_onlineannex2. pdf

[51] Bangladesh, Georgia, India, Indonesia, the Kyrgyz Republic, Malaysia, Mongolia, Pakistan, the Philippines, the Republic of Korea, Sri Lanka, and Thailand.

Box 8.3: Assessing Interbank Contagion During the Global Financial Crisis: Data, Methodology, and Model

The data are bilateral information on cross-economy liability positions collected from Bank for International Settlements (BIS) consolidated banking statistics and locational banking statistics.[a] These data allow an empirical assessment of how shocks transmit through bank exposures on the liability side. The consolidated banking statistics are the consolidated claims of internationally active banks headquartered in 30 BIS reporting economies against 223 counterparty economies.[b, c] Similar to the consolidation approach adopted by financial regulatory supervisors, these statistics include claims of a bank's foreign affiliates, but exclude intragroup positions.[d] Locational banking statistics report the outstanding claims of banks in 43 BIS reporting economies.[e]

Of the counterparty economies, a set of 62 emerging economies is chosen.[f] The list of emerging economies is adopted from Park, Ramayandi, and Shin (2016), Eichengreen and Gupta (2015), and Lim, Mohapatra, and Stocker (2014). To measure the extent to which an emerging

economy's liability side was exposed to borrowing from crisis economies,[g] two indicators are constructed:

$$DE_{i,t}^f = \sum_{j \in C_t} share_{ij,t}^f, \quad share_{ij,t}^f = \frac{fc_{ijt}}{\sum_{k=1}^N fc_{ikt}}$$

$$IDE_{i,t}^f = \sum_j share_{ij,t}^f \cdot DE_{j,t}^f$$

Direct exposure of foreign claims on an emerging economy i at time t to banks in crisis economies, denoted by $DE_{i,t}^f$, is measured by the sum of shares of foreign claims held by all economies that experienced crises. However, the direct measure alone cannot convey the full extent of an economy's exposure to crisis-affected economies—as it neglects the economy's exposure to economies not directly hit by the crisis, but similarly exposed to crisis-affected economies—therefore facing indirect liquidity problems. Consequently, an indirect exposure of foreign claims of an emerging economy i at time t, $IDE_{i,t}^f$, is defined accordingly.

Additionally, direct and indirect exposures of the banking sector,[h] $DE_{i,t}^b$ and $IDE_{i,t}^b$, are constructed to account for the fact that banking sector liabilities play a crucial role in transmitting shocks (for example, see Hahm, Shin, and Shin, 2013). Direct and indirect exposures of short-term maturities,[i] $DE_{i,t}^s$ and $IDE_{i,t}^s$, are constructed using data on claims on maturities with less than 1-year on the counterparty economy. As long-term claims are not easily withdrawn—even by troubled banks—it is more likely that sudden withdrawals of short-term borrowings occur in case the lending economy experiences a credit crunch.

Finally, according to the hypothesis that economies more exposed—directly and indirectly—to banks in crisis economies suffered more from capital outflows during the global financial crisis (GFC), a measure of capital outflows

---

[a]   BIS compiles and publishes two sets of statistics on banks' international positions. Consolidated banking statistics measure banks' country risk exposures by capturing the worldwide consolidated claims of internationally active banks headquartered in BIS reporting economies. Locational banking statistics provide information about the currency composition of bank balance sheets and the geographical breakdown of counterparties by capturing outstanding claims and liabilities of banks located in BIS reporting economies, including intragroup positions between offices within the same banking group.

[b]   In the consolidated banking statistics, claims refer to outstanding loans and holdings of securities by reporting banks. See Park and Shin (2017) for the full list of reporting economies.

[c]   Since the number of the BIS reporting economies is limited—that is, there are other claims of banks with controlling parents located outside the BIS reporting economies—the sum of all claims of these reporting economies against a counterparty would not equal the sum of all liabilities held by the counterparty. However, since the BIS reporting economies include most economies active in international bank loans, actual total foreign claims on a counterpart are not expected to deviate much from the sum of bank claims of just the reporting economies.

[d]   Detailed explanations of the BIS consolidated banking statistics can be found in BIS (2016).

[e]   In 2016, there were 43 reporting economies. However, when the direct and indirect exposures in 2007 are measured, the number with bilateral data available drops to 29. Park and Shin (2017) list reporting economies of locational banking statistics in 2007.

[f]   See Park and Shin (2017) for a full list of emerging economies.

[g]   Crisis-affected economies are defined according to Dates for Banking Crises, Currency Crashes, Sovereign Domestic or External Default (or Restructuring), Inflation Crises, and Stock Market Crashes (Varieties). Carmen Reinhart Author Website. http://www.carmenreinhart.com/data/browse-by-topic/topics/7/ (accessed July 2016)

[h]   These disaggregated data are available in the consolidated banking statistics only on an ultimate risk basis. In the locational banking statistics, bilateral claims on the banking sector are available for total cross-border claims and cross-border loans.

[i]   Short-term claims are available only for consolidated banking statistics international borrowings on an immediate counterparty basis.

Box 8.2 continued

from economy *i* during the GFC, $Koutflow_i$, is defined as follows:

$$Koutflow_i = \frac{TFC_i^{max} - TFC_i^{min}}{TFC_i^{max}}$$

where TFC_i^{max} and TFC_i^{min} are the maximum and the minimum levels of total foreign claims on economy *i* during the period from the first quarter (Q1) of 2007 to Q4 2009. It is assumed that the difference between the maximum and the minimum levels of foreign claims on economy *i* during the period represent the volume of capital outflows from economy *i*. Total foreign claims are measured by adding foreign claims on economy *i* across all reporting economies.

To measure the extent to which capital outflows from emerging economies during the GFC were triggered by direct and indirect exposures vis-à-vis crisis-affected advanced economies, the following regression equation for all three exposure definitions is applied:

$$Koutflow_i = \beta_0 + \beta_1 DE_{i,2007}^j + \beta_2 IDE_{i,2007}^j + \beta_3 X_{i,2007} + \varepsilon_i, j=f,b,s$$

where $DE_{i,2007}^j$ and $IDE_{i,2007}^j$ are measures of direct and indirect exposure in Q4 2007, while $X_{i,2007}$ captures other control variables of economy *i* at time *t*, that include aggravation of current account balances, real exchange rate appreciation before the GFC, increase in domestic credit-to-gross domestic product (GDP) ratio, inflation rate, and real GDP growth rate.[j]

Source: Park and Shin (2017).

are positive and statistically significant, regardless of whether indirect exposure is added, and whether economy-specific control variables ($X_{i,2007}$) are included in the analysis. It is also worth noting that the coefficient of indirect exposure of the banking sector is positive, although it is not statistically significant, when controlling for the full set of other variables. In particular, the addition of sovereign credit rating seems to play a role in mitigating the effect of an economy's indirect exposure. Therefore, Table 8.4 indicates that it is predominantly the banking sector's direct exposure, as opposed to indirect exposure, which explains the capital outflows experienced by emerging economies.[52]

This empirical exercise shows that shocks in advanced economies are transmitted to emerging economies as the credit crunch experienced by troubled banks in turn triggers a run on banks and other entities in emerging economies. The findings underscore the significance of both the degree of an economy's direct and indirect exposures through the banking sector to crisis-affected countries as an important determinant of capital outflows. Hence, these findings suggest that the global banking network of aggregate cross-border lending can be a channel for a global liquidity crunch that can spread financial shocks globally. This liquidity issue of creditor banks can be particularly problematic for emerging market economies, as they rely heavily on foreign borrowing denominated in foreign currency.

The findings are consistent with the conclusions of recent financial contagion studies that highlight the financial vulnerabilities facing economies not directly affected by a crisis—that stem from deleveraging by creditors in crisis-affected economies, and exacerbated by a wider, denser global financial network (see Shin 2009). The results also demonstrate how financial distress can be transmitted from creditor economies to borrowing economies through their funding channels—highlighting the important dimension of the liability side (as in Čihák, Muñoz, and Scuzzarella 2011).

[j] See Eichengreen and Gupta (2015) and Park, Ramayandi, and Shin (2016) for the motivation for including these as explanatory variables.

[52] For more on the impact of direct and indirect exposures of foreign claims and of short-term international borrowings on capital outflows during the GFC, see Online Annexes 2.G and 2.H. https://aric.adb.org/aeir2017_onlineannex2.pdf

Table 8.4: Impact of Direct and Indirect Exposures of the Banking Sector on Capital Outflows during the Global Financial Crisis

Variables	(1) Outflow	(2) Outflow	(3) Outflow	(4) Outflow
Direct exposure of banking sector	0.257*** [0.075]	0.228** [0.085]	0.282*** [0.078]	0.253*** [0.086]
Indirect exposure of banking sector			0.722** [0.285]	0.359 [0.269]
Increase in current account deficit (2004–2007)		-0.006 [0.004]		-0.005 [0.004]
Average change in real exchange rate (% annual, 2003–2007)		-0.676* [0.366]		-0.667* [0.355]
Increase in credit to GDP ratio (2004–2007)		0.005** [0.002]		0.004** [0.002]
GDP growth (% annual, 2007)		-0.017* [0.009]		-0.016 [0.010]
Inflation rate (2007)		-0.023*** [0.008]		-0.022*** [0.008]
Chinn-Ito Index (2007)		0.124** [0.060]		0.126** [0.061]
S&P Sovereign Local Currency Credit Rating (2007)		-0.021** [0.010]		-0.020** [0.010]
Observations	60	49	60	49
R-squared	0.111	0.459	0.212	0.483

*** = significant at 1%, ** = significant at 5%, * = significant at 10%. GDP = gross domestic product. Robust standard errors in brackets.
Notes: The dependent variable is the rate of capital outflows from each emerging economy during the global financial crisis. Measures of direct and indirect exposures are calculated using cross-border claims on the banking sector based on locational banking statistics. See Shin and Park (2017) for more detailed data descriptions.
Source: Park and Shin (2017).

The findings underscore the need for Asia's emerging economies and the region generally to monitor global conditions affecting their external liability side; and ensure adequate foreign currency liquidity coverage.

These findings are highly relevant for policy makers—as they support the idea that cross-border bank lending can serve as an avenue for transmitting global liquidity problems from creditor to borrower economies. They highlight an important channel of contagion and financial vulnerability linked to financial integration and financial interconnectedness.

Even though regional banking has grown in Asia (Remolona and Shim 2015)—underscored by the increase of Asia's cross-border bank liabilities sourced within Asia (from 18.8% in 2011 to 25.7% in 2016)—around three-quarters of Asia's cross-border bank liabilities in 2016 came from external sources, mostly advanced economies (see Table 4.6 in Financial Integration section above).

Even economies not directly hit by a crisis can become vulnerable to its effects—threatening financial stability. Therefore, policies that aim to strengthen regional financial stability and resilience should consider this potential impact. The findings highlight the relevance of considering foreign liability exposure when designing macroprudential policies, capital flow management measures, and financial regulations—both nationally and regionally. While these policies currently focus on the fundamentals of emerging economies, they also need to consider the soundness of lender countries and the cooperation between lender and borrower countries to regulate global SIFIs. As discussed by Ghosh et al. (2014), there is scope for enhanced cooperation on capital flow management measures, not only between source and recipient economies, but also among recipient economies themselves.

Also, the results support the need for emerging economies to closely monitor global financial conditions—in line with Cerutti, Claessens, and Puy (2015). While these results depict the risks of contagion originating from advanced economies, they can equally appear in an expanding regional banking network. As analyzed by Remolona and Shim (2015), some regional banks in Asia have become increasingly important as a future source of systemic risk. Adequately monitoring their cross-border activities and properly supervising these banks will be key to enhancing regional financial resilience.

Macrofinancial Impacts of NPLs and Financial Spillovers across Asia

The recent rise of NPLs in some Asian economies calls for close monitoring due to potential macrofinancial feedback effects and implications for the region's financial stability.

The rise of NPLs needs to be closely monitored. Figure 8.12 describes the dynamics underpinning macroeconomic and financial spillovers, as well as their macrofinancial feedback effects. This conceptual framework captures the interplay between macrofinancial variables and NPLs along with the potential channels of financial spillovers across borders.

NPL ratios have recently begun to rise in several developing Asian economies—an emerging concern due to macrofinancial feedback effects.

NPL ratios in Asia have been trending downward since the AFC—particularly in Southeast Asia, where NPL ratios were 3% or below in 2016 (see Table 8.1). This contrasts starkly against the skyrocketing NPL ratios immediately following the crisis in 1999, when they were well above 30% of all loans in Indonesia and Thailand, 29% in the PRC, and over 10% in India, Malaysia and the Philippines. The improved bank asset quality has been attributed to stronger growth in nominal

Figure 8.12: Macrofinancial Impacts of Nonperforming Loans

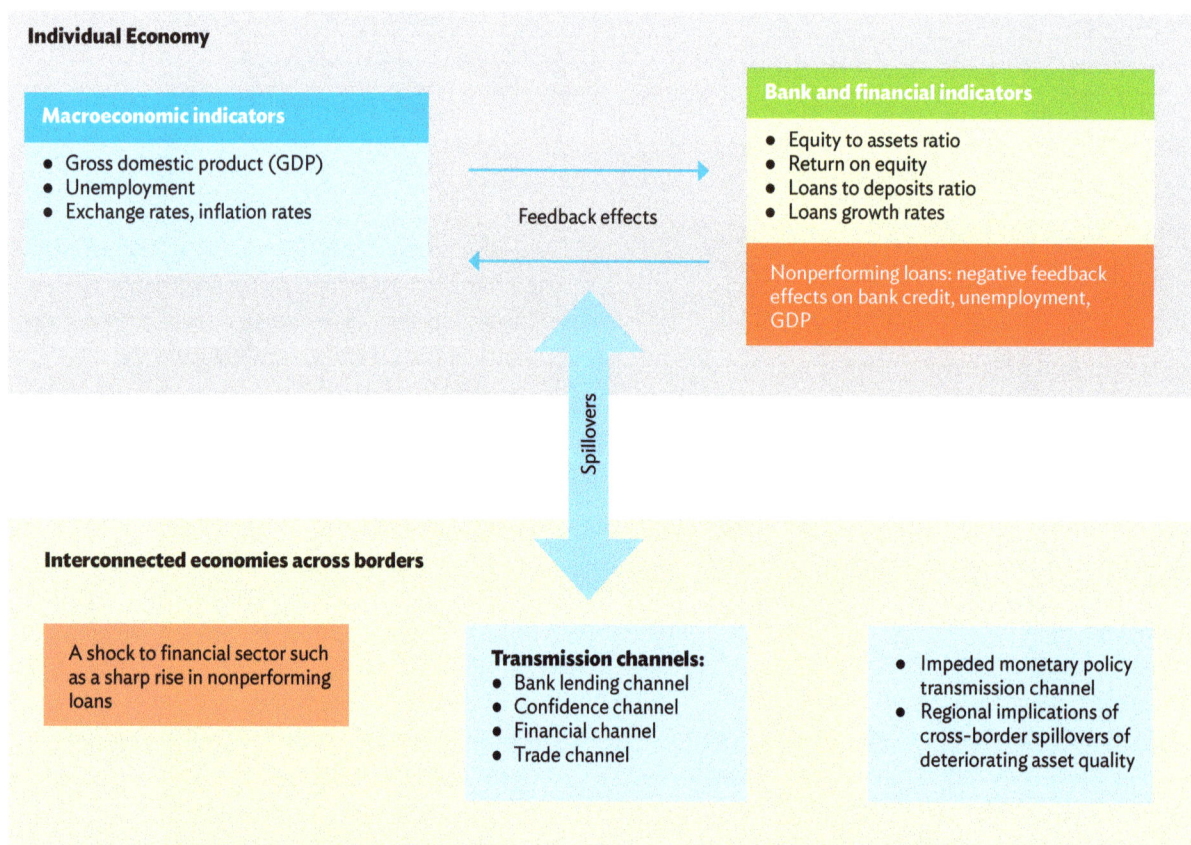

Individual Economy

Macroeconomic indicators
- Gross domestic product (GDP)
- Unemployment
- Exchange rates, inflation rates

Feedback effects

Bank and financial indicators
- Equity to assets ratio
- Return on equity
- Loans to deposits ratio
- Loans growth rates

Nonperforming loans: negative feedback effects on bank credit, unemployment, GDP

Spillovers

Interconnected economies across borders

A shock to financial sector such as a sharp rise in nonperforming loans

Transmission channels:
- Bank lending channel
- Confidence channel
- Financial channel
- Trade channel

- Impeded monetary policy transmission channel
- Regional implications of cross-border spillovers of deteriorating asset quality

Sources: Conceptual framework by ADB, based on Arslanalp, Liao and Seneviratne (2016); Beaton, Myrvoda, and Thompson (2016); Beck, Jakubik, Piloiu (2013); De Bock and Demyanets (2012); Espinoza and Prasad (2010); Klein (2013); Lee and Rosenkranz (2017); Makri, Tsagkanos, Bellas (2014); Martin (2017); Nkusu (2011); Park (2017); Shu, He, Dong, Wang (2016); Swiston and Bayoumi (2008).

incomes and credit, increased financial inclusion, and better supervision of bank credit risk management and underwriting.

However, global headwinds and moderating growth in the PRC in recent years exerted downward pressure on the region's economic conditions. Coupled with greater financial volatility following the start of US monetary policy tightening and financial spillovers from the PRC, bank balance sheets have deteriorated, causing a buildup of NPLs in the region. In particular, since 2010, NPLs—by amount and/or share of total loans—increased in Bangladesh and India (South Asia); Hong Kong, China; Mongolia, and the PRC; (East Asia); and in Cambodia, Indonesia, Singapore, and Thailand (Southeast Asia).[53] This sustained increase is particularly visible in the PRC,[54] India,[55] and Mongolia.

A large sustained NPL buildup could damage the financial sector and likewise lead to a reduction in credit supply and slowdown in overall economic activity. Multiple studies establish a link between deteriorating macroeconomic conditions (as captured by rising unemployment, slower growth, or falling asset prices) and unfavorable financial conditions (such as debt service problems or mounting distressed assets on bank balance sheets) (see Beaton, Myrvoda, Thompson 2016; Beck, Jakubik, and Piloiu 2013; De Bock and Demyanets 2012; Espinoza and Prasad 2010; Klein 2013; Makri, Tsagkanos, Bellas 2014; Nkusu 2011).

Increasing NPL levels reflect weak macroeconomic conditions and excess leverage; and they have harmful feedback effects on the overall economy.

Empirical evidence on the determinants of NPLs in Asia has been limited. And they have not been analyzed from a regional perspective. Nevertheless, there is consensus that two groups of factors determine how NPLs evolve over time. One is overall macroeconomic conditions, which affect borrowers' debt servicing capacity and explain credit risk. There are also bank-specific factors, which focus on variables that can signal or induce risky lending, affecting each bank's NPL level.

Existing studies led to several important insights. First, most studies place greater emphasis on the role of macroeconomic conditions in determining NPLs (as opposed to bank-specific factors), with the analysis performed using aggregate/country-level data. Second, there are very few Asian studies that model NPLs and their macrofinancial feedback effects. Finally, few attempts have been made to control for structural changes such as those relating to the AFC or GFC.

Therefore, a panel VAR analysis of macrofinancial implications of NPLs in emerging Asia offers new insights and significant evidence for the feedback effects of NPLs on real economy and financial variables (Box 8.4). These effects are bidirectional—as macroeconomic conditions impact financial indicators (such as NPLs) and financial conditions in turn affect macroeconomic indicators. In particular, changes in the NPL ratio Granger-cause[56] changes in the policy rate, credit growth, GDP growth, and unemployment (Table 8.5). The other direction of causality also holds as macroeconomic indicators also Granger-cause change in the NPL ratio. Moreover, the panel VAR impulse response functions (Figures 8.13, 8.14) confirm that positive shocks to GDP growth and credit supply both slow NPL ratio growth, while contractionary monetary policy shocks and shocks to unemployment both increase NPL ratio growth. More importantly, rising NPL ratio growth decreases GDP growth, credit supply, and increases the unemployment rate. By magnitude, a one standard deviation shock in NPL ratio would lead to about 0.18 percentage point contraction in GDP growth rate, about 3.61 percentage

---

[53] Based on ADB calculations using NPL data from CEIC; International Monetary Fund. International Financial Statistics. https://imf.org/en/Data; and World Bank. World Development Indicators.http://databank.worldbank.org (all accessed October 2017). For more details, see Table 8.1. and Online Annex 2.I. https://aric.adb.org/aeir2017_onlineannex2.pdf

[54] According to the China Banking Regulatory Commission, the volume of NPLs was equal to CNY433 billion in March 2011, and jumped to as much as CNY1,640 billion in June 2017. Hence, even though the reported NPL ratio still does not exceed 2% in the PRC, the size has almost quadrupled over the last 6 years.

[55] The distressed assets of India's state-owned banks are concentrated in a few dozen large corporate accounts. Concerns over the problem have grown as estimates of bad loans held by three large corporate sector lenders have increased. Bank stress is compounded by a lack of private sector investment, which fell in three quarters of 2016 (Financial Times 2017).

[56] Variable x_t granger causes variable z_t, if z_t can be predicted more efficiently if the information of x_t is taken into account in addition to all other available information.

Box 8.4: Estimating Macrofinancial Implications of Nonperforming Loans: Data, Methodology, and Model

The analysis investigates nonperforming loans (NPLs) in emerging Asia from 1994 to 2014. The study had two goals. First, the determinants of NPLs were analyzed using bank-level and macroeconomic data using a dynamic panel data model framework. Second, the feedback effects of deteriorating bank asset quality (rising NPLs) were examined using a panel vector autoregression (PVAR) model. The latter is explained in more detail below.

The analysis uses panel data of an economy's annual macroeconomic and financial indicators covering 32 economies: Afghanistan; Armenia; Australia; Azerbaijan; Bangladesh; Bhutan; Brunei Darussalam; Cambodia; Georgia; Hong Kong, China; India; Indonesia; Japan; Kazakhstan; the Kyrgyz Republic; the Lao People's Democratic Republic; Malaysia; Mongolia; Myanmar; New Zealand; Pakistan; the People's Republic of China; the Philippines; the Republic of Korea; Samoa; Singapore; Sri Lanka; Tajikistan; Thailand; Turkmenistan; Uzbekistan; and Viet Nam.

The following economy-level data on financial and macroeconomic variables were used:

nplr	NPL ratio defined as the ratio of NPLs to total loans of the economy's overall banking system
Δnplr	Change in NPL ratio
Δloans	Loan growth rate defined as the year-on-year growth rate of loans of the overall banking system
Δgdp	Real gross domestic product (GDP) growth rate
unemployment rate	The number of unemployed as percentage of total labor force
Δunemp	Change in the unemployment rate
Policyrate	Policy rate
Δpolicyrate	Change in policy rate
inf	Inflation rate defined as the year-on-year growth rate of the consumer price index
Δinf	Change in inflation rate

Source: CEIC and Bankscope.

To investigate the feedback effects of NPLs on the real economy, the PVAR model is estimated as

$$Y_{i,t} = \Pi_0 + \sum_{j=1}^{n} \Pi_j Y_{i,t-j} + \varepsilon_{i,t},$$
$$\varepsilon_{i,t} = u_i + e_{i,t}$$

where $Y_{i,t}$ is the vector of endogenous variables, $\varepsilon_{i,t}$ is the composite error term consisting of the economy fixed effects (u_i) and idiosyncratic errors ($e_{i,t}$). In the baseline specification, $Y_{i,t}$ consists of four endogenous variables—$\Delta nplr_{i,t}$, $\Delta loans_{i,t}$, $\Delta unemp_{i,t}$, and $\Delta policyrate_{i,t}$—where subscripts i and t denote economy i and year t, respectively. For robustness checks, the PVAR both in level and first difference forms are estimated and yield qualitatively similar findings. Results of model selection tests developed by Andrews and Lu (2001) reveal that the optimal lag order is one, hence the first lag of each of the four endogenous variables in the estimation are included. Using the programs developed by Abrigo and Love (2015), the PVAR is estimated using generalized method of moments (GMM) techniques to derive consistent estimates of the parameters.

Following Espinoza and Prasad (2010), the identification strategy is based on a Cholesky decomposition with $\Delta policyrate$ appearing first in the ordering, followed by $\Delta loans$, $\Delta unemp$ (Δgdp for specification 2) and finally $\Delta nplr$. This ordering assumes that the NPL ratio can affect unemployment (or economic growth in specification 2) or credit growth only with a lag and not instantaneously. This is consistent with documented empirical evidence that causality runs initially from economic growth to NPLs. For robustness checks, alternative Cholesky orderings proposed by Klein (2013) and De Bock and Demyanets (2012) are tried, which assume NPLs have a contemporaneous effect on GDP growth; unemployment and inflation affect NPLs only with a lag. Qualitatively, the results are similar across alternative Cholesky orderings.

Note: Empirical results have been derived using Stata 13.

Source: Lee and Rosenkranz (2017).

Table 8.5: Results of the Panel Vector Autoregression Granger Causality Test

Regressors Dependent	Baseline Specification				
	Δpolicyrate	Δloans	Δunemp	Δnplr	Joint
Δpolicyrate		0.02	5.24**	3.22*	13.66***
Δloans	0.43		6.72**	28.63***	50.60***
Δunemp	30.30***	9.33***		19.28***	32.94***
Δnplr	3.84**	6.57**	8.05**		17.53***

Regressors Dependent	Specification 2				
	Δpolicyrate	Δloans	Δgdp	Δnplr	Joint
Δpolicyrate		0.06	2.41	5.62**	10.81**
Δloans	0.81		2.78*	29.68***	43.40***
Δgdp	0.76	0.29		3.45*	6.74*
Δnplr	6.51**	0.22	15.56***		20.10***

*** = significant at 1%, ** = significant at 5%, * = significant at 10%. Empirical results are derived using Stata 13.
Source: Lee and Rosenkranz (2017).

Figure 8.13: Orthogonalized Impulse Response Functions—Baseline Specification

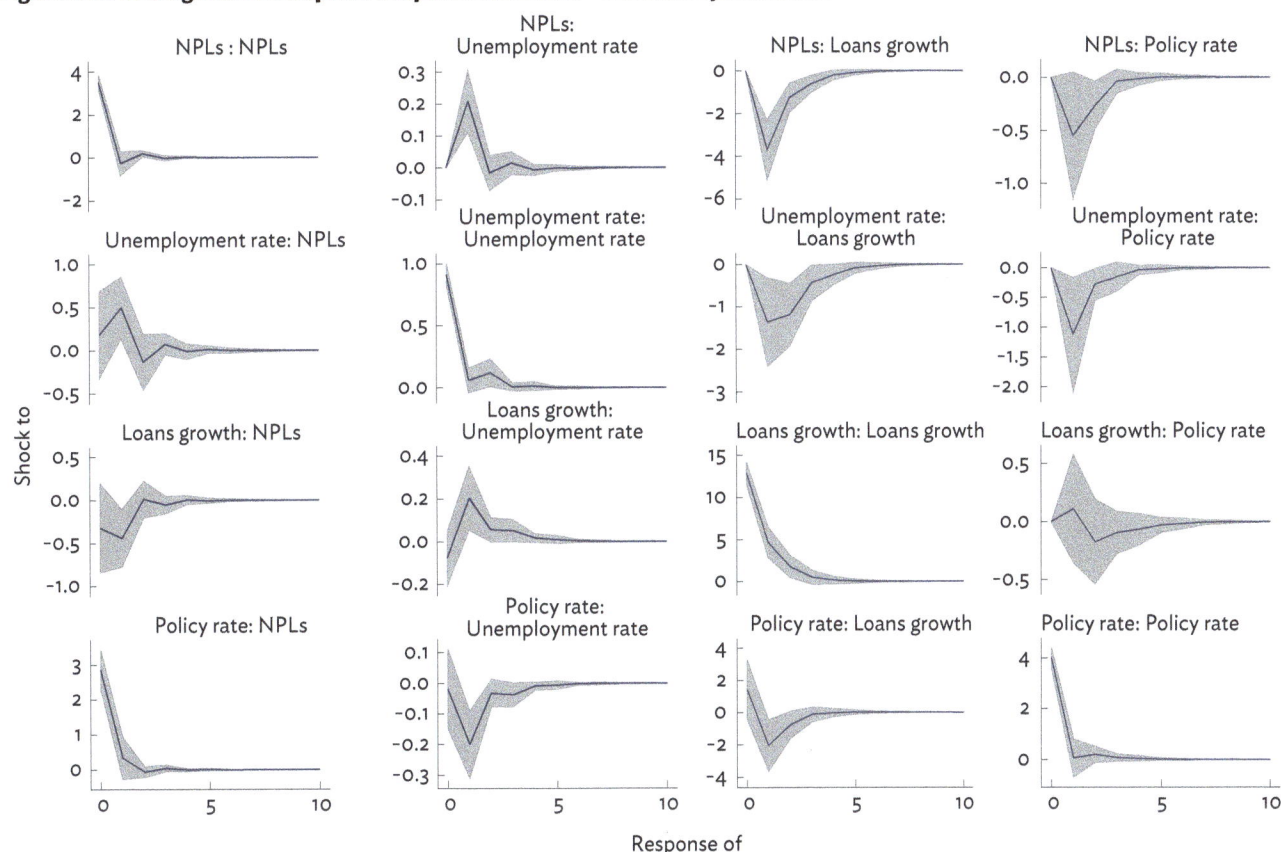

CI = confidence interval, GDP = gross domestic product, IRF = impulse response functions, NPLs = nonperforming loans. Responses are denoted in percentage points.
Note: 95% CI are generated by Monte Carlo draws with 5000 repetitions. Empirical results are derived using Stata 13.
Source: Lee and Rosenkranz (2017).

124   Asian Economic Integration Report 2017

Figure 8.14: Orthogonalized Impulse Response Functions—Specification 2

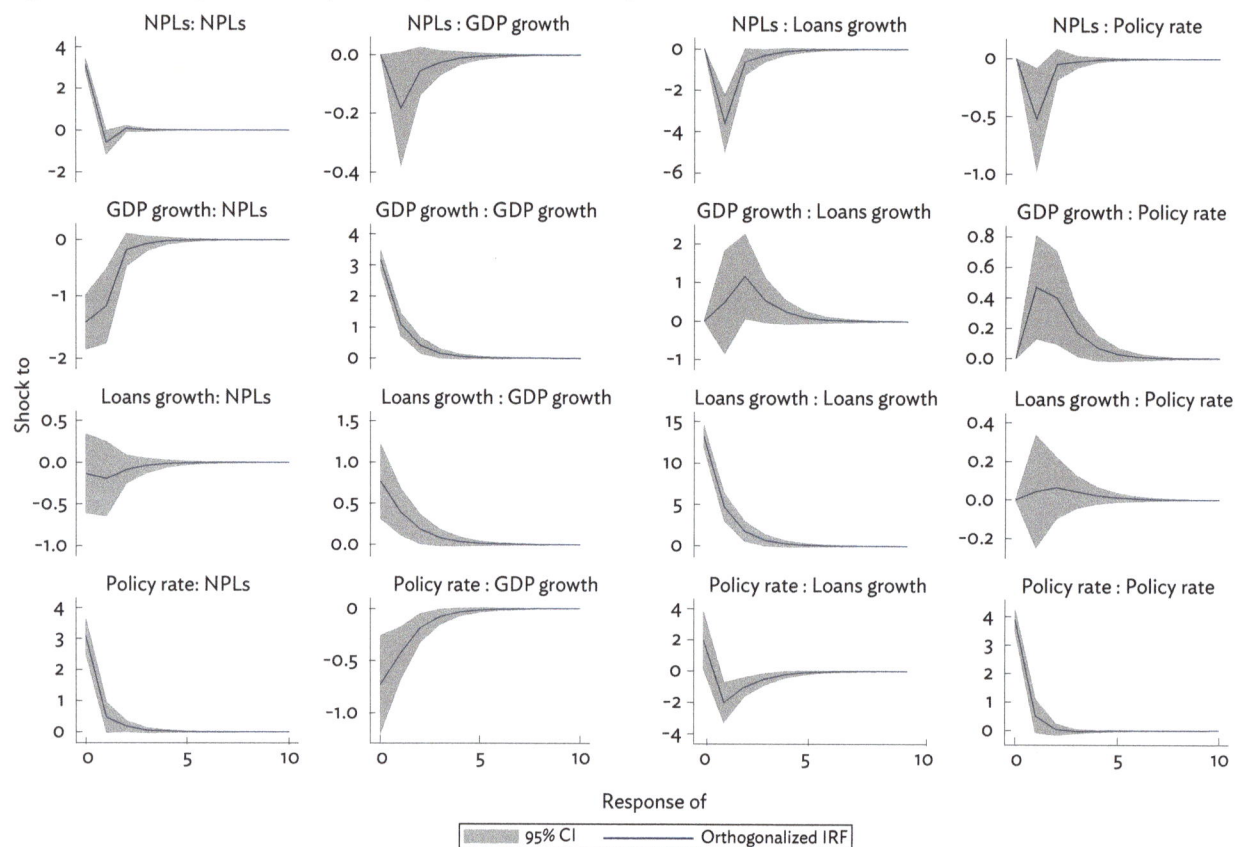

CI = confidence interval, GDP = gross domestic product, IRF = impulse response functions, NPLs = nonperforming loans. Responses are denoted in percentage points.
Note: 95% CI are generated by Monte Carlo draws with 5000 repetitions. Empirical results are derived using Stata 13.
Source: Lee and Rosenkranz (2017).

point decline in the loan growth rate, and about 0.21 percentage point rise in unemployment after 1 year.[57]

The macrofinancial impact of NPLs may spill over to other economies, transmitted through various channels.

In an increasingly integrated global financial system, financial shocks can be transmitted across borders with greater speed and frequency. The cross-border transmission of the impact of NPLs operates through various channels: (i) cross-border bank lending, (ii) changes in investor confidence, (iii) changes in bank asset (or liability) value due to financial market fluctuations, and (iv) a trade channel where lower growth in high NPL economies translates into lower import demand (Martin 2017, IMF 2015).

Recent experience in Europe demonstrates the negative impact of a large overhang of distressed assets weighing on domestic bank balance sheets is not confined to high-NPL economies, but can extend to the region as a whole.

The euro area's recent experience with distressed assets shows the systemic implications of NPLs and illustrates how NPL problems can spread across financially integrated markets. Largely as a legacy of the European sovereign debt crisis, the buildup and slow resolution of NPLs was exacerbated by (i) demand-and supply-side impediments,[58] (ii) structural and regulatory

---

[57] Over 3 years, a one percentage point shock to the in NPL ratio leads to a cumulative effect of about 0.1 percentage point contraction in the GDP growth rate, about 1.5 percentage point decline in loans growth, and about 0.1 percentage point pickup in unemployment after a year.

[58] These include, respectively, information asymmetry, inefficient and uncertain debt enforcement frameworks, licensing requirements, and restrictions on transferability of loans on the demand-side; and an unwillingness to realize losses, first-mover disadvantage, and the high cost of debt recovery not recognized in NPL book values on the supply side (Fell, Grodzicki, Martin, and O'Brien 2016; Martin 2017).

impediments (such as a lack of transnational supervisory structures in fiscal monitoring, bank supervision and resolution), and (iii) less-developed distressed asset markets in Europe compared with the US (to effectively and preemptively address the problem), among others. As the euro area experience shows, the negative impact of a high stock of distressed assets weighing on bank balance sheets is not confined to high-NPL economies, but can extend to the region as whole (see Martin 2017; Buckley, Avgouleas, and Arner 2017).

Through the various channels mentioned, increasing NPL levels could (i) negatively impact the flow of cross-border lending, (ii) damage market sentiment of the region as a whole, (iii) have negative wealth effects, and (iv) lead to a deterioration in affected countries' macroeconomic conditions, lowering import demand for others' exports (Martin 2017). The systemic implication of NPLs is a potential cause for concern.[59] One recent example in response includes policy discussions on a European blueprint for national asset management companies (AMCs).[60] In Asia—with ADB's support— the International Public Asset Management Company Forum (IPAF)[61] was established in 2013. IPAF members share knowledge and experience on how to best deal with distressed assets from both national and regional perspectives—with an emphasis on facilitating NPL markets as part of Asia's broader financial safety nets.

Broadly, the cross-border and systemic implication of NPLs underscores the need for policy makers to swiftly and effectively manage and respond to a buildup of distressed assets. The national and regional mechanisms underlying distressed asset resolution—in particular NPLs—are important for safeguarding financial stability. While it is critical to establish and strengthen national resolution mechanisms, regional cooperation can help advance more effective strategies for identifying and implementing national NPL resolution mechanisms and developing distressed asset markets.

Conclusions and Policy Considerations

Twenty years after the AFC, Asia stands strong—with more flexible exchange rates, healthier external and fiscal positions, stronger regulations, deeper capital markets, and better regional financial cooperation mechanisms.

However, despite these visible improvements, the region was severely (if briefly) affected by the GFC 10 years later. This highlights the need for the region to identify and address the gaps between existing policies stemming from lessons learned from the AFC and emerging challenges since the AFC.

This thematic chapter has sought to identify and analyze both existing and newly emerging challenges that pose potential risks to financial stability in developing Asia, and to discuss lessons drawn from past crises. These lessons are distilled and briefly summarized below, complemented by possible policy considerations.

Past financial crises highlighted financial sector weaknesses and served as the impetus for crisis-affected economies to undertake needed reforms.

The AFC showed how a financial crisis can undercut economic development and how currency and maturity mismatches can lead to the buildup of troubled assets and disrupt financial systems. In response to the crisis, badly affected economies such as Indonesia, the Philippines, the Republic of Korea, and Thailand, undertook a wide array of reforms (Table 8.6). These included: (i) strengthening financial supervision and macroprudential regulations to address NPLs and restore banking sector confidence, (ii) adopting measures to stem short-term capital outflows and raising interest rates to reduce investor flight, (iii) establishing more flexible exchange rate regimes, and (iv) instituting a broader set of reforms to restructure the banking sector and develop and deepen capital markets.

---

[59]   See presentation of Martin on 30 May 2017, http://k-learn.adb.org/system/files/materials/2017/05/201705-resolution-nonperforming-loans.pdf

[60]   See the 3 February 2017 speech by ECB Vice President Vítor Constâncio, https://www.ecb.europa.eu/press/key/date/2017/html/sp170203.en.html. See also ESRB (2017) and Fell, Grodzicki, Martin and O'Brien (2017).

[61]   See IPAF website: https://ipaf.adb.org/

Table 8.6 Selected National and Regional Policy Responses to the Asian Financial Crisis and the Global Financial Crisis

	Causes	Policy Responses	
		National	**Regional**
Asian Financial Crisis	• **Trigger event:** currency devaluation in Thailand • **Causes:** nature of foreign borrowing (currency and maturity mismatches), structural financial sector weaknesses, de-facto dollar pegs, region-wide loss of confidence that triggered capital flow reversals, the collapse of asset prices, putting bank and corporate balance sheets in disrepair.	• **Monetary policy:** Intervention in the foreign exchange market to defend currency and avoid sharp loss of confidence (INO, KOR, MAL, PHI); transition to more flexible exchange rate regimes; open market sales of Central Banks to sterilize capital inflows (KOR, MAL, THA) (2005–2008); raising of reserve requirements (INO [2004], KOR [2000, 2006]) • **Capital controls** to stem short-term capital flows (MAL [1998]), reserve requirements on foreign exchange transactions (THA [2006]), liberalization of resident outflows to counteract large capital inflows (KOR, MAL, PHI, THA, VIE) (2005–2007) • **Prudential policies:** caps on LTV ratio (HKG [2000–2001], KOR [2002–2006], PHI [2002], PRC [2004–2006], SIN [2005], THA [2003]); caps on DTI (HKG [2000], KOR [2005–2006], PRC [2004]); housing-related countercyclical capital requirements (IND [2004], KOR [2002], MAL [2005]); loan-loss provisioning (IND [2005–2006], KOR [2002], PHI [2000–2001]); consumer loan measures (THA [2004–2005]); limits to forward foreign currency contracts offered to nonresidents (INO [2001]); limits on net open currency position (KOR [2006]); limits to short-term borrowing by banks (INO [2005]) • **Other policy measures:** strengthening financial supervision and resolution mechanisms: measures/mechanisms to resolve nonperforming loans (via AMCs) (INO, KOR, MAL, PRC, THA); capital account liberalization (KOR)—lifting regulations on capital inflows (1998–1999), developing local foreign exchange market (2002), relaxing controls on overseas investments (2005, 2006)	• **ASEAN+3 Economic Review and Policy Dialogue (ERPD)** established in 2000 to support joint regional economic surveillance through peer review and policy dialogue. • Regional mechanism for liquidity support and crisis management **(ASEAN+3 Chiang Mai Initiative 2000])** • Local currency bond market development **(ASEAN+3 Asian Bond Markets Initiative [2002])** **Global** • International regulatory response: **Financial Stability Forum, Group of Twenty (G-20) FMM, Basel II**
Global Financial Crisis	• **Trigger event:** default of US subprime mortgages • **Causes:** Excessive borrowing and lending, poorly functioning credit markets, misaligned incentives, disconnect between regulatory structures and the financial system, international transmission of systemic risks	• **Monetary policy:** Foreign exchange market intervention to soften currency volatility (INO, KOR, MAL, PHI) (2008); increasing reserve requirements (INO, PHI, TAP, THA) • **Capital flow management measures and capital controls:** limits on net open positions of banks (INO, THA); minimum holding periods for foreign ownership of government bonds (INO [2010]); liberalization of resident outflows to counteract large capital inflows (KOR, MAL, PHI, THA, VIE) • **Macroprudential policies:** caps on LTV ratio (HKG [2009–2013], IND [2010, 2013], INO [2012–2013], KOR [2008–2012], MAL [2011], PRC [2007–2011], SIN [2010–2013], TAP [2010], THA [2009]); caps on DTI (HKG [2010–2013], KOR [2007–2012], SIN [2013], TAP [2010, 2014]); special stamp duty on properties sold (HKG [2010], SIN [2010]); restrictions on foreign exchange derivatives (KOR [2010]); withholding tax on foreign investor's interest income from bond investment (KOR [2011]); levy on noncore foreign currency liabilities to reduce capital flow volatility (KOR [2011]); housing-related countercyclical capital requirements (HKG [2013], IND [2010], MAL [2011], THA [2010–2012]); loan-loss provisioning (IND [2008–2010], PRC [2010]); consumer loan measures (INO [2012], SIN [2013], THA [2007]); countercyclical capital requirements (IND [2008], MAL [2011], PRC [2010]); minimum holding periods (INO [2010])	**Regional** • Regional mechanism for liquidity support and macroeconomic and financial surveillance **(Chiang Mai Initiative Multilateralisation [CMIM] [2010], ASEAN+3 Macroeconomic Research Office [2011])** **Global** • International regulatory response: **Financial Stability Board (FSB), G-20 and FSB post-crisis regulatory reforms, Basel III;** Introduction of resolution standards or structural and resolution legislation by G-20 and FSB

AMCs = asset management companies; DTI = debt to income; HKG = Hong Kong, China; IND = India; INO = Indonesia; KOR = Republic of Korea; LTV = loan to value; MAL = Malaysia; PHI = Philippines; PRC = People's Republic of China; SIN = Singapore; TAP = Taipei,China; THA = Thailand; VIE = Viet Nam.
Sources: ADB compilation based on Akinci and Olmstead-Rumsey (2015); Arner (2011); Buckley, Avgouleas, and Arner (2017); Lee, Asuncion, and Kim (2015); Lee, Gaspar, and Villaruel (2017); Lee (2016); and Villafuerte (2017).

The region's crisis experiences underscored the need for regional cooperation in risk identification, mitigation, and response.

Asian policy makers should remain vigilant and work collectively to enhance financial resilience and safeguard financial stability. The three financial disruptions led to tightened supervisory structures and augmented regulatory standards—such as higher levels of capital and liquidity reserves. Other financial reforms included an overhaul of banking governance and better risk management measures.

Regional responses to the AFC consisted of both bilateral and multilateral assistance to crisis-affected economies and the furthering of regional cooperation initiatives. Immediately following the crisis, leaders from ASEAN+3 held regional dialogues on the measures required to bolster stability of the region's financial systems. Several major regional initiatives were established to strengthen regional financial safety nets, enhance financial resilience, and develop capital markets in the region—including the ASEAN+3 Economic Review and Policy Dialogue, the ASEAN+3 CMI and its later Multilateralisation (CMIM), its associated ASEAN+3 Macroeconomic Research Office (AMRO), and the ASEAN+3 Asian Bond Markets Initiative (ABMI) (see Figure 8.15 for a chronological overview of Asia's financial integration initiatives).

While crisis responses noticeably improved macroeconomic and financial management in the region, emerging Asia continues to face significant long-term challenges that could undermine regional financial stability.

The analyses in the preceding sections provided an overview for various pockets of financial fragility facing the region. Against the backdrop of increasing financial interconnectedness and procyclicality of financial cycles, recent trends of: (i) rising private sector debt and deteriorating asset quality, (ii) continued heavy reliance on foreign currency (particularly US dollar-) denominated debt, and (iii) limited domestic capital market-based financial solutions are among those vulnerabilities that could potentially destabilize Asia's financial systems and hinder long-term economic development.

The empirical exercises conducted underscore the challenges to Asia's financial stability. There are several important findings: (i) over the past 20 years, Asian financial markets have grown more interconnected both

within the region and across the globe; (ii) growing financial interconnectedness can increase vulnerabilities to external shocks, financial contagion, or liquidity risks stemming from cross-border bank lending; (iii) continued high reliance on US dollar-denominated funding has significant implications for the transmission of global financial conditions to domestic financial and macroeconomic conditions; and (iv) a sustained increase in NPLs can lead to a reduction in credit supply and slowdown in overall economic activity.

Lessons drawn from the crises and the results of empirical analyses highlight the importance of enhancing financial market resilience to safeguard Asia's financial stability. This can only work through the interplay between adequate national policies/frameworks and efforts to continue and facilitate regional cooperation. In an increasingly interconnected global financial network, financial resilience cannot be achieved in isolation; it requires cross-border cooperation.

Maintaining sound macroeconomic fundamentals is a strong prerequisite for financial stability and resilience.

Sound macroeconomic conditions—healthy external and fiscal positions, exchange rate flexibility, a well-regulated and strong financial system, and adequate foreign exchange reserves—are central to financial resilience and economic growth. These also serve as a buffer against future crises and help soften the impact of external shocks. Targeted microprudential and macroprudential policies to curb financial excess are also needed to maintain financial stability and fiscal sustainability. Given the rapidly globalizing financial landscape, important considerations for prudential supervision include: (i) strengthening bank capacity to manage foreign currency liquidity risk—for example, through monitoring and implementing a foreign currency liquidity coverage ratio; (ii) consolidating supervision; (iii) ensuring adequate communication between central banks and other financial supervisors; and (iv) regulating SIFIs.

Figure 8.15: Asia's Financial Integration Initiatives—Chronology

AMRO = ASEAN+3 Macroeconomic Research Office, ASEAN = Association of Southeast Asian Nations.
Source: Park et al. (2017)

Asian policy makers need to further strengthen their national regulatory and supervisory frameworks, along with their institutional capacities.

Regulatory policy gaps and weaknesses in financial markets and systems leave room for excessive leverage and risk-taking—often through off-balance sheet activities—leading to the buildup of systemic risk. Thus, strengthening and broadening the scope of regulation and oversight is essential. While the AFC triggered the emergence of micro-prudential regulation—ensuring the safety and soundness of each significant financial institution in the system—the GFC highlighted the importance of a comprehensive macroprudential policy framework. The GFC exposed the possible

buildup of systemic risk stemming from SIFIs in tightly interconnected financial systems.

A key crisis lesson is the urgent need to strengthen macroprudential regulation and supervision in the region.

Authorities should consider establishing and implementing an effective macroprudential policy framework to address two dimensions of system-wide risks: (i) a buildup of a systemic risk over time (the "time dimension") and (ii) a spillover and contagion of risk across different financial sectors and systems (the "cross-sectional dimension"). Macroprudential policies can be useful in dampening the procyclicality of the financial system. Countercyclical provisions, capital and liquidity buffers, and balance sheet instruments such as leverage ratios, limits on debt-to-income and loan-to-value ratios are good examples.

Past crises have furthermore underscored the need for a foreign currency funding condition to macroprudential policies. As the AFC demonstrated, currency mismatches are a major source of risk. Given Asia's heavy reliance on US dollar-denominated debt, the region could augment existing macroprudential policy tools with, for example, a foreign currency liquidity coverage ratio. This policy tool could help the banking sector strengthen resilience against external shocks, especially during times of financial distress.

More developed and regionally integrated banking sectors and financial markets can improve the efficiency of resource allocation to the real economy.

Asia's funding limitations—due to insufficient capital market-based financing solutions and reliance on US dollar funding—suggests that its vast amounts of regional savings could be better channeled into more productive investments. For example, there is about $4.4 trillion invested in Asia's pension funds, $5.1 trillion with insurers, and several large social security and public pension reserve funds. Yet, potential investors must often restrain investments due to concerns over political risk, weak regulatory systems, the legal environment, governance standards, and undeveloped capital markets. More developed and regionally integrated banking and financial markets can improve the efficiency of resource allocation to the real economy.

While local currency bonds outstanding in ASEAN+3 increased threefold—from $6.6 trillion in 2002 to $19.8 trillion by the end of 2016—challenges remain. To meet the region's financing needs, local currency bond markets must improve market efficiency, broaden their investor base, deepen secondary markets, and integrate more regionally. Developing local currency bond markets will also help diversify funding sources, reduce concentrated funding risks, and provide long-term finance opportunities for investors—vital for financing long-term infrastructure projects. Regional efforts like the ABMI continue to help promote the development of regional capital markets, which can help avoid maturity and currency mismatches.

Strengthening policy dialogue and cooperation both globally and regionally is essential for enhancing Asia's financial resilience.

Asia's financial markets are increasingly open, interconnected, and vulnerable to external shocks. Approaching the challenges from a regional perspective helps build financial resilience. For example, a regional cooperation mechanism on macroprudential policy frameworks could be valuable for safeguarding financial stability in the region. Existing high-level policy forums—such as ASEAN, ASEAN+3, or the Asia-Pacific Economic Cooperation forums—are useful venues for regional dialogue. Strengthening the CMIM and its AMRO surveillance unit should also be considered to help monitor potential liquidity risks and slow the spread of shocks across the region's economies.

Several options can be considered to strengthen the CMIM and AMRO to bolster financial safety nets: (i) the CMIM's operability needs to be enhanced and clearly communicated to members; (ii) current callable capital can be complemented by paid-in capital to improve market sentiment over members' CMIM commitments; (iii) paid-in capital could be further leveraged by issuing bonds, thereby increasing CMIM capacity and enabling it to respond to financial crises affecting the region's larger economies; (iv) increased capacity could also offer scope for widening the CMIM's mandate—in particular, CMIM resources could be utilized to recapitalize systemically important banks in the region; and (v) strengthening AMRO's role as regional macroeconomic surveillance unit and enhancing CMIM efficacy by increasing the IMF de-linked portion can be considered.

Regional cooperation to develop effective resolution mechanisms for distressed assets of cross-border financial institutions is an important part of broader financial safety net arrangements.

With greater financial integration, banks increasingly operate internationally. Growing regional banking activities and institutions—possibly of systemic importance—underpin the need to discuss regional regulatory cooperation, including resolution mechanisms for interconnected regional banks—such as Qualified Asian Banks. In this highly interconnected environment, the failure of a single regional bank could have a considerable negative impact on economies in emerging Asia. Measures that identify and effectively deal with vulnerabilities in SIFIs would thus be key to reducing systemic risk and their associated moral hazards. Regional cooperation to develop effective resolution mechanisms for distressed assets of cross-border financial institutions can also complement national efforts to address NPLs efficiently and sustainably. In addition, developing both distressed asset markets and market infrastructure nationally can deepen financial markets and enhance market resilience, thereby contributing to strengthening multilayered financial safety nets.

Supervisory colleges for regionally active foreign banks can be an effective regional cooperation tool to strengthen cross-border supervision in Asia.

As highlighted above, the systemic importance of foreign banks in Asia is growing. Stable funding through foreign bank credit supply channels to a host economy remains a key issue for financial stability. Supervisory colleges for regionally active foreign banks can be an effective regional cooperation tool to strengthen cross-border supervision in Asia. They can enhance understanding and oversight of the sources and transmission channels of systemic risks and shocks.

Continued improvement of Asia's financial market infrastructure by establishing cross-border collateral arrangements could strengthen the region's multilayer financial safety nets and bolster financial market development.

Appropriate risk mitigation measures and multilayer regional financial safety nets are needed to adequately respond to heightened cross-border banking activity. In particular, cross-border collateral arrangements are needed to supply regional banks with liquidity from their home central banks by pledging assets held by branches in another economy. These measures have been discussed by the Cross-Border Settlement Infrastructure Forum under ASEAN+3. Proposals have been raised concerning the establishment of linkages among central securities depositories (CSD) and central banks (CSD-

RTGS[62] Linkages) in the region. CSD-RTGS Linkages are expected to support the routinization of cross-border collateral arrangements and the efficient use of the region's high-quality government bonds as collateral. This will help reduce local currency liquidity risks among cross-border banks in the region and develop local currency bond markets, thereby promoting the region's financial development and resilience (see Box 4.1, page 47).

Background Papers

R.P. Buckley, E. Avgouleas, and D.W. Arner. 2017. Twenty Years of International Financial Crises: What Have We Learned and What Still Needs to Be Done? Background paper for Asian Economic Integration Report 2017 Theme Chapter on "The Era of Financial Interconnectedness: How Can Asia Strengthen Financial Resilience?" Manuscript.

S. Claessens. 2017. Financial Cycles and Crises in Asia. Background paper for Asian Economic Integration Report 2017 Theme Chapter on "The Era of Financial Interconnectedness: How Can Asia Strengthen Financial Resilience?" Manuscript.

M. Dungey, B. Chowdhury, M. Kangogo, M.A. Sayeed, and V. Volkov. 2017a. The Changing Network of Financial Market Linkages: The Asian Experience. Background paper for Asian Economic Integration Report 2017 Theme Chapter on "The Era of Financial Interconnectedness: How Can Asia Strengthen Financial Resilience?" Manuscript.

J. Lee and P. Rosenkranz. 2017. Nonperforming Loans in Asia: Determinants and Macro Financial Linkages. Background paper for Asian Economic Integration Report 2017 Theme Chapter on "The Era of Financial Interconnectedness: How Can Asia Strengthen Financial Resilience?" Manuscript.

C.Y. Park and K. Shin. 2017. A Contagion through Exposure to Foreign Banks during the Global Financial Crisis. *ADB Economics Working Paper.*No. 516. Manila: Asian Development Bank.

---

[62] A "CSD-RTGS Linkage" connects national CSDs and real time gross settlement (RTGS) systems operated by central banks.

J. Villafuerte. 2017. Managing Capital Flows to Emerging Asia. Background paper for Asian Economic Integration Report 2017 Theme Chapter on "The Era of Financial Interconnectedness: How Can Asia Strengthen Financial Resilience?" Manuscript.

References

M.R.M. Abrigo and I. Love. 2015. Estimation of Panel Vector Autoregression in Stata: A Package of Programs. http:// paneldataconference2015.ceu.hu/Program/ MichaelAbrigo.pdf

ADB. 2014. *Asian Economic Integration Monitor April2014*. Manila.

———. Climate Change Resilience in Asia's Cities (infographic). https://www.adb.org/news/infographics/ climate-change-resilience-asias-cities

O. Akinci and J. Olmstead-Rumsey. 2015. How Effective are Macroprudential Policies? An Empirical Investigation. *International Finance Discussion Papers*. No. 1136. Washington, DC: Board of Governors of the Federal Reserve System.

N. Ananchotikul, S. Piao, and E. Zoli. 2015. Drivers of Financial Integration—Implications for Asia. *IMF Working Papers*. No. 15/160. Washington, DC: International Monetary Fund.

T. Anderson and C. Hsiao. 1982. Formulation and Estimation of Dynamic Models Using Panel Data. *Journal of Econometrics*. 18 (1). pp. 47–82.

D.W.K. Andrews and B. Lu. 2001. Consistent Model and Moment Selection Procedures for GMM Estimation with Application to Dynamic Panel Data Models. *Journal of Econometrics*. 101 (1). pp. 123-164.

D.W. Arner. 2009. The Global Credit Crisis of 2008: Causes, Consequences, and Implications for International Finance. *The International Lawyer*. 43 (91).pp. 91-136.

———. 2011. Adaptation and Resilience in Global Financial Regulation. *North Carolina Law Review*. 109 (89).pp. 1579-1627.

D.W. Arner, E. Avgouleas, and E.C. Gibson. 2017. Overstating Moral Hazard: Lessons from Two Decades of Financial Crises. *University of Hong Kong Faculty of Law Research Paper*. No. 2017/003. Hong Kong, China: University of Hong Kong.

S. Arslanalp, W. Liao, S. Piao, and D. Seneviratne. 2016. [People's Republic of] China's Growing Influence on Asian Financial Markets. *IMF Working Paper*. No. 15/173. Washington, DC: International Monetary Fund.

E. Avgouleas. 2012. *Governance of Global Financial Markets: The Law, the Economics, the Politics*. UK: Cambridge University Press.

Bank for International Settlements. 2016. *BIS Statistical Bulletin*. Basel.

K. Beaton, A. Myrvoda, S. Thompson. 2016. Nonperforming Loans in the ECCU: Determinants and Macroeconomic Impact. *IMF Working Paper*. No. 15/229. Washington, DC: International Monetary Fund.

R. Beck, P. Jakubik, and A. Piloiu. 2013. Nonperforming Loans: What Matters in Addition to the Economic Cycle? *European Central Bank Working Paper*. No. 1515. Frankfurt: European Central Bank.

S. Bhattarai, A. Chatterjee, and W.Y. Park. 2015. Effects of US Quantitative Easing on Emerging Market Economies. *Federal Reserve Bank of Dallas Globalization and Monetary Policy Institute Working Paper*. No. 255. Dallas: Federal Reserve Bank of Dallas.

M. Billio, M. Getmansky, A.W. Lo, and L. Pelizzon. 2012. Econometric Measures of Connectedness and Systemic Risk in the Finance and Insurance Sectors. *Journal of Financial Economics*. 104 (3). pp. 535-559.

O. Blanchard, R. Rajan, K. Rogoff, and L. H. Summers, eds. 2016. *Progress and Confusion: The State of Macroeconomic Policy*. Cambridge, MA: MIT Press.

C. Borio and P. Lowe. 2002. Assessing the Risk of Banking Crises. *BIS Quarterly Review*. December. pp. 43-54. Basel.

E. Cerutti, S. Claessens, and D. Puy. 2015. Push Factors and Capital Flows to Emerging Markets: Why Knowing Your Lender Matters More Than Fundamentals. *IMF Working Paper*. No. 15/127. Washington, DC: International Monetary Fund.

R. Chang and A. Velasco. 2001. A Model of Financial Crises in Emerging Markets. *The Quarterly Journal of Economics*. 116 (2). pp. 489-517.

Q. Chen, A. Filardo, D. He and F. Zhu. 2011. International Spillovers of Central Bank Balance Sheet Policies. Contributed paper for the Joint Bank of Thailand and the Bank for International Settlements Conference on "Central bank balance sheets in Asia and the Pacific: the policy challenges ahead". Chiang Mai. 12-13 December.

M. Čihák, S. Muñoz, and R. Scuzzarella. 2011. The Bright and the Dark Side of Cross-Border Banking Linkages. *IMF Working Paper*. No. 11/186. Washington, DC: International Monetary Fund.

S. Claessens, M.A. Kose, and M. Terrones. 2011. How Do Business and Financial Cycles Interact? *Journal of International Economics*. 87 (1). pp.178–90.

J.C. Cuaresma and T. Slacík. 2007. On the Determinants of Currency Crises: The Role of Model Uncertainty. *Working Papers in Economics and Statistics*. No. 2008-03. Innsbruck: University of Innsbruck.

R.D. De Bock and A. Demyanets. 2012. Bank Asset Quality in Emerging Markets: Determinants and Spillovers. *IMF Working Paper*. No. 12/71.Washington, DC: International Monetary Fund.

P. De Grauwe. 2011. The Governance of a Fragile Eurozone. *CEPS Working Document*. No. 346. Brussels: Centre for European Policy Studies.

D.W. Diamond and P.H. Dybvig. 1983. Bank Runs, Deposit Insurance, and Liquidity. *Journal of Political Economy*. 91 (3). pp. 401-419.

F.X. Diebold and K. Yilmaz. 2009. Measuring Financial Asset Return and Volatility Spillovers, with Application to Global Equity Markets. *The Economic Journal*. 119 (534). pp. 158-171.

————. 2014. On the Network Topology of Variance Decompositions: Measuring the Connectedness of Financial Firms. *Journal of Econometrics*. 182 (1). pp. 119-134.

M.H. Dungey, R. Fry, and V.L. Martin. 2006. Correlation Contagion, and Asian evidence. *Asian Economic Papers*. 5 (2). pp. 32-72.

M.H. Dungey, G. Milunovich, S. Thorp, and M. Yang. 2015. Endogenous Crisis Dating and Contagion Using Smooth Transition Structural GARCH. *Journal of Banking and Finance*. 58. pp. 71-79.

M.H. Dungey, D.J. Harvey, and V. Volkov. 2017b. The Changing International Network of Sovereign Debt and Financial Institutions. *Discussion Paper Series*. No. 2017-04. Hobart, TAS: University of Tasmania.

B. Eichengreen and P. Gupta. 2015. Tapering Talk: The Impact of Expectations of Reduced Federal Reserve Security Purchases on Emerging Markets. *Emerging Markets Review*. 25 (C). pp. 1–15.

R. Espinoza and A. Prasad. 2010. Nonperforming Loans in the GCC Banking System and their Macroeconomic Effects. *IMF Working Paper*. No. 10/224. Washington, DC: International Monetary Fund.

G.B. Estrada, M. Noland, D. Park, and A. Ramayandi. 2015. Financing Asia's Growth. *ADB Economics Working Paper*. No. 438. Manila: Asian Development Bank.

European Systemic Risk Board. 2017. Resolving Nonperforming Loans in Europe. *ESRB Reports*. No. 2017. Frankfurt: European Systemic Risk Board.

J. Fell, M. Grodzicki, R. Martin, E. O'Brien. 2016. Addressing Market Failures in the Resolution of Nonperforming Loans in the euro area. *Financial Stability Review November 2016*. Frankfurt: European Central Bank.

J. Fell, M. Grodzicki, R. Martin, and E. O'Brien. 2017. A Role for Systemic Asset Management Companies in Solving Europe's Nonperforming Loan Problems. *European Economy: Banks, Regulation, and the Real Sector*. pp. 71-85.

Financial Stability Board. 2015. *Global Shadow Banking Monitoring Report 2015*. Basel.

Financial Stability Board. 2017. *Global Shadow Banking Monitoring Report 2016*. Basel.

J. M. Fleming. 1962. Domestic Financial Policies under Fixed and under Floating Exchange Rates. *IMF Staff Papers*. 9 (3). pp. 369-380.

Financial Times. 2017. New Delhi Under Pressure for Bolder Action on Bad Loan Malaise. 15 May.

R.P. Flood and P.M. Garber. 1984. Collapsing Exchange-rate Regimes: Some Linear Examples. *Journal of International Economics*. 17 (1-2). pp. 1-13.

A.R. Ghosh, M.S. Qureshi, N. Sugawara. 2014. Regulating Capital Flows at Both Ends: Does It Work? *IMF Working Paper*. No. 14/188.Washington, DC: International Monetary Fund.

M. Goswami and S. Sharma. 2011. The Development of Local Debt Markets in Asia. *IMF Working Paper*. No. 11/132. Washington, DC: International Monetary Fund.

J.H. Hahm, H.S. Shin, and K. Shin. 2013. Noncore Bank Liabilities and Financial Vulnerability. *Journal of Money, Credit, and Banking*. 45 (1). pp. 3–36.

B. Hoffmann, I. Shim, and H.S. Shin. 2017. Sovereign Yields and the Risk-taking Channel of Currency Appreciation. *BIS Working Papers*. No. 538. Basel: Bank for International Settlements.

International Monetary Fund. 2015. *Regional Economic Outlook: Asia and the Pacific – Stabilizing and Outperforming Other Regions.* Washington, DC.

G.L. Kaminsky and C.M. Reinhart. 1999. The Twin Crises: The Causes of Banking and Balance-of-Payments Problems. *American Economic Review*. 89 (3). pp. 473-500.

J.I. Kim. 2014. The International Transmission of Monetary Policy: [Republic of] Korea's Experience. Contributed paper for the Bank for International Settlements Meeting of Senior Officials from Central Banks on the Transmission of Unconventional Monetary Policy to the Emerging Markets. Basel. 6-7 March.

N. Klein. 2013. Nonperforming Loans in CESEE: Determinants and Impact on MacroeconomicPerformance. *IMF Working Paper*. No. 13/72. Washington, DC: International Monetary Fund.

P. Krugman. 1979. A Model of Balance-of-Payments Crises. *Journal of Money, Credit and Banking*. 11(3). pp. 311-325.

_____. 1999. Balance Sheets, the Transfer Problem, and Financial Crises. *International Tax and Public Finance* . 6 (4). pp 459–472.

M. Lee, R.C. Asuncion, J. Kim. 2015. Effectiveness of Macroprudential Policies in Developing Asia: An Empirical Analysis. *ADB Economics Working Paper*. No. 439. Manila: Asian Development Bank.

J.J. Lim, S. Mohapatra, and M. Stocker. 2014. Tinker, Taper, QE, Bye? The Effect of Quantitative Easing on Financial Flows to Developing Countries. *Policy Research Working Paper*. No. 6820. Washington, DC: World Bank.

V. Makri, A. Tsagkanos, and A. Bellas. 2014. Determinants of Nonperforming Loans: The Case of Eurozone. *Paneconomicus*. 2. pp. 193-206.

R. Martin. 2017. The Resolution of Nonperforming Loans. Presentation at the International Public Asset Management Company Forum Research Dissemination Workshop. Manila. 30 May.

A. Mian, A. Sufi, E. Verner. 2017. Household Debt and Business Cycles Worldwide. *The Quarterly Journal of Economics*. 132 (4). pp. 1755–1817.

S. Morris and H.S. Shin. 1998. Unique Equilibrium in a Model of Self-Fulfilling Currency Attacks. *American Economic Review*. 88 (3). pp. 587-597.

R.A. Mundell. 1963. Capital Mobility and Stabilization Policy under Fixed and Flexible Exchange Rates. *The Canadian Journal of Economics and Political Science*. 29 (4). pp. 475-485.

M. Nkusu. 2011. Nonperforming Loans and Macrofinancial Vulnerabilities in Advanced Economies. *IMF Working Paper*. No. 11/161. Washington, DC: International Monetary Fund.

M. Obstfeld. 1994. The Logic of Currency Crises. *NBER Working Paper*. No. 4640. Cambridge, MA: National Bureau of Economic Research.

_____. 1996. Models of Currency Crises with Self-Fulfilling Features. *European Economic Review*. 40. pp.1037-1047.

C.Y. Park. 2017. Decoupling Asia Revisited. *ADB Economics Working Paper*. No. 506. Manila: Asian Development Bank.

C.Y. Park, J. Lee, J. Villafuerte, and P. Rosenkranz. 2017. 20 Years after the Asian Financial Crisis: Lessons Learned and Future Challenges. *ADB Briefs*. No. 85. Manila: Asian Development Bank.

D. Park, A. Ramayandi, and K. Shin. 2016. Capital Flows During Quantitative Easing and Aftermath: Experiences of Asian Countries. *Emerging Markets Finance and Trade*. 52 (4). pp. 886–903.

M. Pesaran and C. Yang. 2016. Econometric Analysis of Production Networks with Dominant Units. *CESifo Working Paper*. No. 6141. Munich:CESifo Group Munich.

J. Lee. 2016. Recent Developments in Capital Flows and Policy Challenges. Presentation at the ADB-BSP Inception Workshop. Manila. 12 April.

C.M. Reinhart. Dates for Banking Crises, Currency Crashes, Sovereign Domestic or External Default (or Restructuring), Inflation Crises, and Stock Market Crashes (Varieties). http://www.carmenreinhart.com/data/browse-by-topic/ topics/7/ (accessed July 2016).

C.M. Reinhart and V. R. Reinhart. 2009. Capital Flow Bonanzas: An Encompassing View of the Past and Present. *NBER Working Paper Series.* No. 14321. Cambridge, MA: National Bureau of Economic Research.

E. Remolona and I. Shim. 2015. The Rise of Regional Banking in Asia and the Pacific. *BIS Quarterly Review.* September 2015. pp. 119-134.

V. Constâncio. 2017. Resolving Europe's NPL Burden: Challenges and Benefits. Speech at Bruegel's event on "Tackling Europe's Nonperforming Loans Crisis: Restructuring Debt, Reviving Growth". Brussels. 3 February.

H. Rey. 2013. Dilemma not Trilemma: The Global Financial Cycle and Monetary Policy Independence. In Proceedings of the 2013 Federal Reserve Bank of Kansas City Economic Symposium at Jackson Hole. pp. 285-333.

P.L. Shimpalee and J.B. Breuer. 2006. Currency Crises and Institutions. *Journal of International Money and Finance.* 25 (1). pp. 125-145.

H.S. Shin. 2009. Reflections on Northern Rock: The Bank Run that Heralded the Global Financial Crisis. *Journal of Economic Perspectives.* 23 (1). pp. 101–119.

C. Shu, D. He, J. Dong, and H. Wang. 2016. Regional Pull vs. Global Push Factors: China and US Influence on AsiaPacific Financial Markets. *BIS Working Papers.* No. 579. Basel: Bank for International Settlements.

K. Slowikowski. 2016. ggrepel: Repulsive Text and Label Geoms for 'ggplot2'. R package version 0.6.5. https://CRAN.R-project.org/package=ggrepel.

S. Sugisaki. 1998. Economic Crises in Asia. Address at the 1998 Harvard Asia Business Conference, Harvard Business School. Cambridge, MA. 30 January.

A. Swiston and T. Bayoumi. 2008. Spillovers across NAFTA. *IMF Working Paper.* No. 08/3. Washington, DC: International Monetary Fund.

A.M. Taylor. 2015. Credit, Financial Stability, and the Macroeconomy. *Annual Review of Economics.* 7 (1). pp. 309- 339.

H. Wickham. 2009. *ggplot2: Elegant Graphics for Data Analysis.* New York: Springer-Verlag.

World Bank. 1998. *Global Development Finance 1998: Analysis and Summary Tables.* Washington, DC.

Annex

Annex 8.1: Chronology of Financial Crises, Theories, and Policy Advice

Financial crises can be classified into three main types. The first, sovereign debt crises, are rooted in the inability to repay sovereign (or government) debt owed to foreign creditors. Examples include the Latin American debt crisis of the early 1980s or the more recent debt crises in Europe, particularly Greece, which started toward the end of 2009, intensifying in 2010. The second, balance of payments (or currency) crises, occur due to an unsustainable balance of payments deficit with a drop in foreign exchange reserves—often followed by devaluation in a fixed exchange rate regime. Examples include India's 1991 currency crisis, Mexico's Tequila crisis in 1994, and the 1997/98 Asian financial crisis (AFC). The last type, banking crises, emerge more frequently and are due to bank runs and panics that affect banking activity. The most prominent examples include the United States savings and loan crisis in the 1980s and 1990s, the AFC and 1998 banking crisis in the Russian Federation.

Theories of currency crises fall under four generations, and highlight respectively weak macrofundamentals, self-fulfilling expectations, structural imbalances, and institutional factors. First generation models of currency crises are motivated by a series of events where fixed exchange rate regimes collapsed following speculative attacks—as occurred during the breakdown of the Bretton Wood global system in the early 1970s or the Latin American debt crisis in the 1980s. These crises were often preceded by excessive credit expansions, ongoing fiscal deficits, rising debt levels, or falling reserves as governments tried to maintain a fixed exchange rate regime. Seminal authors include Krugman

(1979) and Flood and Garber (1984), who introduced a "shadow floating exchange rate" to extend the basic model by Krugman.

Second generation models were pioneered by Obstfeld (1994, 1996) following the collapse of the European Exchange Rate Mechanism in the early 1990s. These crises followed from speculative attacks and self-fulfilling expectations in multiple equilibria—as speculators forced the government to abandon an existing fixed-exchange rate regime by attacking its foreign currency reserves—maintaining the fixed exchange rate becomes too costly. Extensions of this model were undertaken by Morris and Shin (1998) and De Grauwe (2011).

While the first and second generation currency crisis literature focused on the government alone, third generation models connect currency crises to models of banking crises and credit friction. The AFC largely motivated this generation of models, spurring extensive research on how the rapid deterioration of balance sheets from asset price fluctuations (or banking crises) can precipitate currency crises—hence "twin crises" (Kaminsky and Reinhart 1999). A clear feature of these crises is the combination of a collapse of fixed exchange rate regimes, capital flow reversals, bankruptcies of financial institutions, and credit crunches. Relevant references include Krugman (1999), who models balance sheet effects of devaluation due to a currency mismatch; and Chang and Velasco (2001), who consider

double mismatches of currency and liquidity exposures as per the Diamond and Dybvig (1983) bank run model.

In the fourth generation of models, currency crises are said to be defined by institutional factors (Cuaresma and Slacík 2007, Shimpalee and Breuer 2006). The models identify features of the institutional environment that set the stage for the buildup of macroeconomic imbalances, which subsequently give rise to crises. They also highlight the roles of rule of law and contract enforcement, protection of shareholder and creditor rights, regulatory frameworks, and the socioeconomic environment.

Policy responses are largely a function of crisis type. Measures to respond to sovereign debt crises include debt restructuring and relief initiatives involving refinancing and rescheduling, debt reduction, and debt conversion. Balance of payments or currency crisis responses include the adoption of flexible exchange rates, creation of foreign reserve buffers, and currency swap arrangements. Policy pronouncements following banking crises have included capital adequacy ratios (Basel I, 1988), prudential regulation and supervision (Basel II, 2004), and systemic risk and macroprudential policies (Basel III, 2010).

A summary of financial crises including a timeline along with the corresponding financial theories and policy advice is illustrated in Figure 8A.1.

Figure 8A.1: Chronology of Financial Crises, Theories, and Policy Advice

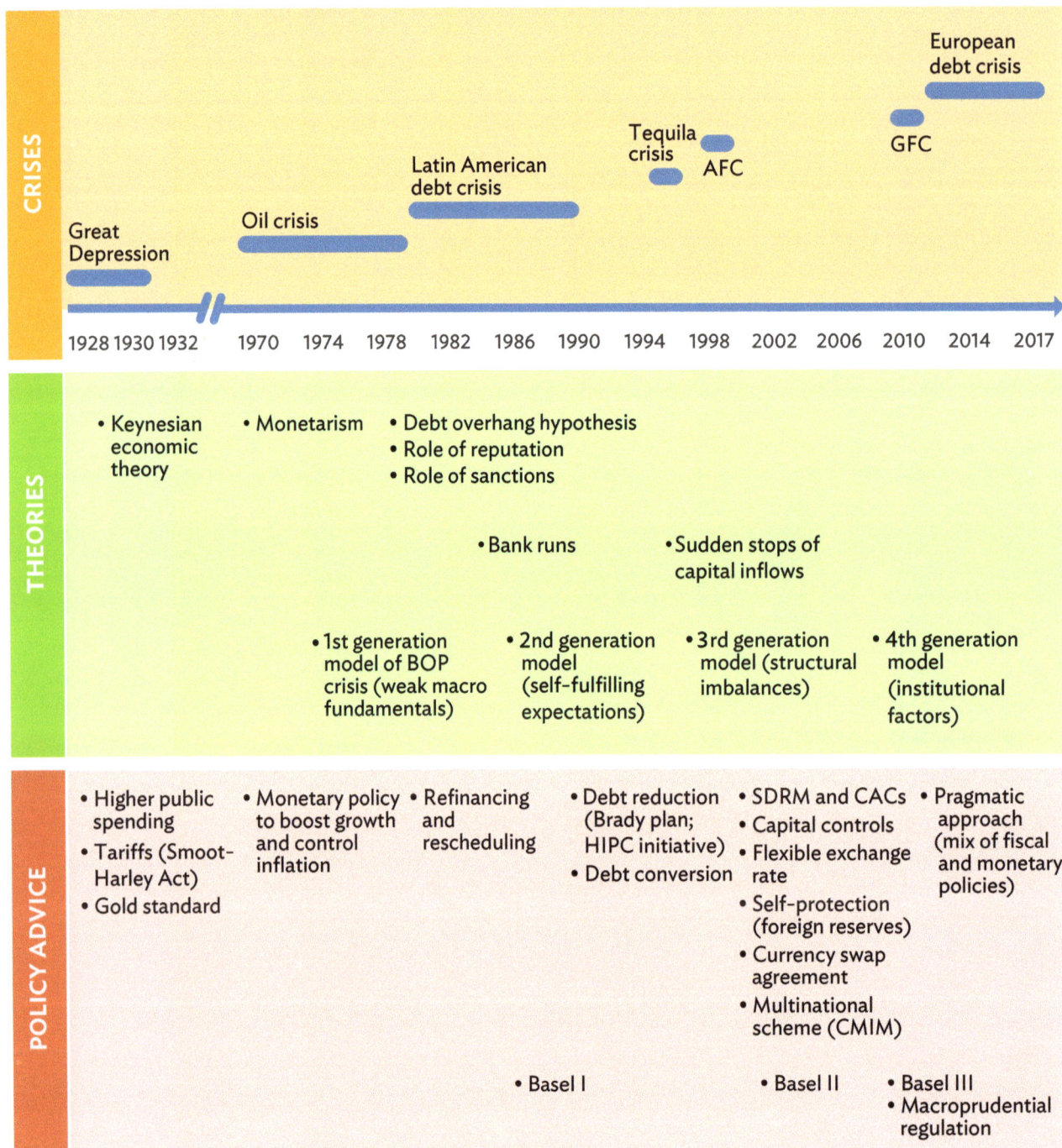

AFC = Asian financial crisis, BOP = balance of payments, CACs = collective action clauses, CMIM = Chiang Mai Initiative Multilateralisation, GFC = global financial crisis, HIPC = heavily indebted poor countries, SDRM = sovereign debt restructuring mechanism.
Source: Park et al. (2017)

09

Statistical Appendix

Statistical Appendix

The statistical appendix is comprised of 11 tables that present selected indicators on economic integration covering the 48 regional members of the Asian Development Bank (ADB). The succeeding notes describe the country groupings and the calculation procedures undertaken.

Regional Groupings

- Asia consists of the 48 regional members of ADB.
- Developing Asia refers to Asia excluding Australia, Japan, and New Zealand.
- European Union (EU-28) consists of Austria, Belgium, Bulgaria, Croatia, Cyprus, Czech Republic, Denmark, Estonia, Finland, France, Germany, Greece, Hungary, Ireland, Italy, Latvia, Lithuania, Luxembourg, Malta, the Netherlands, Poland, Portugal, Romania, Slovak Republic, Slovenia, Spain, Sweden, and the United Kingdom.

Table Descriptions

Table A1: Regional Integration Indicators—Asia (% of total)

The table provides a summary of regional integration indicators for three areas: trade and investment, capital (equity and bond holdings), and people movement (migration, remittances and tourism); and for Asian subregions, including ASEAN+3 (including Hong Kong, China). Cross-border flows within and across subregions are shown as well as total flows with Asia and the rest of the world. The definition of each indicators are provided in the description below.

Table A2: Trade Share—Asia (% of total trade)

It is calculated as $(t_{ij}/T_{iw})*100$, where t_{ij} is the total trade of economy "i" with economy "j" and T_{iw} is the total trade of economy "i" with the world. A higher share indicates a higher degree of regional trade integration.

Table A3: FTA Status—Asia

It is the number and status of bilateral and plurilateral free trade agreements (FTA) with at least one of the Asian economies as signatory. FTAs only proposed are excluded. It covers FTAs with the following status: Framework Agreement signed—the parties initially negotiate the contents of a framework agreement, which serves as a framework for future negotiations; Negotiations launched—the parties, through the relevant ministries, declare the official launch of negotiations or set the date for such, or start the first round of negotiations; Signed but not yet in effect—parties sign the agreement after negotiations have been completed, however, the agreement has yet to be implemented; and Signed and in effect—provisions of FTA come into force, after legislative or executive ratification.

Table A4: Time to Export and Import—Asia (number of hours)

Time to export (import) data measures the number of hours required to export (import) by ocean transport, including the processing of documents required to complete the transaction. It covers time used for documentation requirements and procedures at customs and other regulatory agencies as well as the time of inland transport between the largest business city and the main port used by traders. Regional aggregates are weighted averages based on total exports or imports.

Table A5: Logistics Performance Index—Asia (% to EU)

Logistics Performance Index scores are based on the following dimensions: (i) efficiency of border control and customs process; (ii) transport and trade-related infrastructure; (iii) competitively priced shipments;

(iv) ability to track and trace consignments; and (v) timeliness of shipments. Regional aggregates are computed using total trade as weights. A score above (below) 100 means that it is easier (more difficult) to export or import from that economy compared to EU.

Table A6: Cross-Border Portfolio Equity Holdings Share—Asia (% of total cross-border equity holdings)

It is calculated as $(E_{ij}/E_{iw})*100$ where E_{ij} is the holding of economy "i" of the equity securities issued by economy "j" and E_{iw} is the holding of economy "i" of the equity securities issued by all economies except those issued in the domestic market. Calculations are based solely on available data in the Coordinated Portfolio Investment Survey (CPIS) database of the International Monetary Fund (IMF). Rest of the world includes equity securities issued by international organizations defined in the CPIS database and "not specified (including confidential) category". A higher share indicates a higher degree of regional integration.

Table A7: Cross-Border Portfolio Debt Holdings Share—Asia (% of total cross-border debt holdings)

It is calculated as $(D_{ij}/D_{iw})*100$ where D_{ij} is the holding of economy "i" of the debt securities issued by partner "j" and D_{iw} is the holding of economy "i" of the debt securities issued by all economies except those issued in the domestic market. Calculations are based solely on available data in the CPIS database of the IMF. ROW includes debt securities issued by international organizations defined in the CPIS database and "not specified (including confidential) category". A higher share indicates a higher degree of regional integration.

Table A8: FDI Inflow Share—Asia (% of total FDI inflows)

It is calculated as $(F_{ij}/F_{iw})*100$ where F_{ij} is the foreign direct investment (FDI) received by economy "i" from economy "j" and F_{iw} is the FDI received by economy "i" from the world. Figures are based on net FDI inflow data. A higher share indicates a higher degree of regional integration. The bilateral FDI database was constructed using data from the United Nations Conference on Trade and Development (UNCTAD), ASEAN Secretariat, Eurostat, Organisation for Economic Co-operation and

Development, and national sources. For countries with missing data from 2013 to 2016, the bilateral flows were estimated as follows: For each economy "i", the GDP share of the FDI received from economy "j" is computed using the latest data point available. This share is then multiplied to the GDP of economy "i" to get the annual amount of FDI inflow from country "j" for each year up to 2016. For 2015 and 2016, the Republic of Korea's bilateral FDI inflows were estimated using the share of each partner "j" in the Ministry of Trade, Industry and Energy's FDI arrival database. But for FDI inflow from the People's Republic of China and the US, actual net FDI inflows from Bank of Korea from 2014 to 2016 were used.

Table A9: Remittance Inflows Share—Asia (% of total remittance inflows)

It is calculated as $(R_{ij}/R_{iw})*100$ where R_{ij} is the remittance received by economy "i" from partner "j" and R_{iw} is the remittance received by economy "i" from the world. Remittances refer to the sum of the following: (i) workers' remittances which are recorded as current transfers under the current account of the IMF's Balance of Payments (BOP); (ii) compensation of employees which includes wages, salaries, and other benefits of border, seasonal, and other nonresident workers and which are recorded under the "income" subcategory of the current account; and (iii) migrants' transfers which are reported under capital transfers in the BOP's capital account. Transfers through informal channels are excluded.

Table A10: Outbound Migration Share—Asia (% of total outbound migrants)

It is calculated as $(M_{ij}/M_{iw})*100$ where M_{ij} is the number migrants of economy "i" residing in economy "j" and M_{iw} is the number of all migrants of economy "i" residing overseas. This definition excludes those traveling abroad on a temporary basis. A higher share indicates a higher degree of regional integration.

Table A11: Outbound Tourism Share—Asia (% of total outbound tourists)

It is calculated as $(TR_{ij}/TR_{iw})*100$ where TR_{ij} is the number of nationals of economy "i" traveling as tourists in economy "j" and TR_{iw} is the total number of nationals of economy "i" traveling as tourists overseas. A higher share indicates a higher degree of regional integration.

Table A1: Regional Integration Indicators—Asia

	Movement in Trade and Investment				Movement in Capital				People Movement					
	Trade (%) 2016		FDI (%) 2016		Equity Holdings (%) 2016		Bond Holdings (%) 2016		Migration (%) 2015		Tourism (%) 2015		Remittances (%) 2016	
Within Subregions														
ASEAN+3 (including HKG)[a]	47.0	▲	57.8	▲	16.3	▼	9.9	▼	40.0	▲	72.3	▼	33.0	▼
Central Asia	7.0	▲	2.9	▼	0.0	▲	0.0	–	9.3	▼	38.7	▲	6.2	▼
East Asia	36.9	▼	53.5	▲	11.5	▼	6.7	▼	34.6	▼	59.2	▼	35.6	▼
South Asia	5.8	▲	0.6	▲	0.3	▼	2.2	▲	26.2	▼	11.9	▼	9.2	▼
Southeast Asia	22.8	▼	23.7	▲	7.4	▲	7.9	▲	34.1	▼	69.5	▼	14.3	▲
The Pacific and Oceania	6.9	▲	8.2	▼	5.0	▼	1.1	▲	56.3	▲	20.2	▲	31.4	▲
Across Subregions														
ASEAN+3 (including HKG)[a]	10.8	▲	5.2	▲	3.2	▼	5.8	▲	8.8	▲	5.5	▲	6.9	▼
Central Asia	24.1	▼	11.4	▲	11.7	▲	15.0	▲	0.8	▼	1.8	▼	0.6	▼
East Asia	18.9	▲	8.2	▲	3.2	▲	7.3	▲	14.3	▲	15.5	▲	15.2	▲
South Asia	33.2	▲	36.6	▼	21.1	▲	9.6	▼	5.8	▲	30.8	▼	5.8	▲
Southeast Asia	45.2	▼	42.5	▲	32.2	▼	17.1	▼	14.6	▼	21.2	▼	13.6	▼
The Pacific and Oceania	59.8	▼	27.0	▼	10.8	▼	9.0	▲	5.4	▼	37.6	▲	12.8	▼
TOTAL (within and across subregions)														
Asia	**57.3**	▲	**55.3**	▲	**19.0**	▼	**15.3**	▼	**36.7**	▼	**72.5**	▼	**28.1**	▲
ASEAN+3 (including HKG)[a]	57.8	▲	63.0	▲	19.5	▲	15.7	▼	48.8	▲	77.7	▼	39.9	▼
Central Asia	31.1	▼	14.3	▲	11.8	▲	15.0	▲	10.0	▼	40.5	▲	6.9	▼
East Asia	55.9	▲	61.7	▲	14.7	▼	14.0	▼	48.9	▼	74.7	▲	50.8	▼
South Asia	39.1	▲	37.2	▼	21.4	▼	11.8	▼	32.0	▼	42.7	▼	14.9	▼
Southeast Asia	67.9	▼	66.1	▲	39.6	▼	25.0	▼	48.7	▲	90.7	▼	27.9	▼
The Pacific and Oceania	66.8	▼	35.2	▼	15.8	▼	10.1	▲	61.7	▲	57.7	▼	44.2	▲
With the rest of the world														
Asia	**42.7**	▼	**44.7**	▼	**81.0**	▲	**84.7**	▲	**63.3**	▲	**27.5**	▲	**71.9**	▼
ASEAN+3 (including HKG)[a]	42.2	▼	37.0	▼	80.5	▲	84.3	▲	51.2	▼	22.3	▲	60.1	▲
Central Asia	68.9	▲	85.7	▼	88.2	▼	85.0	▼	90.0	▲	59.5	▼	93.1	▲
East Asia	44.1	▼	38.3	▼	85.3	▲	86.0	▲	51.1	▲	25.3	▼	49.2	▲
South Asia	61.0	▼	62.8	▲	78.6	▲	88.2	▲	68.0	▲	57.3	▲	85.1	▲
Southeast Asia	32.1	▲	33.9	▼	60.4	▲	75.0	▲	51.3	▼	9.3	▲	72.1	▲
The Pacific and Oceania	33.2	▲	64.8	▲	84.2	▲	89.9	▼	38.3	▼	42.3	▲	55.8	▼

▲ = increase from previous period; ▼ = decrease from previous period; – = no change from previous period.

HKG = Hong Kong, China.

[a] Includes ASEAN (Brunei Darussalam, Cambodia, Indonesia, the Lao People's Democratic Republic, Malaysia, Myanmar, the Philippines, Singapore, Thailand, and Viet Nam) plus the People's Republic of China; Hong Kong, China; Japan; and the Republic of Korea.

Trade—national data unavailable for Bhutan, Kiribati, Nauru, Palau, Timor-Leste, and Tuvalu; no data available on the Cook Islands, the Marshall Islands, and the Federated States of Micronesia.

Equity and Bond holdings—based on investments from Australia, Bangladesh (start from 2013); Hong Kong, China; India; Indonesia; Japan; Kazakhstan; the Republic of Korea; Malaysia; New Zealand; Pakistan; and Palau (start from 2015); the Philippines; Singapore; and Thailand. Africa: Reporters are Liberia (start from 2012), Mauritius, and South Africa; Latin America: Reporters are Argentina; Bahamas, The; Barbados (start from 2003); Bolivia (start from 2011); Brazil; Chile; Colombia; Costa Rica; Honduras (start from 2014); Mexico (start from 2003); Panama; Uruguay; and Venezuela, Republica Bolivariana de; North America: Reporters are the United States and Canada; euro area / European Union: Reporters are Austria; Belgium; Bulgaria; Cyprus; Czech Republic; Denmark; Estonia; Finland; France; Germany; Greece; Hungary; Ireland; Italy; Latvia; Lithuania (start from 2009); Luxembourg; Malta; Netherlands, The; Poland; Portugal; Romania; Slovak Republic; Slovenia (start from 2009); Spain; Sweden; and United Kingdom, The. Middle East: Reporters are Bahrain, Egypt, Kuwait (start from 2003), Lebanon, and Saudi Arabia (start from 2013). Otherwise, data start from 2001. Intraregional share not comparable to previously released issue due to data availability.

Migration—share of migrant stock to total migrants in 2015 (compared with 2010).

Tourism—share of outbound tourists to total tourists in 2014 (compared with 2013).

Remittances—share of inward remittances to total remittances in 2015 (compared with 2010).

Sources: ADB calculations using data from ASEAN Secretariat; Asia Regional Integration Center, Asian Development Bank; CEIC; International Monetary Fund. Direction of Trade Statistics. http://imf.org/en/data (accessed July 2017); International Monetary Fund. Coordinated Portfolio Investment Survey. http://cpis.imf.org (accessed September 2017); Organisation for Economic Co-operation and Development; Department of Economic and Social Affairs, United Nations. Trends in International Migrant Stock. http://www.un.org/en/development/desa/population/migration/data/estimates2/estimates15.shtml (accessed July 2017); United Nations World Tourism Organization; and International Monetary Fund.World Economic Outlook Database October 2016. http://www.imf.org/external/pubs/ft/weo/2016/02/ (accessed June 2017).

Table A2: Trade Shares, 2016—Asia (% of total world trade)

Reporter	Asia	of which		EU	US	ROW
		PRC	**Japan**			
Central Asia	**31.1**	**15.8**	**1.7**	**29.3**	**2.6**	**37.0**
Armenia	20.8	9.1	1.0	23.6	2.4	53.1
Azerbaijan	23.0	5.5	1.6	34.9	3.1	38.9
Georgia	21.4	6.1	1.6	28.8	2.4	47.4
Kazakhstan	23.9	12.7	1.8	39.0	3.1	34.1
Kyrgyz Republic	50.7	29.0	0.4	6.0	2.9	40.4
Tajikistan	35.2	14.1	0.2	10.3	1.0	53.4
Turkmenistan	59.9	44.0	3.4	15.9	1.0	23.2
Uzbekistan	46.3	21.3	1.0	12.0	2.1	39.6
East Asia	**55.9**	**15.6**	**6.1**	**12.4**	**13.0**	**18.8**
China, People's Rep. of	47.2	–	7.4	14.8	14.1	23.9
Hong Kong, China	77.6	49.7	4.8	7.7	6.9	7.8
Japan	55.9	21.6	–	11.9	16.0	16.2
Republic of Korea	56.9	23.4	8.0	10.9	12.2	20.0
Mongolia	70.0	59.6	4.2	15.1	1.8	13.1
Taipei,China	71.5	30.3	10.4	8.4	10.9	9.1
South Asia	**39.0**	**12.4**	**2.5**	**15.1**	**9.5**	**36.4**
Afghanistan	71.6	15.3	3.5	1.3	1.0	26.0
Bangladesh	43.8	15.0	3.5	23.7	6.8	25.7
Bhutan	97.7	0.4	0.9	1.6	0.2	0.5
India	36.0	11.2	2.2	14.0	10.1	39.8
Maldives	65.3	12.5	1.0	10.6	2.4	21.7
Nepal	86.1	9.7	0.8	3.3	2.0	8.6
Pakistan	44.2	22.5	3.1	17.2	8.0	30.6
Sri Lanka	50.8	8.0	4.1	18.8	12.0	18.4
Southeast Asia	**67.9**	**16.3**	**8.9**	**10.4**	**9.5**	**12.1**
Brunei Darussalam	83.2	4.7	24.3	3.1	11.5	2.1
Cambodia	61.8	22.4	5.9	19.8	10.1	8.4
Indonesia	70.2	17.0	10.4	9.0	8.4	12.4
Lao PDR	95.0	28.3	2.0	2.8	0.5	1.7
Malaysia	69.1	15.9	7.9	9.8	9.0	12.1
Myanmar	91.3	36.8	6.9	3.7	1.3	3.7
Philippines	70.2	15.0	14.8	9.2	11.1	9.5
Singapore	69.3	13.5	5.6	11.1	8.7	10.9
Thailand	66.1	16.1	12.5	9.7	8.9	15.2
Viet Nam	61.8	19.6	8.0	12.3	13.1	12.8
The Pacific	**76.5**	**15.6**	**5.8**	**14.5**	**3.1**	**5.8**
Fiji	83.1	12.9	6.0	4.7	7.4	4.8
Kiribati	91.1	6.1	7.6	2.1	2.0	4.8
Marshall Islands	49.8	21.3	0.0	43.8	1.0	5.5
Micronesia, Fed. States of	38.1	3.8	3.9	0.4	24.4	37.1
Nauru	76.1	2.1	7.9	0.8	1.8	21.3
Palau	51.1	13.9	19.4	4.7	24.3	19.9
Papua New Guinea	88.3	12.9	8.7	7.4	1.8	2.5
Samoa	82.5	11.6	4.6	1.3	9.5	6.7
Solomon Islands	89.8	43.4	3.0	6.7	1.5	2.1
Timor-Leste	86.6	21.1	2.2	5.4	2.0	6.0
Tonga	33.9	3.0	2.1	1.5	3.4	61.2
Tuvalu	65.2	0.4	4.6	1.1	5.2	28.4
Vanuatu	77.4	9.0	4.4	13.1	4.5	5.0
Oceania	**66.3**	**25.8**	**9.5**	**14.8**	**9.3**	**9.6**
Australia	67.0	26.9	10.1	14.9	9.0	9.1
New Zealand	62.3	19.7	6.6	14.0	11.1	12.6
Asia	**57.3**	**15.9**	**6.5**	**12.5**	**11.7**	**18.5**
Developing Asia	**57.0**	**14.7**	**7.2**	**12.5**	**11.3**	**19.3**

EU = European Union, Lao PDR = Lao People's Democratic Republic, PRC = People's Republic of China, ROW = rest of the world, US = United States.
Source: ADB calculations using data from International Monetary Fund. Direction of Trade Database. https://www.imf.org/en/Data (accessed July 2017).

Table A3: FTA Status, 2017—Asia

Economy	Under Negotiation		Signed but not yet In Effect	Signed and In Effect	Total
	Framework Agreement signed	Negotiations launched			
Central Asia					
Armenia	0	2	0	11	13
Azerbaijan	0	0	0	10	10
Georgia	0	0	2	11	13
Kazakhstan	0	4	0	11	15
Kyrgyz Republic	0	2	0	11	13
Tajikistan	0	0	0	8	8
Turkmenistan	0	0	0	6	6
Uzbekistan	0	0	0	10	10
East Asia					
China, People's Rep. of	0	7	1	16	24
Hong Kong, China	0	3	0	4	7
Japan	0	8	1	15	24
Republic of Korea	0	10	0	16	26
Mongolia	0	0	0	1	1
Taipei,China	1	1	0	7	9
South Asia					
Afghanistan	0	0	0	2	2
Bangladesh	0	2	1	3	6
Bhutan	0	1	0	2	3
India	1	14	0	13	28
Maldives	0	1	1	1	3
Nepal	0	1	0	2	3
Pakistan	0	7	1	10	18
Sri Lanka	0	3	0	5	8
Southeast Asia					
Brunei Darussalam	0	2	1	8	11
Cambodia	0	2	0	6	8
Indonesia	0	7	1	9	17
Lao PDR	0	2	0	8	10
Malaysia	1	5	2	14	22
Myanmar	1	3	0	6	10
Philippines	0	3	1	7	11
Singapore	0	9	2	20	31
Thailand	1	8	0	13	22
Viet Nam	0	5	1	10	16
The Pacific					
Cook Islands	0	1	1	2	4
Fiji	0	1	1	3	5
Kiribati	0	1	1	2	4
Marshall Islands	0	1	1	3	5
Micronesia, Fed. States of	0	1	1	3	5
Nauru	0	1	1	2	4
Palau	0	1	1	2	4
Papua New Guinea	0	1	1	4	6
Samoa	0	1	1	2	4
Solomon Islands	0	1	1	3	5
Tonga	0	1	1	2	4
Tuvalu	0	1	1	2	4
Vanuatu	0	1	1	3	5
Oceania					
Australia	0	7	2	12	21
New Zealand	0	6	2	11	19

FTA = free trade agreement, Lao PDR = Lao People's Democratic Republic.

Notes:

(i)   Framework Agreement signed: The parties initially negotiate the contents of a framework agreement (FA) , which serves as a framework for future negotiations.

(ii) Negotiations launched: The parties, through the relevant ministries, declare the official launch of negotiations or set the date for such, or start the first round of negotiations.

(iii) Signed but not yet in effect: Parties sign the agreement after negotiations have been completed. However, the agreement has yet to be implemented.

(iv) Signed and in effect: Provisions of FTA come into force, after legislative or executive ratification.

Source: ADB. Asia Regional Integration Center FTA Database. https://aric.adb.org/fta (accessed August 2017).

Table A4: Time to Export and Import—Asia (hours)

	Time to Export		Time to Import			Time to Export		Time to Import	
	2015	2016	2015	2016		2015	2016	2015	2016
Central Asia	**191**	**190**	**73**	**71**	Lao PDR	228	228	230	230
Armenia	41	41	43	43	Malaysia	58	58	82	82
Azerbaijan	69	62	73	68	Myanmar	288	288	168	280
Georgia	62	16	39	17	Philippines	114	114	168	168
Kazakhstan	265	261	8	8	Singapore	14	14	38	38
Kyrgyz Republic	51	41	73	73	Thailand	62	62	54	54
Tajikistan	141	141	234	234	Viet Nam	143	108	170	138
Turkmenistan	–	–	–	–	**The Pacific**	**137**	**137**	**157**	**153**
Uzbekistan	286	286	285	285	Cook Islands	–	–	–	–
East Asia	**37**	**37**	**92**	**93**	Fiji	112	112	76	76
China, People's Rep. of	47	47	158	158	Kiribati	96	96	144	144
Hong Kong, China	20	20	20	20	Marshall Islands	84	84	144	144
Japan	25	25	43	43	Micronesia, Fed. States of	62	62	91	91
Republic of Korea	14	14	7	7	Nauru	–	–	–	–
Mongolia	230	230	163	163	Palau	270	270	252	252
Taipei,China	48	48	88	88	Papua New Guinea	138	138	192	192
South Asia	**157**	**152**	**333**	**323**	Samoa	75	75	109	109
Afghanistan	291	276	432	420	Solomon Islands	170	170	145	145
Bangladesh	247	247	327	327	Timor-Leste	129	129	144	144
Bhutan	14	14	13	13	Tonga	220	220	98	98
India	150	144	350	344	Tuvalu	–	–	–	–
Maldives	90	90	161	161	Vanuatu	110	110	174	174
Nepal	83	75	114	109					
Pakistan	141	134	294	276	**Oceania**	**43**	**43**	**41**	**40**
Sri Lanka	119	119	130	130	Australia	43	43	43	43
Southeast Asia	**74**	**69**	**108**	**105**	New Zealand	41	41	26	26
Brunei Darussalam	288	280	192	188					
Cambodia	180	180	140	140	**Asia**	**53**	**52**	**115**	**114**
Indonesia	125	114	243	232	**Developing Asia**	**56**	**54**	**123**	**121**

– = data unavailable, Lao PDR = Lao People's Democratic Republic.

Notes: Time to export/import data measures the number of hours required to export/import by ocean transport, including the processing of documents required to complete the transaction. It covers time used up for documentation requirements and procedures at customs and other regulatory agencies as well as the time of inland transport between the largest business city and the main port used by traders. Regional aggregates are weighted averages based on total exports or imports.

Source: ADB calculations using data from World Bank. Doing Business Database. http://www.doingbusiness.org (accessed July 2017).

Table A5: Logistics Performance Index Scores—Asia (% to EU)

	2012	2014	2016		2012	2014	2016
Central Asia	**63.7**	**66.6**	**57.3**	Lao PDR	65.7	61.8	52.4
Armenia	67.4	69.2	55.9	Malaysia	91.8	92.9	86.9
Azerbaijan	65.2	63.4	–	Myanmar	62.2	58.2	62.4
Georgia	72.9	64.9	59.7	Philippines	79.5	77.7	72.4
Kazakhstan	70.8	69.8	69.8	Singapore	108.4	103.6	105.1
Kyrgyz Republic	61.9	57.2	54.7	Thailand	83.5	88.7	82.6
Tajikistan	60.0	65.4	52.3	Viet Nam	79.0	81.6	75.5
Turkmenistan	–	59.6	56.1	**The Pacific**	**56.0**	**57.6**	**55.9**
Uzbekistan	64.8	62.0	61.0	Cook Islands	–	–	–
East Asia	**97.5**	**94.8**	**95.8**	Fiji	63.6	65.9	58.7
China, People's Rep. of	92.4	91.4	92.9	Kiribati	–	–	–
Hong Kong, China	108.3	99.0	103.2	Marshall Islands	–	–	–
Japan	103.4	101.3	100.7	Micronesia, Federated States of	–	–	–
Republic of Korea	97.1	94.9	94.3	Nauru	–	–	–
Mongolia	59.1	61.0	63.6	Palau	–	–	–
Taipei,China	97.4	96.2	93.8	Papua New Guinea	62.4	62.9	63.7
South Asia	**75.0**	**77.5**	**80.3**	Samoa	–	–	–
Afghanistan	60.4	53.5	54.3	Solomon Islands	63.4	67.0	61.3
Bangladesh	–	66.3	67.6	Timor-Leste	–	–	–
Bhutan	66.2	59.3	58.9	Tonga	–	–	–
India	80.8	79.7	86.7	Tuvalu	–	–	–
Maldives	66.9	71.1	63.7	Vanuatu	–	–	–
Nepal	53.5	67.0	60.3				
Pakistan	74.3	73.1	74.1	**Oceania**	**96.9**	**98.0**	**94.7**
Sri Lanka	72.3	69.7	–	Australia	97.9	98.6	96.2
Southeast Asia	**90.5**	**90.2**	**85.9**	New Zealand	89.9	94.3	85.9
Brunei Darussalam	–	–	72.8				
Cambodia	67.3	70.9	71.0	**Asia**	**93.3**	**92.2**	**92.1**
Indonesia	77.4	79.7	75.7	**Developing Asia**	**79.2**	**79.9**	**80.2**

– = unavailable, EU = European Union, Lao PDR = Lao People's Democratic Republic.
Source: ADB calculations using data from World Bank. Logistics Performance Index. https://lpi.worldbank.org (accessed July 2017).

Table A6: Cross-Border Equity Holdings, 2016—Asia (% of total cross-border equity holdings)

Reporter	Asia	of which PRC	of which Japan	EU	US	ROW
Central Asia	**11.8**	**0.0**	**8.7**	**24.9**	**52.4**	**10.9**
Armenia	–	–	–	–	–	–
Azerbaijan	–	–	–	–	–	–
Georgia	–	–	–	–	–	–
Kazakhstan	11.8	0.0	8.7	24.9	52.4	10.9
Kyrgyz Republic	–	–	–	–	–	–
Tajikistan	–	–	–	–	–	–
Turkmenistan	–	–	–	–	–	–
Uzbekistan	–	–	–	–	–	–
East Asia	**16.5**	**8.4**	**1.0**	**15.9**	**23.5**	**44.1**
China, People's Rep. of	37.8	0.0	4.2	15.2	32.5	14.5
Hong Kong, China	26.9	23.3	0.9	11.7	3.0	58.3
Japan	6.3	0.7	0.0	17.7	32.1	43.8
Republic of Korea	19.9	4.2	6.1	23.0	46.5	10.5
Mongolia	70.0	0.4	0.0	12.4	12.7	4.9
Taipei,China	–	–	–	–	–	–
South Asia	**21.4**	**13.3**	**0.2**	**32.7**	**28.7**	**17.2**
Afghanistan	–	–	–	–	–	–
Bangladesh	100.0	0.0	0.0	0.0	0.0	0.0
Bhutan	–	–	–	–	–	–
India	22.8	14.4	0.3	34.7	31.0	11.5
Maldives	–	–	–	–	–	–
Nepal	–	–	–	–	–	–
Pakistan	0.7	0.0	0.0	8.9	0.3	90.2
Sri Lanka	–	–	–	–	–	–
Southeast Asia	**39.6**	**12.7**	**5.3**	**10.3**	**26.0**	**24.0**
Brunei Darussalam	–	–	–	–	–	–
Cambodia	–	–	–	–	–	–
Indonesia	13.6	5.3	0.2	44.3	3.4	38.6
Lao PDR	–	–	–	–	–	–
Malaysia	46.6	1.6	0.6	8.2	39.4	5.8
Myanmar	–	–	–	–	–	–
Philippines	11.9	0.6	0.1	52.1	33.7	2.3
Singapore	39.7	14.2	5.9	9.1	25.0	26.2
Thailand	24.5	2.2	3.1	43.9	23.7	8.0
Viet Nam	–	–	–	–	–	–
The Pacific	**–**	**–**	**–**	**–**	**–**	**–**
Cook Islands	–	–	–	–	–	–
Fiji	–	–	–	–	–	–
Kiribati	–	–	–	–	–	–
Marshall Islands	–	–	–	–	–	–
Micronesia, Fed. States of	–	–	–	–	–	–
Nauru	–	–	–	–	–	–
Palau	–	–	–	–	–	–
Papua New Guinea	–	–	–	–	–	–
Samoa	–	–	–	–	–	–
Solomon Islands	–	–	–	–	–	–
Timor-Leste	–	–	–	–	–	–
Tonga	–	–	–	–	–	–
Tuvalu	–	–	–	–	–	–
Vanuatu	–	–	–	–	–	–
Oceania	**15.8**	**1.1**	**4.7**	**18.0**	**45.8**	**20.4**
Australia	13.1	1.2	4.8	19.1	47.2	20.6
New Zealand	36.1	0.3	4.0	10.4	35.0	18.5
Asia	**20.1**	**8.1**	**2.2**	**15.3**	**26.7**	**37.9**
Developing Asia	**31.4**	**15.4**	**3.2**	**12.8**	**18.0**	**37.8**

– = unavailable, EU = European Union, Lao PDR = Lao People's Democratic Republic, PRC = People's Republic of China, ROW = rest of the world, US = United States.
Source: ADB calculations using data from International Monetary Fund. Coordinated Portfolio Investment Survey. http://cpis.imf.org (accessed September 2017).

Table A7: Cross-Border Debt Holdings, 2016—Asia (% of total cross-border debt holdings)

Reporter	Asia	PRC	Japan	EU	US	ROW
		of which				
Central Asia	**15.0**	**0.1**	**6.7**	**24.3**	**51.5**	**9.1**
Armenia	–	–	–	–	–	–
Azerbaijan	–	–	–	–	–	–
Georgia	–	–	–	–	–	–
Kazakhstan	15.0	0.1	6.7	24.3	51.5	9.1
Kyrgyz Republic	–	–	–	–	–	–
Tajikistan	–	–	–	–	–	–
Turkmenistan	–	–	–	–	–	–
Uzbekistan	–	–	–	–	–	–
East Asia	**14.8**	**3.7**	**1.5**	**27.4**	**42.1**	**15.7**
China, People's Rep. of	30.9	0.0	2.1	9.4	38.2	21.4
Hong Kong, China	45.9	22.5	8.7	17.1	21.8	15.2
Japan	7.5	0.2	0.0	30.8	46.2	15.5
Republic of Korea	17.3	3.3	3.1	21.5	45.7	15.5
Mongolia	43.0	0.9	0.0	4.7	2.1	50.1
Taipei,China	–	–	–	–	–	–
South Asia	**11.8**	**2.3**	**2.3**	**44.3**	**31.4**	**12.5**
Afghanistan	–	–	–	–	–	–
Bangladesh	14.1	3.0	2.6	57.8	15.5	12.5
Bhutan	–	–	–	–	–	–
India	0.6	0.0	0.0	0.2	99.2	0.0
Maldives	–	–	–	–	–	–
Nepal	–	–	–	–	–	–
Pakistan	20.3	0.0	6.4	2.9	11.3	65.5
Sri Lanka	–	–	–	–	–	–
Southeast Asia	**25.0**	**4.2**	**0.7**	**11.8**	**34.0**	**29.2**
Brunei Darussalam	–	–	–	–	–	–
Cambodia	–	–	–	–	–	–
Indonesia	28.3	3.2	0.1	31.1	23.6	16.9
Lao PDR	–	–	–	–	–	–
Malaysia	61.8	1.7	1.7	9.0	17.2	12.0
Myanmar	–	–	–	–	–	–
Philippines	41.4	3.8	3.6	9.1	37.7	11.8
Singapore	21.8	4.2	0.0	11.8	36.0	30.4
Thailand	50.0	7.8	14.2	8.0	7.0	35.0
Viet Nam	–	–	–	–	–	–
The Pacific	**0.0**	**0.0**	**0.0**	**0.0**	**100.0**	**0.0**
Cook Islands	–	–	–	–	–	–
Fiji	–	–	–	–	–	–
Kiribati	–	–	–	–	–	–
Marshall Islands	–	–	–	–	–	–
Micronesia, Fed. States of	–	–	–	–	–	–
Nauru	–	–	–	–	–	–
Palau	0.0	0.0	0.0	0.0	100.0	0.0
Papua New Guinea	–	–	–	–	–	–
Samoa	–	–	–	–	–	–
Solomon Islands	–	–	–	–	–	–
Timor-Leste	–	–	–	–	–	–
Tonga	–	–	–	–	–	–
Tuvalu	–	–	–	–	–	–
Vanuatu	–	–	–	–	–	–
Oceania	**10.1**	**1.4**	**5.1**	**28.8**	**32.5**	**28.5**
Australia	10.7	1.6	5.2	31.8	37.2	20.3
New Zealand	5.6	0.0	4.2	8.0	0.0	86.4
Asia	**15.9**	**3.6**	**1.7**	**25.3**	**40.5**	**18.3**
Developing Asia	**31.9**	**9.9**	**4.1**	**14.8**	**31.9**	**21.4**

– = unavailable, EU = European Union, Lao PDR = Lao People's Democratic Republic, PRC = People's Republic of China, ROW = rest of the world, US = United States.
Source: ADB calculations using data from International Monetary Fund. Coordinated Portfolio Investment Survey. http://cpis.imf.org (accessed September 2017).

Table A8: FDI Inflow Share, 2016—Asia

Reporter	Partner Asia	of which PRC	Japan	EU	US	ROW
Central Asia	14.3	6.0	2.3	56.6	16.6	12.5
Armenia	0.2	0.0	0.0	119.1	4.3	-23.6
Azerbaijan	0.1	0.1	0.1	4.8	0.3	94.8
Georgia	38.9	1.6	0.5	28.4	2.7	30.0
Kazakhstan	22.6	10.6	5.2	118.4	37.8	-78.8
Kyrgyz Republic	19.9	14.5	0.0	19.5	1.1	59.5
Tajikistan	49.2	49.2	0.0	0.0	0.0	50.8
Turkmenistan	–	–	–	–	–	–
Uzbekistan	–	–	–	–	–	–
East Asia	**61.7**	**10.6**	**5.4**	**15.4**	**4.9**	**18.0**
China, People's Rep. of	31.2	24.8	2.8	11.1	0.4	57.3
Hong Kong, China	76.9	-1.1	–	104.8	50.6	-132.3
Japan	51.2	11.1	12.8	46.1	30.9	-28.2
Republic of Korea	-15.4	-5.4	-0.8	-43.3	-1.4	160.1
Mongolia	86.0	–	7.3	2.6	2.6	8.8
Taipei,China	22.4	3.0	4.2	86.2	1.7	-10.3
South Asia	**37.2**	**1.7**	**11.6**	**19.3**	**5.9**	**37.6**
Afghanistan	16.5	16.5	–	-5.0	–	88.6
Bangladesh	44.4	1.2	2.1	19.6	3.0	33.0
Bhutan	-118.2	–	–	-28.9	0.0	247.0
India	37.8	0.6	13.0	18.8	5.9	37.6
Maldives	0.0	–	0.0	-8.6	0.0	108.6
Nepal	9.4	8.1	1.3	0.0	0.0	90.6
Pakistan	31.5	25.2	2.1	49.4	13.5	5.6
Sri Lanka	26.3	2.6	-0.6	-6.9	0.0	80.6
Southeast Asia	**66.1**	**9.1**	**13.8**	**28.6**	**11.5**	**-6.2**
Brunei Darussalam	44.9	0.0	2.3	117.6	-1.5	-61.0
Cambodia	92.0	26.2	10.4	10.1	2.8	-4.9
Indonesia	597.1	11.2	184.8	-8.0	-19.3	-469.8
Lao PDR	108.7	79.8	5.0	1.8	0.4	-10.8
Malaysia	75.6	8.9	9.2	13.7	8.2	2.6
Myanmar	94.4	9.4	0.7	38.3	2.0	-34.7
Philippines	54.9	0.2	33.3	18.2	17.0	9.9
Singapore	33.2	8.7	0.5	47.3	15.2	4.3
Thailand	445.5	16.4	231.9	-273.2	21.4	-93.7
Viet Nam	55.9	7.7	10.6	4.4	1.6	38.1
The Pacific	**–**	**–**	**–**	**–**	**–**	**–**
Cook Islands	–	–	–	–	–	–
Fiji	112.7	29.6	3.8	2.8	–	–
Kiribati	–	–	–	–	–	–
Marshall Islands	0.0	0.0	0.0	197.1	–	–
FSM	–	–	–	–	–	–
Nauru	–	–	–	–	–	–
Palau	16.7	0.0	16.7	–	–	–
Papua New Guinea	–	–	–	–	–	–
Samoa	67.5	52.3	15.2	32.5	–	–
Solomon Islands	121.9	0.0	0.0	0.0	–	–
Timor-Leste	–	–	–	–	–	–
Tonga	–	–	–	–	–	–
Tuvalu	–	–	–	–	–	–
Vanuatu	74.0	8.9	-7.6	7.8	–	–
Oceania	**30.4**	**5.7**	**15.0**	**20.2**	**16.9**	**32.5**
Australia	30.3	6.0	15.8	21.9	17.5	30.3
New Zealand	33.0	0.0	-0.8	-14.0	3.0	77.9
Asia	**55.3**	**8.7**	**8.6**	**20.8**	**8.1**	**15.8**
Developing Asia	**57.7**	**9.3**	**8.1**	**18.6**	**5.9**	**17.7**

– = unavailable, EU = European Union, FSM = Federated States of Micronesia, FDI = foreign direct investments, Lao PDR = Lao People's Democratic Republic, PRC = People's Republic of China, ROW = rest of the world, US = United States.
Sources: ADB calculations using data from Association of Southeast Asian Nations Secretariat; CEIC; Eurosatat. Balance of Payments; Organisation for Economic Co-operation and Development; and United Nations Conference on Trade and Development. Bilateral FDI Statistics. http://unctad.org/en/Pages/Home.aspx (all accessed July 2017).

Table A9: Remittance Inflows Share, 2016—Asia (% of total remittance inflows)

Reporter	Asia	of which Japan	EU	US	ROW
Central Asia	**6.9**	**0.0**	**8.2**	**2.7**	**82.2**
Armenia	4.4	0.0	10.5	13.9	71.2
Azerbaijan	24.3	0.0	3.4	2.0	70.3
Georgia	9.2	0.0	16.7	2.4	71.7
Kazakhstan	4.2	0.0	22.1	0.6	73.1
Kyrgyz Republic	4.7	0.0	12.8	0.7	81.9
Tajikistan	12.3	0.0	4.3	0.9	82.5
Turkmenistan	–	–	–	–	–
Uzbekistan	–	–	–	–	–
East Asia	**42.9**	**7.9**	**8.9**	**27.5**	**20.7**
China, People's Rep. of	22.7	0.0	11.5	30.7	35.2
Hong Kong, China	39.7	0.0	13.1	34.9	12.4
Japan	16.9	26.4	4.5	44.9	33.7
Republic of Korea	44.9	0.0	19.8	0.4	35.0
Mongolia	45.9	6.6	9.0	25.4	19.7
Taipei,China	–	–	–	–	–
South Asia	**14.8**	**0.2**	**9.5**	**11.8**	**63.9**
Afghanistan	31.7	0.0	7.7	2.2	58.3
Bangladesh	34.9	0.2	5.5	3.4	56.2
Bhutan	95.2	0.0	0.0	0.0	4.8
India	12.5	0.2	8.6	17.0	61.9
Maldives	50.0	0.0	0.0	0.0	50.0
Nepal	20.9	0.0	3.0	4.7	71.4
Pakistan	5.2	0.2	13.9	6.7	74.2
Sri Lanka	16.2	0.6	19.0	3.1	61.7
Southeast Asia	**25.4**	**2.5**	**9.8**	**31.2**	**33.6**
Brunei Darussalam	–	–	–	–	–
Cambodia	67.8	0.3	7.4	21.4	3.4
Indonesia	39.1	0.7	4.6	2.8	53.6
Lao PDR	74.7	0.0	4.2	20.0	1.1
Malaysia	88.8	0.5	4.3	3.8	3.2
Myanmar	66.2	0.0	0.7	5.4	27.7
Philippines	14.6	3.5	7.0	33.9	44.5
Singapore	–	–	–	–	–
Thailand	32.4	4.5	25.2	27.7	14.7
Viet Nam	18.0	1.4	15.4	56.3	10.2
The Pacific	**58.8**	**0.0**	**2.0**	**25.3**	**13.9**
Cook Islands	–	–	–	–	–
Fiji	59.6	0.0	3.1	23.1	14.1
Kiribati	50.0	0.0	0.0	50.0	0.0
Marshall Islands	3.7	0.0	0.0	92.6	3.7
Micronesia, Fed. States of	0.0	0.0	0.0	70.8	29.2
Nauru	–	–	–	–	–
Palau	0.0	0.0	0.0	50.0	50.0
Papua New Guinea	90.9	0.0	0.0	9.1	0.0
Samoa	64.4	0.0	0.0	12.9	22.7
Solomon Islands	90.0	0.0	0.0	5.0	5.0
Timor-Leste	93.8	0.0	6.2	0.0	0.0
Tonga	57.1	0.0	0.0	39.5	3.4
Tuvalu	75.0	0.0	0.0	0.0	25.0
Vanuatu	20.8	0.0	8.3	4.2	66.7
Oceania	**37.6**	**2.4**	**36.4**	**13.1**	**12.8**
Australia	28.7	2.7	41.8	14.9	14.6
New Zealand	83.6	0.5	9.1	3.8	3.5
Asia	**25.2**	**2.9**	**9.6**	**20.7**	**44.5**
Developing Asia	**24.9**	**3.0**	**9.3**	**20.5**	**45.3**

– = unavailable, EU = European Union, Lao PDR = Lao People's Democratic Republic, ROW = rest of the world, US = United States.
Source: ADB calculations using data from World Bank. World Bank Migration and Remittances Data. http://www.worldbank.org/en/topic/migrationremittancesdiasporaissues/brief/migration-remittances-data (accessed July 2017).

Table A10: Outbound Migration Share, 2015—Asia (% of total outbound migrants)

Reporter	Asia	Partner of which PRC	Japan	EU	US	ROW
Central Asia	**10.0**	**0.0**	**0.0**	**15.1**	**1.9**	**72.9**
Armenia	18.8	0.0	0.0	9.1	9.1	63.0
Azerbaijan	15.1	0.0	0.0	3.7	1.7	79.4
Georgia	11.9	0.0	0.0	20.4	2.9	64.8
Kazakhstan	1.6	0.0	0.0	26.8	0.6	70.9
Kyrgyz Republic	4.0	0.0	0.0	12.4	0.7	82.9
Tajikistan	7.9	0.0	0.0	5.5	0.7	85.8
Turkmenistan	2.8	0.0	0.0	4.2	0.9	92.2
Uzbekistan	23.2	0.0	0.0	3.7	1.8	71.3
East Asia	**37.0**	**3.4**	**8.5**	**9.6**	**27.5**	**25.9**
China, People's Rep. of	47.5	0.0	6.8	9.9	22.0	20.5
Hong Kong, China	15.9	26.0	0.0	11.9	21.5	50.7
Japan	22.0	0.9	0.0	17.0	43.3	17.7
Republic of Korea	8.9	8.0	22.3	4.2	47.7	39.2
Mongolia	32.6	0.0	0.0	27.4	0.0	40.1
Taipei,China	0.0	0.0	0.0	0.0	0.0	0.0
South Asia	**31.8**	**0.1**	**0.1**	**8.6**	**7.2**	**52.4**
Afghanistan	34.6	0.0	0.0	5.9	1.3	58.1
Bangladesh	51.8	0.1	0.1	5.3	2.6	40.3
Bhutan	89.3	0.0	0.0	4.0	0.0	6.7
India	21.8	0.1	0.1	7.7	12.6	57.9
Maldives	73.9	0.0	0.0	17.3	0.0	8.8
Nepal	52.9	0.0	0.0	4.7	4.6	37.8
Pakistan	28.6	0.1	0.2	14.3	5.5	51.6
Sri Lanka	20.7	0.3	0.6	22.0	2.9	54.4
Southeast Asia	**46.1**	**0.8**	**1.8**	**7.9**	**20.3**	**25.7**
Brunei Darussalam	75.6	0.0	0.0	14.0	0.0	10.4
Cambodia	77.0	0.0	0.3	6.1	14.1	2.8
Indonesia	43.4	1.0	0.7	4.7	2.5	49.5
Lao PDR	80.1	0.0	0.0	3.6	14.9	1.4
Malaysia	88.0	0.3	0.4	5.3	3.5	3.2
Myanmar	88.1	0.0	0.0	0.8	3.6	7.5
Philippines	9.1	1.4	4.0	9.2	35.7	46.1
Singapore	65.1	0.0	0.7	18.5	10.0	6.5
Thailand	27.3	1.8	4.8	28.5	27.6	16.6
Viet Nam	20.7	1.1	2.8	15.2	50.9	13.3
The Pacific	**64.9**	**0.0**	**0.0**	**3.3**	**18.2**	**13.6**
Cook Islands	99.9	0.0	0.0	0.0	0.0	0.0
Fiji	63.1	0.0	0.0	3.5	19.9	13.5
Kiribati	93.5	0.0	0.0	4.3	0.0	2.2
Marshall Islands	1.9	0.0	0.0	0.1	93.9	4.1
Micronesia, Fed. States of	3.4	0.0	0.0	0.5	36.7	59.4
Nauru	97.3	0.0	0.0	1.5	0.0	1.3
Palau	12.3	0.0	0.0	7.7	0.0	80.0
Papua New Guinea	46.5	0.0	0.0	33.7	0.0	19.8
Samoa	70.2	0.0	0.0	0.8	14.9	14.1
Solomon Islands	89.6	0.0	0.0	10.3	0.0	0.1
Timor-Leste	89.1	0.0	0.0	10.7	0.0	0.2
Tonga	64.7	0.0	0.0	0.8	31.3	3.1
Tuvalu	77.6	0.0	0.0	2.0	0.0	20.4
Vanuatu	22.6	0.0	0.0	12.0	0.0	65.4
Oceania	**59.2**	**0.4**	**0.9**	**25.0**	**8.2**	**7.6**
Australia	23.8	1.0	1.7	47.0	14.8	14.5
New Zealand	82.5	0.0	0.4	10.6	3.8	3.1
Asia	**34.0**	**0.8**	**1.9**	**9.6**	**13.2**	**43.2**
Developing Asia	**33.7**	**0.8**	**2.0**	**9.3**	**12.9**	**44.0**

– = unavailable, EU = European Union, Lao PDR = Lao People's Democratic Republic, PRC = People's Republic of China, ROW = rest of the world, US = United States.
Source: ADB calculations using data from United Nations. Department of Economic and Social Affairs, Population Division. International Migrant Stock 2015. http://www.un.org/en/development/desa/population/migration/data/index.shtml (accessed July 2016).

Table A11: Outbound Tourism Share, 2015—Asia (% of total outbound tourists)

Reporter	Asia	of which PRC	of which Japan	EU	US	ROW
Central Asia	**39.4**	**1.1**	**-**	**0.6**	**0.2**	**59.8**
Armenia	61.1	-	-	0.6	0.3	38.1
Azerbaijan	35.0	-	-	0.4	0.1	64.5
Georgia	22.0	-	-	1.8	0.3	75.9
Kazakhstan	27.8	3.1	-	0.9	0.3	71.0
Kyrgyz Republic	60.7	1.8	-	0.0	0.1	39.2
Tajikistan	17.9	-	-	0.1	0.1	82.0
Turkmenistan	15.4	-	-	0.2	0.2	84.3
Uzbekistan	63.6	-	-	0.2	0.3	35.9
East Asia	**30.9**	**38.0**	**5.8**	**5.8**	**3.6**	**59.8**
China, People's Rep. of	55.5	-	5.5	7.9	2.9	33.7
Hong Kong, China	4.1	86.3	1.7	0.3	0.1	95.4
Japan	43.3	11.2	-	16.8	16.8	23.0
Republic of Korea	34.8	19.2	17.3	10.4	7.6	47.2
Mongolia	8.7	65.2	1.3	0.1	0.8	90.4
Taipei,China	25.0	36.2	24.2	3.3	2.9	68.8
South Asia	**37.4**	**4.5**	**0.8**	**6.3**	**6.0**	**50.2**
Afghanistan	20.4	-	-	1.0	0.4	78.3
Bangladesh	72.5	-	0.4	0.1	1.5	25.9
Bhutan	87.7	-	-	5.4	2.8	4.0
India	34.6	5.5	0.8	9.2	8.4	47.8
Maldives	96.4	-	-	0.1	0.1	3.3
Nepal	57.4	8.1	4.7	0.2	3.9	38.5
Pakistan	12.1	3.6	0.3	3.6	2.7	81.6
Sri Lanka	64.9	5.7	1.7	0.1	1.8	33.2
Southeast Asia	**81.1**	**6.4**	**3.2**	**1.3**	**1.2**	**16.4**
Brunei Darussalam	98.6	-	0.2	0.0	0.1	1.2
Cambodia	97.4	-	1.1	0.0	0.4	2.2
Indonesia	75.1	5.8	2.2	1.3	1.0	22.6
Lao PDR	99.5	-	0.2	0.0	0.1	0.4
Malaysia	77.5	9.9	2.8	2.1	0.7	19.7
Myanmar	93.6	-	2.5	0.2	0.9	5.3
Philippines	53.8	15.8	4.2	1.5	3.8	40.9
Singapore	89.8	4.6	1.6	1.4	0.8	8.0
Thailand	78.5	6.6	8.2	1.4	1.0	19.1
Viet Nam	91.1	-	4.1	0.3	2.2	6.4
The Pacific	**82.9**	**-**	**-**	**0.5**	**4.4**	**12.3**
Cook Islands	96.9	-	-	0.2	0.5	2.5
Fiji	85.5	-	-	0.5	8.6	5.3
Kiribati	80.7	-	-	1.0	4.2	14.1
Marshall Islands	45.2	-	-	0.4	-	54.4
Micronesia, Fed. States of	9.6	-	-	0.6	-	89.8
Nauru	93.1	-	-	1.9	2.5	2.6
Palau	11.0	-	-	0.9	-	88.1
Papua New Guinea	96.1	-	-	0.3	2.0	1.5
Samoa	73.2	-	-	0.5	-	26.3
Solomon Islands	91.2	-	-	1.1	2.9	4.8
Timor-Leste	-	-	-	-	-	-
Tonga	88.0	-	-	0.2	10.3	1.5
Tuvalu	92.3	-	-	0.7	5.2	1.8
Vanuatu	78.2	-	-	0.4	1.3	20.1
Oceania	**50.9**	**4.1**	**2.3**	**23.2**	**9.5**	**16.5**
Australia	47.0	4.2	2.5	26.0	9.6	17.4
New Zealand	67.9	3.7	1.5	10.7	8.7	12.7
Asia	**41.6**	**26.4**	**4.5**	**5.5**	**3.4**	**49.5**
Developing Asia	**41.0**	**28.6**	**4.9**	**3.8**	**2.1**	**53.1**

- = unavailable, EU = European Union, Lao PDR = Lao People's Democratic Republic, PRC = People's Republic of China, ROW = rest of the world, US = United States.
Source: ADB calculations using data from World Tourism Organization. 2017. Tourism Statistics Database.

www.ingramcontent.com/pod-product-compliance
Lightning Source LLC
Chambersburg PA
CBHW041120280326
41928CB00061B/3463